RACIAL IMMANENCE

Racial Immanence

Chicanx Bodies beyond Representation

Marissa K. López

NEW YORK UNIVERSITY PRESS
New York

NEW YORK UNIVERSITY PRESS
New York
www.nyupress.org

© 2019 by New York University
All rights reserved

References to Internet websites (URLs) were accurate at the time of writing. Neither the author nor New York University Press is responsible for URLs that may have expired or changed since the manuscript was prepared.

Library of Congress Cataloging-in-Publication Data
Names: López, Marissa K., author.
Title: Racial immanence: chicanx bodies beyond representation / Marissa K. López.
Description: New York : New York University Press, 2019. | Includes bibliographical references and index.
Identifiers: LCCN 2018046201| ISBN 9781479807727 (cl : alk. paper) | ISBN 9781479813902 (pb : alk. paper)
Subjects: LCSH: American literature—Mexican American authors—History and criticism. | Race in literature. | Ethnicity in literature. | Mexican Americans in literature.
Classification: LCC PS153.M4 L665 2019 | DDC 810.9/86872073—dc23
LC record available at https://lccn.loc.gov/2018046201

New York University Press books are printed on acid-free paper, and their binding materials are chosen for strength and durability. We strive to use environmentally responsible suppliers and materials to the greatest extent possible in publishing our books.

Manufactured in the United States of America

10 9 8 7 6 5 4 3 2 1

Also available as an ebook

Como todo, pa' mis hijos, quienes me enseñaron el milagro de mi propio cuerpo

Go on, indulge your senses
(Lower defenses)
Skip the simulation
Dare to live in your body
(You won't be sorry)
It's a thrilling sensation
—Alice Bag, "Incorporeal Life"

CONTENTS

Introduction. Santa Anna's Wooden Leg and Other Things about the Chicanx Body; or, What Are We Really Talking about When We Talk about Chicanx Literature?   1

1. RACE: Dagoberto Gilb's Phenomenology   25

2. FACE: Cecile Pineda's Spectacular Blank Slate   57

3. PLACE: Authenticity, Metaphor, and AIDS in Gil Cuadros and Sheila Ortiz Taylor   91

4. WASTE: The Trash Fiction of Alejandro Morales, Beatrice Pita, and Rosaura Sánchez   119

Coda. Accordions of Abjection: Genealogies of Chicanx Punk   151

Acknowledgments   159

Notes   161

Works Cited   173

Index   183

About the Author   191

Introduction

Santa Anna's Wooden Leg and Other Things about the Chicanx Body; or, What Are We Really Talking about When We Talk about Chicanx Literature?

> You know, you have a lot of academics and you have a lot of politicians, and you have a lot of people sitting around saying, there's no such thing as a Latino identity. And then . . . you look around and you're like, "Nah that's nonsense." I think that I belong, and you all belong, to a moment when our community is knitting a larger identity in a really interesting and nuanced way. It completely escapes the politicians and the intellectuals.
> —Junot Díaz

In conversation with hosts Felix Contreras and Jasmine Garsd on NPR's music podcast *alt.Latino*, Junot Díaz, a Dominican American author, argues that despite diversities of class, race, and geography, there is still a tie that binds US Latinxs. That was not the case in the 1980s, he continues, when he was growing up listening to primarily English-language hip-hop. In 2016, Díaz marvels, his young goddaughters have plenty of Spanish-language music in their collections and feel free to embrace the salsa, merengue, and bachata upon which Díaz and his friends turned their backs in their youth.

For Díaz this is a sign of something that politicians and intellectuals cannot see, something that transcends market shares and voting blocs. To those, for example, who would argue that a Cuban American politician from Florida could never speak to the concerns of, let alone be embraced by, Chicanx activists in the Southwest, Díaz presents the language of music and the intangible filiations it conjures.[1] There is something that unites us all, Díaz asserts, even though Latinxs come from many different places. But what is this thing that evades the intellectual's grasp? What does nuanced knitting entail, and what is Díaz referring to when he talks about "identity"? What, most importantly, are the stakes of, and what role do the arts play in, pulling "identity" together?

These questions motivate *Racial Immanence*. In the following chapters I explore what it means to talk about Chicanx literature in a political and intellectual climate that minimizes at the same time it dangerously maximizes the value of human difference. Despite increasingly visible state violence against people of color as we move further into the twenty-first century, many still believe that the election of an African American president in 2008 heralded the dawn of a post-racial United States, a belief the US Supreme Court reinforced in *Shelby County v. Holder* (2013). "Our country has changed," wrote Chief Justice John Roberts in the majority opinion for that case (Roberts).[2] Critical theory has changed, too. Having confronted the internal contradictions of humanism, scholars now explore the posthuman. The planetary consciousness of the anthropocene, cyborgs, technoculture, and the formal utopias of object-oriented ontology are all philosophical domains where race, ethnicity, and inequality appear to have little purchase.

Alongside these political and intellectual attempts to render raced bodies invisible or insignificant, the number of Latinx bodies in the United States has been steadily increasing. In 2014 Latinxs accounted for 17.3 percent of the total US population, compared to just 6.5 percent in 1980 (Stepler and Brown). Latinxs are currently the largest minority group in the United States, and by 2060 the US Census Bureau expects Latinxs to make up 28.6 percent of the total US population (US Census Bureau). This population growth, moreover, has since the early 2000s been fueled more by US births than by immigration, inflammatory rhetoric notwithstanding. Latinxs are a constitutive and increasingly unavoidable segment of the US population, and they are overwhelmingly (63.9 percent) of Mexican origin (Stepler and Brown).

These statistics have, since the 1980s, motivated a range of projects— political, commercial, and intellectual—aimed at generating knowledge about this growing population. The data motivate me as well and illuminate my approach to untangling the questions raised by Díaz's observations about Latinx identity and the stakes of Latinx cultural production. Data show both that there are many Latinxs in the United States and that our numbers will continue to grow. We must, therefore, pay attention to Latinx voices, and, comprising the significant majority they do, in the general population if not in academia, Chicanx voices can be taken as illustrative, if not exemplary, of broader Latinx trends.[3] Beyond pure numbers, though, the historical, social, and political connections between the United States and Mexico condition twenty-first century *latinidad*. I am thinking here specifically of the militarization of the US-Mexico border, which I turn to in the fourth and final chapter of this book, and the structural impact it has had on what it means to be Latinx (not just Chicanx) in the United States, regardless of national origin. If for no other reason than this, it behooves us to attend to Chicanx voices in particular. But how can we listen if, as Díaz contends, Chicanxs and Latinxs are speaking at inaccessible frequencies? How do we—and why should we—attend to the invisible and the inaudible?

Problems

Our current strategies for reading literature by people of color do not directly answer this challenge. In *The Social Imperative*, for example, Paula Moya argues that textual analysis is key to racial understanding. In her introduction she describes being "challenged by faculty colleagues working in the social and natural sciences to demonstrate how literary criticism might contribute to an understanding of" race and gender, and even to explain "the value of literary criticism for the production of knowledge generally" (1). This she connects to a general sense of the humanities in crisis, especially in literary studies, where scholars struggle with increasing doubts that "literature or its criticism can provide the keys to our liberation" (5). In response to this crisis Moya proposes a return to basic principles, asserting the value of close reading "in the context of a changing American society in which literacy about race and ethnicity will be needed more than ever" (5). Close reading, she argues, is key to understanding how "race, ethnicity, gender, and sexuality structure individual experience and identity," and this, in her final analysis, is why it is important to read and study literature (6).

Moya believes that literature has ideological impact because close reading influences a reader's perception of the worlds and peoples represented in a text. While scholars of Chicanx and Latinx literature may not all share Moya's faith in close reading's ability to promote "racial literacy" (6), they do tend to share her assumption that literature represents things in the world and that one of its primary functions is to communicate these things to readers.[4] This is what I mean when I refer to "reading representationally" or "reading for representation," and in *Racial Immanence* I argue that such an interpretive mode marks a division between reader and text that can preclude meaningful engagement.

While Moya asserts that race must be represented in order to be understood, Mel Chen argues the opposite. In *Animacies*, a study of the "alchemical magic of language," Chen shows how language forms, hierarchizes, and coerces matter (23). "Words more than signify; they affect and effect," writes Chen (54). Language, that is, does not just reflect the world; it makes, breaks, and shapes it. In a parallel theoretical vein, both Walter Benn Michaels and Jodi Melamed see representational reading as an impediment to social change. To read as Moya suggests performs a version of what Michaels in *The Beauty of a Social Problem* calls "neoliberal aesthetics," which he defines as a way of looking that reduces art to its subject, to "hierarchies of vision" that occlude their underlying economic conditions (63). Melamed makes a similar argument in *Represent and Destroy* when she notes that "liberal terms of difference have depoliticized economic arrangements" by shifting the meaning of race away from material inequalities toward representational otherness (xvii). As Michaels links this to developments in aesthetic theory, Melamed similarly associates this formal anti-racism with literary multiculturalism as practiced in US universities that, she argues, destroys the potential of anti-racist knowledge (xi).

These pitfalls notwithstanding, I believe that we *can* attend to race without destroying it. To do so, however, we must reimagine the relationship between bodies, words, and the world. In any given moment of reading, texts are doing so much more than representing experiences, the appreciation of which will produce better, more empathic citizens. Reading for representation anticipates learning what we already think we know. By contrast, the works I bring together in *Racial Immanence* gesture rather than represent, and gestures, as Juana María Rodríguez reminds readers, "are where the literal and the figurative copulate" (4); gesture "highlights intentions, process, and practice over objectives and certainty" (Rodríguez 5). The bodies encountered in *Racial Immanence* gesture; they do not look, behave, or signify as anticipated. In these deviations they disrupt the temporality of expectation; they force a lingering that redefines politics as "something we await" rather than "something we arrive at," to borrow Sandra Ruiz's formulation (337).

In the following pages, for example, I read race as the unseen, unheard, and ineffable unifier that Díaz describes. The artifacts I explore are less interested, however, in the visible, external signs of race and more in the materiality of race as a physical condition of experience. My interest in matter continues a lively conversation around the multiple significances of race and ethnicity begun by Michael Omi and Howard Winant when they first published *Racial Formation in the United States* in 1986. As they make abundantly clear in their now classic and foundational study, race is both a process and product of modernity. It is, they assert, an idea, a "fundamental concept that has profoundly shaped, and continues to shape, the history, polity, economic structure, and culture of the United States" (106). In their third edition Omi and Winant admit that "the body was largely under theorized in our earlier accounts" (viii), but their more recent attempts to foreground the racial body rely on the ocular dimensions of race, on how the visual differences between bodies acquire social meaning through racial projects (109). While I concur with Omi and Winant that race is as pervasive and consequential as the air we breathe, I am not content to see bodies as passive and inert objects of racial formation. Omi and Winant understand bodies as "visually read and narrated in ways that draw upon an ensemble of symbolic meanings and associations" (111), but I prefer to grant the body and biology more active agency in the making of race.

For many years, though, and for good reason, scholars have operated under the assumption that race is not biological. It is a slippery slope from materiality to colonial eugenics, as Omi and Winant remind readers (24). To navigate that slipperiness, I take inspiration from Michael Hames-García, who wonders "what race might be beyond a means for oppression and exploitation" (331). Taking as a starting point the assumption that the body "is an agential reality with its own causal role in making meaning," Hames-García explores the mutual constitution of biology and culture in order to argue a biological theory of race as a temporally variable phenomenon that emerges from the interplay of matter and socioeconomic forces (327). Likewise, I read the body not as a sign, or token, of subjectivity but as something more like the oscillation of current and voltage upon which, as Jane Bennett describes in *Vibrant Matter*, the US electrical grid is based (26). Race, in this analogy, is like the play of active and reactive power guiding the rhythms of current and voltage, intangible, but very, very real.

Omi and Winant, similarly, say that they "cannot dismiss race as a legitimate category of social analysis by simply stating that race is not real" (110). Race has real social consequences, they argue, even if it lacks a biological root; for them, race is both "located on the body" and "the means by which power is 'made flesh'" (247). Like Omi and Winant, I see race as both noun and verb but understand it to be *in* rather than *on* the body. Race, this is to say, might not be locatable in the biological real, but it is nevertheless, I argue, a form of physical, affective experience that catalyzes personal and political change in the world. If race is merely an abstraction of geopolitical power, and the human body is a mutable, historically contingent phenomenon, then what, I ask in *Racial Immanence*, to make of the attention to disease, disability, abjection, and sense experience increasingly visible in Chicanx visual, verbal, and performing arts at the turn of the 1980s into the 1990s? What can this attention to physicality tell us about the real, political stakes of Latinx cultural production?

Answering questions like these demands a reading method that neither privileges nor essentializes the distinction between reader and text, that sees their imbrication and understands that Díaz's "larger identity" is a red herring. Though it has received the most critical attention, identity is not what matters in Díaz's Pulitzer Prize–winning tour de force *The Brief Wondrous Life of Oscar Wao* (2007), which explores the history of the Dominican Republic through a science fiction–obsessed Dominican American protagonist. The titular Oscar is *ni de allí ni de allá*, from neither here nor there, steeped in US popular culture but living always in the shadow of his skin and the story of his mother's country. Oscar's identity is a distraction from the real matter of *latinidad*, which asserts itself less as a matter of content than of form.

The Brief Wondrous Life of Oscar Wao suffers, charmingly, from a near total lack of nuance. It tells the reader exactly what to think of it, Oscar, and the Dominican Republic in didactic prose and with even more aggressive footnotes glossing the action and explaining the many historical and popular culture references. Even after the novel's publication Díaz did not stop unpacking for his readership, annotating, for example, sections of the novel online.[5] These notes enjoyed a warm reception in the popular and scholarly press, but they can be read as obfuscating just as much as they reveal. What if we thought about them as resisting, rather than inviting, interpretation?

Díaz's footnotes in *The Brief Wondrous Life of Oscar Wao* prioritize the act as much as the subject of writing, and on *alt.Latino* Díaz emphasizes the knitting as much as the knitted. His formulation shifts the focus of the conversation from object to action. This is the same move that political theorist Cristina Beltrán makes in *The Trouble with Unity* when she titles her conclusion "Latino Is a Verb." People identified as Latinx, she writes, "do *not* represent a preexisting community just waiting to emerge from the shadows. Instead 'Latino politics' is best understood as a form of enactment, a democratic moment in which subjects create new patterns of commonality and contest unequal forms of power" (157). On the one hand, Beltrán sounds here like one of Díaz's clueless intellectuals; on the other hand, her discussion of "enactment" as creating new modes of political community grants import to Díaz's knitting and provides a new way of understanding his politics of form.

In *Racial Immanence* I attend to form as a mode of political action along the lines Beltrán describes. My primary vehicle for these explorations is the human body and the role it plays in Chicanx cultural production at the turn of the 1980s into the 1990s. Of course, artists attended to the body *before* the 1980s, but bodily meditations increase so significantly by the end of the twentieth century that, in addition to establishing a genealogy of corporeal musings, *Racial Immanence* asks what about this period prompts such marked attention to physicality in Chicanx arts. By theorizing Chicanx artists' uses of the body, *Racial Immanence* makes a historical argument about how Chicanx cultural production responds to late twentieth-century neoliberal encroachments on the economic, political, and social lives of communities of color. In so doing, I also put forward different models for thinking through how "Chicanx" and "Latinx" signify in the twenty-first century and how these concepts can be socially and politically leveraged.

Abstractions

Interlude 1: The Leg
The Battle of San Juan de Ulúa began in the early morning hours of December 5, 1838, when the French navy landed 1,500 men on the shore at Veracruz. It led to a decisive French victory in the 1837–1838 "Pastry War" between France and Mexico.[6] In the frenzy of the fight, General Antonio López de Santa Anna, commander of the Mexican forces at Veracruz, was severely wounded in his left leg with shrapnel from a cannonball that also killed his horse. The leg was amputated below the knee the next day and returned to Mexico City, where it was blessed with a Te Deum and buried (East, "Wooden Leg" 51). Some time after that, Santa Anna visited the New York City offices of Charles Bartlett, a prosthetics manufacturer, who built a custom-designed leg for the general (Carl Johnson 1).

It was a beautiful leg made of lightweight, easy-to-maneuver cork, and fitted with a swivel joint at the ankle to allow for natural range of motion (Carl Johnson 3). Santa Anna was surely sorry to lose it on April 18, 1847, when Samuel Rhoades, John Gill, and Abraham Waldron, members of the Fourth Illinois Infantry, stole it at the Battle of Cerro Gordo during the 1846–1848 US-Mexico War.[7] The Fourth Infantry was assigned to attack Santa Anna's troops, who held a key mountain pass blocking the US Army's advance into Mexico City. Santa Anna escaped the surprise attack, but was forced to desert his carriage, which held, along with his leg, $18,000 in gold and a lunch of roast chicken. Upon discovery of the carriage, Rhoades, Gill, and Waldron ate the chicken, turned the gold over to their superior officers, and took the leg back to Illinois as a spoil of war.

Santa Anna's amputated leg suffered the vagaries of his political misfortunes. After he lost political power, the leg was reportedly stolen from its tomb, dragged through city streets, and left at a garbage dump (East, "Cork Leg" 169). His prosthetic leg, however, remained in private, US hands for decades, enjoying adventures of its own. Its captors charged ten cents a head to view it in Illinois, but the leg also apparently traveled. Correspondence suggests that it was displayed in London's Crystal Palace (East, "Cork Leg" 169) and news reports indicate that P. T. Barnum had it on view in his American Museum in the years immediately following the war (Harris 62). The State of Illinois gained possession in the early twentieth century, and the leg received little attention until 1942, when the state assembly passed a resolution to return the leg to Mexico. This much-protested resolution was never carried out. Instead, the leg was put into storage until 1974, when the Illinois National Guard included it in a mobile historical display that traveled to Washington, DC, in observance of the American Bicentennial (Carl Johnson 5). After that it was put on permanent display in the Illinois adjutant general's office in Springfield, in which city visitors today can see Santa Anna's wooden leg presented in a diorama replicating its scene of capture at the Illinois State Military Museum.

The story of Santa Anna's wooden leg comprises most of the elements of my argument in *Racial Immanence*. The leg could be read as a parable of US-Mexico relations, but Mexico has its own conflicted relationship with Santa Anna and never launched an aggressive campaign for the leg's repatriation. The leg on display in Illinois, moreover, is prosthetic, not flesh of Santa Anna's flesh, and it was made in the United States. The Fourth Illinois Infantry captured a representation of a representation (figure I.1). P. T. Barnum presented America with a vision of its desire to possess a Mexico of its own manufacture, undermined by the ambiguous "nature" of the leg and the controversial character of the man to whom it was attached. The leg, therefore, cannot be read representationally. Let us consider it instead as an occasion to accept Hames-García's invitation to think of race beyond subjection and disempowerment, to see the prosthetic limb as an unknowable illusion, a shade of human form that cannot be grasped, the circulation of which knits other objects together in ever-shifting patterns of the real.

A key question for me in *Racial Immanence*, then, is whether or not it is possible to think of race as something more than a human construct, to see Santa Anna's leg as something other than a surrogate limb. What if, I wonder, inspired by the artists gathered within these pages, race is something real and material that nevertheless eludes language? Can we think of race without subjection? Can we imagine the body—can we imagine Santa Anna's leg—not as indexing a racially managed subject but as an object among objects? How does Chicanx cultural production help us think of race as something that exceeds the individual, and what are the political and ethical implications of that imagining?

Figure I.1. A life-sized diorama at the Illinois State Military Museum in Springfield, of US soldiers capturing Mexican general Antonio López de Santa Anna's wooden leg. Photo courtesy of the author.

To explore these questions, in writing *Racial Immanence* I have had to fight my own desire to interpret; I have instead forced myself to linger in the experience of reading to sense how *chicanidad* is not represented but produced in moments of textual engagement. Rather than make meaning, I have tried to honor texts' resistance to interpretation. Modeling a transportable method, I have crafted readings as moments of what political scientist William Connolly theorizes as "emergent causality." He defines this as "the dicey process by which new entities and processes periodically surge into being" (179). Doing this, I have responded to Antonio Viego's call in *Dead Subjects* for revised notions of ethnic subjectivity that are "guided by the refusal of what we are currently made to be" (29).[8] We should not, Viego argues, expect twenty-first-century Latinxs to act like or be guided by the behavior of historical Latinx subjects. He sees Latinx studies projects as motivated by a desire to root the future in a continuation of the past, a move that he says "drains the future into the past and burrows the past into the future" (22). Such historicist expectations produce, according to Viego, "dead subjects" unable to move forward in time, whereas he advocates for the flourishing of Latinx subjectivities that refuse to perform institutionally recognized *latinidad*.

Santa Anna's leg, I contend, refuses to perform the drama of the US-Mexico border. Such refusals, I argue, are where the progressive potential of Chicanx and Latinx cultural production lies. *Latinidad* rests on a set of social expectations that must be upended if *latinidad* is to be anything other than an ethnic performance dictated by an Anglo-dominant majority.[9] If, as Connolly argues, political change relies on intervening in *how* people perceive the world, rather than on changing *what* they perceive, *latinidad* must create moments of experiential dissonance wherein Latinxs refuse, in Viego's words, "what we are currently made to be" (29).[10] Viego finds that dissonance in Lacan's refutation of ego psychology; for Cristina Beltrán, embodied political action is crucially dissonant; and Juana María Rodríguez reads queer gestures, either literal movements of the body or figurative manipulations of "how energy and matter flow in the world," as dissonantly performative (4). Such moments disrupt the temporality of expectations; they render the future perennially surprising, impeding linearity and suspending time.[11]

That suspension can be the work of *latinidad*. Parallel efforts can also be made in Latinx studies if scholars create moments of intellectual dissonance wherein we refuse to look at and for that which our institutions have come to expect. Viego argues that "Latino," a famously empty signifier eluding specific class and race distinctions, occupies a liminal time between a future knowledge and an always already knowing. "The temporal paradox," explain Joshua Guzmán and Christina León, "collapses the demand for knowledge with an anticipation that forecloses any serious encounter with the object" (271). The now of *latinidad* is always already lost, constantly performing itself in the present moment of Anglo consumption, allowed neither past nor future.

Guzmán and León conjure "another 'now' for *latinidad*" (263) and in *Racial Immanence* I answer their summons to linger in the ambivalent present of *latinidad*, "to slow down the work of understanding *latinidad* and instead to dwell in the space of its many times and places" (272). To linger in the now of *latinidad* is to draw back from the desire to know and to turn toward the appreciation of an embodied present that does not necessarily point toward a future understanding. Lingering means embracing the future contingent as an emergent causality that halts the linear flow of an appreciation of the other that already knows what it wants to know.

Instead of learning what they already know, readers of *Racial Immanence* will witness the objects gathered herein fostering networks of connection that deepen human attachment to the material world. Readers will be challenged to think of text as a physical engagement and to see reading as a process of connection rather than interpretation. To consider reading as merging with the stuff of the world opens the door, as I explain more fully in my final chapter, to an ethics of shared vulnerability that reimagines the political.

Methods

Interlude 2: The Zine

In 2015 Maricón Collective, a group of queer artists and activists from East Los Angeles, produced a limited run of exact replicas of the first two issues of Joey Terrill's *Homeboy Beautiful*. Maricón Collective were known as public historians who organized community-building dance parties with publicity materials featuring its members' queer Chicanx art. They produced a zine of their own, but with the *Homeboy Beautiful* reissues, they paid homage to a pioneering queer Chicanx artist.

Terrill's life, explains Richard T. Rodríguez, "represents a remarkable archive of Chicano, gay male cultural and political engagement consistently ignored or rendered nonexistent by revisionist scholars and activists" (467). Since the 1960s Terrill has performed politics through his art and activism, building, as Rodríguez describes, a "repertoire of interlocking lived, artistic, and activist practices" that made it possible to be queer and Latinx in the public sphere (467). *Homeboy Beautiful*, which Terrill printed and circulated in the late 1970s, was one such performance.

A tongue-in-cheek satire of popular women's magazines, *Homeboy Beautiful* includes segments on fashion such as, in issue 2, "Leather for Homegirls" and a "Homeboy Makeover" in which a group of homeboys kidnap "Joseph Cornish," an Anglo librarian, and make him over so he looks like a "native of Lincoln Heights." Included are photos of a violent beating described as massages to Cornish's back and neck with a two-by-four and "fancy footwork to ease away tension in the pec area." There is an advice column, and, in issue 2, there are journalistic pieces like "Exposé: E.L.A. Terrorism," in which Santo, an investigative journalist, embeds with a "radical homeboy terrorist group" engaged in "White-people kidnappings!!!!" In this photo essay the group kidnaps a couple from their home in West Los Angeles. The group finishes the couple's board game before taking them back to East Los Angeles and forcing them to eat tortillas, chilies, and menudo. They are then made to watch Spanish-language television before the group leaves the couple dazed and confused on the streets of East Los Angeles.

The violent silliness of issue 2 culminates in the takeover of the *Homeboy Beautiful* editorial offices by the "homo-homeboy terrorists," who put up political banners and spray-paint slogans across the walls. "We the Homo-Homeboys of Los Angeles," they declare, will hold the *Homeboy Beautiful* editor hostage until "we feel that *Homeboy Beautiful* magazine sincerely attempts to represent the 'ambiente' of Homo-Homeboys in their publication." Even as the zine pushes against Anglo-dominant representations of *chicanidad*—placing a newspaper clipping declaring, "In case you hadn't heard, *Chicanismo* has come of age" next to an announcement, "Next Issue: Passing into White Society"—it recognizes intra-communal tensions over hetero- and homonormativity.

Even as it makes these explicit arguments about representation, the zine's overall playfulness and convoluted narratives of undermined editorial control make it difficult to read as an argument for accurate reflections of a community. Even as it offers imagistic and textual windows onto queer Chicanx life, those words and images drip with a sarcasm that highlights representational struggles rather than represented objects. *Homeboy Beautiful* does not, in other words, represent queer *chicanidad* so much as it performs the struggle for survival and visibility. Maricón Collective's exact copies of Terrill's originals, by extension, do not so much assert a genealogy of queer *chicanidad* as argue that the struggle for visibility continues in the twenty-first century in terms not so different from Terrill's in the 1970s.

Because Maricón Collective's copies of Terrill's zine do not use the past moment of Terrill's production to anchor a progress narrative leading to their present-day Chicanx cultural expression, their twenty-first-century

Figure I.2. Maricón Collective, *Homeboy Beautiful* cover (reissue 2), undated. Illustrator unknown. © Maricón Collective. Courtesy of the UCLA Chicano Studies Research Center.

reissues of *Homeboy Beautiful* linger in an eternal now of queer *chicanidad* (figure I.2). The collective performs a perpetually self-ironizing struggle for visibility that anticipates never arriving at the moment of being seen. This refusal of linear time is also present in the content of the original zine; for instance, issue 2 opens with an editorial apology for its own lateness, refuses the coming of age of "*Chicanismo*," has no formal indications of its date of issue save for references to California propositions 6 and 13, and characters in vignettes are usually late or pressed for time, operating—like the zine itself—beyond the bounds of temporal expectation.[12] *Homeboy Beautiful* awaits itself, and Maricón Collective's reissues are an iterative performance of a performance of lingering.

As a genre, zines demand reading that lingers, that focuses on process over product, on representational strategies rather than represented objects. Zines, as Stephen Duncombe explains, are "noncommercial, nonprofessional, small-circulation magazines," which their creators produce, publish, and distribute by themselves (6). They are products of passion that "communicate the range, however wide or narrow, that makes up the personal interests of the publisher" (Duncombe 10). Zines are a means without end; nonnarrative, noncommercial, they are modes of creative self-expression requiring, according to Todd Honma, neither technical skill nor adherence to any particular ideology or aesthetic. Zines are often thought of as individual endeavors, but they can be, as Honma argues, important community-building tools that promote a "participatory culture, in which everyone is encouraged to contribute according to their own capacities towards a shared collective experience." Terrill's *Homeboy Beautiful* and Maricón Collective's reissues function both ways, as individual expression that is then cultivated, continued, and circulated by and through a collective of artists, activists, and community members.

To read *Homeboy Beautiful* as a work of Chicanx literature, then, demands considering the zine not as a representation of queer *chicanidad* but as both archive and actant of a particular social movement. This mode of reading must be nonrepresentational while also recognizing that Chicanx texts often have *real* stakes that matter in the *real* world. In *Racial Immanence* I limn this contradiction with a way of reading built around how racialized bodies flicker between indexical and materialist understandings of language. *Homeboy Beautiful*, to illustrate, hovers, with words and images, between meaning and mattering, yet the zine's investments in race and gender linger. It remains socially and politically aware, that is, but refuses to clearly signify. That refusal makes sense only if we read in a way that brings both text and the human body into the fleshy folds of the stuff of the world.

I do this in *Racial Immanence* by mediating a philosophical argument between object-oriented ontology (OOO) and new materialism, whose disagreements open a radical space in which it is possible to read literature by people of color for things besides representation. OOO insists on the reality of things that can be neither known nor seen, but it flattens the work of language and prevents readers from achieving any great textual insight. New materialist theories of language, on the other hand, greatly expand our textual imaginations but offer no way to appreciate the significance of *chicanidad*. In this introduction I represent these fields in the work of Graham Harman and Karen Barad, respectively. From their points of tension and overlap I draw the building blocks of my own method.

A cornerstone of my approach is to insist on the reality of race despite its lack of genetic basis.[13] Omi and Winant do this as well, but Harman's work makes possible a consideration of race beyond the bounds of human sociality, and Barad offers the tools for keeping race rooted in the material world. Things exist whether or not we know about them, says Harman, rejecting the notion that things that cannot be thought do not, for all intents and purposes, exist. In fact, Harman writes, "the vast majority of relations in the universe do not involve human beings" (*Immaterialism* 6). If we thought of race as one such relation, it might be possible to read a Chicanx text, for example, for the ways it consciously resisted all attempts to "know" it instead of expecting it to teach readers something about Mexican Americans. Harman calls this "a *weird* [as opposed to naïve] realism" in which things actively resist interpretation ("Hammer" 187). Harman sees this as a form of what he calls "withdrawal," a denial of substantive connection between words, things, and reality. This keeps him from seeing texts as active agents in the world, however, and leads to his substituting language games for textual analysis ("Hammer" 201).

Karen Barad, on the other hand, with whom Harman takes explicit issue (*Immaterialism* 14, 16), postulates "intra-action" over "interaction" as a way of understanding the relationship between words and entities. "Why," she asks, "do we think that the existence of relations requires relata?" (130). What are the political and metaphysical stakes, she wonders, of dissolving the discrete boundaries around words? "Discursive practices are not . . . linguistic representations," Barad contends, thus reimagining language as an agential intra-action catalyzing the emergence of matter into time-limited discursive practices (139). Barad rejects Harman's distinction between ontology and epistemology, arguing that knowledge is gained not through observation but through embodied presence, by being in the world.

Drawing on both Barad and Harman, but mindful of their significant differences, in *Racial Immanence* I read in a mode best described as "choratic." Doing so, I extend Rebekah Sheldon's generative work on "chora," which Plato describes in the *Timaeus* as both the place *in which* and the stuff *from which* a supreme craftsman formed the universe. "Chora's" status as both space and stuff has long puzzled philosophers.[14] Sheldon's contribution to this conversation is to deploy "choratic reading" as a strategy for discussing the "emergent property" of matter that works "in the gaps between its actants" but "slips the noose" of language (Sheldon 209). This is, at bottom, what I mean to evoke with "racial immanence," a method of reading choratically that emphasizes form as both the matter and energy of text.

"Racial immanence," which receives a fuller explication in my first chapter, entails understanding race as animating the infolding of matter that coalesces into the cultural production at hand, as both constituting and being constituted by text. Reconceived in this way, language, human bodies, and all the matter of the world become intra-actional performances. *Homeboy Beautiful* appears as enacting political struggle rather than representing politicized subjects. Reading representationally stakes political claims built around subjectivity, rights, and human agency. What is the impact on reading, then, if we, as Guzmán, León, Beltrán, and Connolly do, pursue a radically different understanding of politics as affective moments of lingering and potentiality in productive tension? This brings me to the question I pose in my introduction's subtitle: what *are* we talking about when we talk about Chicanx literature?

In *Racial Immanence* I treat texts as things rather than objects, not as things that represent other things, but as things in and of themselves. *Homeboy Beautiful*, for instance, forces a reading of itself as a thing that enacts and performs political struggle without resolution; it is an event that asks us to broaden the scope of actions that constitute "reading," and it embodies the kinds of resistance to neoliberal aesthetics that runs as a thread through my chapters. To read it and the various other things gathered within these pages, I take as my methodological starting point Bruno Latour's challenge in "Why Has Critique Run out of Steam?" to revivify criticism by shifting our attention away from matters of fact to matters of concern. "What if," Latour asks, "explanations resorting automatically to power, society, discourse had outlived their usefulness?" (229).

What would it mean to read Chicanx literature, then, if not as verbally indexing the ways that oppressed social subjects experience power? Such a reading strategy requires thinking of literary texts not as reflective objects consumed by reflecting subjects, but as events in and of themselves that exist in and make the world.

I build readings that eschew a distinction between subjects and objects in favor of considering texts as "things" as Latour defines them: as either object, event, or place, as a "gathering" or an "issue" that launches a "multifarious inquiry" into the nature and motivations of a particular coming together. *Homeboy Beautiful*, to illustrate, does not represent actual queer Chicanxs from the 1970s. It deploys highly ironized stereotypes who sometimes appear in frame but sometimes, as in the case of "Homeboy Makeover" from issue 2, remain largely off-stage to indicate their status as figments of an Anglo-American imaginary. In the zine, queer Chicanx concerns linger in the province of text and drawing, awaiting their emergence into the photographic real, just as the broader queer political debates hover in the background of issue 2 as so many spray-painted slogans signaling a political future at which queer Chicanxs have not yet arrived and adumbrating a political present in which they are not fully seen. Their invisibility, though, is rendered not as disempowerment but as an effect of intra-communal struggles over the plurality of queer *chicanidad* reminiscent of Beltrán's insistence on the impossibility of Latinx politics.

Homeboy Beautiful makes room for a queer Chicanx future that had not in 1978, and still has not as of this writing, arrived. In bringing the zine together with Santa Anna's leg to introduce the things in my chapters, I aim to critique, as Latour suggests, not as "one who debunks, but as one who assembles" ("Critique" 246). The interludes in which I present the leg and the zine suspend the time of reading to invite reflection, to encourage looking without interpreting. I have avoided analyzing the leg and zine in favor of appreciating them as events, as flashpoints illuminating my methodology and gesturing toward the theories that ground it. These interludes also indicate how I am thinking about the human body in this book, as stuff existing in synergistic relation to other stuff, not bound by narrative constraints. This approach—critique by assemblage—proffers a way to think about Chicanx cultural production as doing something other than reflecting history or subjectivity. Approaching texts as events and bodies as confederations of things pushes us to think about what else Chicanx literature might be doing.

I write "something other than reflecting history," but it is true that the literary texts at the core of *Racial Immanence* emerged in the late 1980s and early 1990s, which also saw the consolidation of a "Hispanic" middle class in the United States and the promotion of the "Decade of the Hispanic." This was a time of high visibility and increased rhetoric around Latinx concerns, but also a time of decreasing household incomes and heightened political antagonism (Stepler and Brown). In literary historical terms, this period corresponds with the emergence of queer *mestizaje* in the very influential writings of Cherríe Moraga, Gloria Anzaldúa, and others whose work depicts subjects in contradistinction to bourgeois white heteronormativity. While Anzaldúa does write extensively about the unruly body as a conduit for philosophical revisions of subjectivity—as I discuss in chapter 4—she remains most known, valued, and anthologized for the queer subject she ushered into print. In bringing together a very different set of texts from the same moment, by contrast, I propose another way of characterizing this period of Chicanx literary history. The authors in *Racial Immanence* respond to the corporate consolidation of "Hispanic" identities not by asserting counter-subjectivities but by undermining representation and visibility as political and aesthetic strategies.

Praxis

I tease out this undermining in my readings by connecting textual bodies to a series of extralinguistic objects. Though the literary works I discuss were produced mainly in the 1980s and 1990s, the material objects in my study trace a chronological sweep from fifteenth-century Aztec stone carvings to twenty-first-century Chicanx punk rocker Álvaro del Norte's accordion. My argument in *Racial Immanence* works both chronologically and by accretion, simultaneously providing and interrupting a temporal structure by unfolding a specific historical period into interlocking moments of lingering. First, I trace a microhistory of racialized objects, beginning with the central premise that objects always resist, in one way or another, the desire to own them. Though this looks different at different points in time, from it can be extrapolated an enduring truth about our inability to know "things."

I follow this idea through a series of accretive chapters that reimagine political community and the work of reading and writing. Communities comprise bodies, and *Racial Immanence* is about how bodies create choratic networks that are both in and of the world. In each chapter the body is an occasion to linger, and in these moments the intersections of race with time, visuality, the planet, and the extraterrestrial are figured anew. Attending to the machinations of the body, I argue across my readings, posits the body as a portal through which the imbrications of the political and the aesthetic can be reconceived. In this I have been inspired by Stacy Alaimo's germinal work on transcorporeality, her neologism for the ways "the human is always intermeshed with the more-than-human world" (*Bodily Natures* 2). I turn to Alaimo most explicitly in chapter 3's discussion of AIDS and the Latinx political imaginary, but her influence is apparent across the entirety of this book.

Chapter 1 takes up the work of Dagoberto Gilb and the compromised bodies that inhabit his fiction. Here I am interested in the relationship between sensation and language in Gilb's work and how bodies produce their own temporality, their own lingering moments during which race becomes an immanent condition of his protagonists' experience of time. I frame my analysis with a discussion of the discovery in 1790 of the Aztec calendar stone in Mexico City. There is no clear anthropological consensus on the purpose or meaning of the stone's markings, which convey time as well as events of geologic, religious, and political significance. In its fusing of time and space, the stone allows me to present temporality and materiality as intertwined and race as the chora from which these concepts issue in Gilb's fiction.

These ideas ground my explorations of the body in the remaining three chapters. In chapter 2 I postulate the body as mediator of form as well as stuff. Reading Cecile Pineda's novel *Face* (1985) together with contemporary art and commercial photography, I argue that the body is both form itself and a thing through which form passes; it mediates between forms by being both the subject and the structure of the photographs in the novel and the photo projects I read alongside *Face*. In addition to choratically mediating things and forms, the body marks a crisis of signification in my reading of Chicanx AIDS fiction in chapter 3.

There, my framing object is barbasco, the wild Mexican yam from which synthetic hormones were first derived, thus enabling the development of, among other things, oral contraceptives. In addition to interrupting the linear time of heterosexual reproduction, barbasco's size, root structure, and resistance to commercial cultivation occasion a rethinking of indigeneity and global markets. I use this reimagined indigeneity as a lens through which to read Gil Cuadros's and Sheila Ortiz Taylor's depictions of the body as mediating sex, death, and the roots of culture in *City of God* (1994) and *Coachella* (1998) respectively.

Chapter 4, finally, moves from Cuadros's and Taylor's earthly concerns to ponder the body's mediation of technology and the extraterrestrial. Using the work of contemporary Mexican digital installation artist Rafael Lozano-Hemmer's idea of "participation platforms" to ground my reading of two Chicanx science fiction novels—Alejandro Morales's *The Rag Doll Plagues* (1992) and *Lunar Braceros*, by Rosaura Sánchez and Beatrice Pita (2009)—in chapter 4 I explore how bodies interact with and mediate geographic, planetary, and political spaces. In chapter 3 I consider what it means to ground the body in specific places or to depict bodies as being out of place, but the novels in chapter 4 inspire an exploration of what it means for the body to both physically constitute and be physically constituted by space.

Situating the body as an object among objects, my chapters create a material archive, a network through which to reimagine the racialized body. Each chapter advances a way of reading the body in relation to different epistemes—time, form, planetary consciousness, and bio- and cyber-technology—that bring us back to at the same time they appear to move us away from racial considerations. I offer, within these pages, a way of reading that sees the body as doing something other than representing a set of racialized experiences. Santa Anna's wooden leg may be directly tied to the experiences of a specific community, but racial immanence and the ways of reading that it makes possible are transportable.

To illustrate that claim, and by way of closing, I turn to *King of the Hill*, the animated series about the Hill family, their friends, and their adventures in the fictional town of Arlen, Texas, which ran on the Fox network from 1997 to 2009. "The Final Shinsult," the thirtieth episode of *King of the Hill*, aired on March 15, 1998, just a few years after the implementation of the North American Free Trade Agreement (NAFTA) in 1994.[15] In "The Final Shinsult," Santa Anna's leg is making a cross-country tour of the United States before being returned to Mexico, and Arlen will be its last stop. Bobby Hill's middle school is performing a play about the leg and planning a field trip to visit it at the Arlen Museum. Bobby's father, Hank, convinces his own father, Cotton, to help chaperone the trip. Cotton, who has recently failed an eye exam to renew his driver's license, is thrown into even more of a rage when he learns of the leg. "You see, Bobby," he yells, "your daddy's generation is giving away everything we fought for!" The "Shinsult" of the episode's title refers to Cotton's anger about the leg as well as the ongoing humor the series finds in Cotton's diminutive stature. "A man who gave his shins to win the Second World War," explains Hank's friend Dale, "has earned the right to drive an automobile."

Later in the episode, the museum director stops the school bus as it is leaving and accuses the children of having stolen the now-missing leg. Hank heaves a beleaguered sigh and tells the children that he will now close his eyes and wants to see the leg when he opens them. He turns his head and opens his eyes to gaze into the distance, where he sees Dale and Cotton sneaking away from the museum. Cotton has Santa Anna's leg strapped to one of his own, the other is strapped to Dale's, and the two men hobble toward Dale's car as if competing in a three-legged race. When Hank later confronts them, Cotton and Dale refuse to tell Hank where the leg is, revealing, after Hank leaves, the leg's hiding place on a makeshift altar in a broom closet, sporting a fuzzy pink slipper, surrounded by holiday lights and empty beer bottles.

When the police finally come for the leg, Cotton tells them, as he resists arrest, "I need that leg for leverage in my negotiations with the Mexican government!" The leg is, however, eventually returned to Mexico in a ceremony at the Arlen Museum. City officials formally hand the leg to a retired Mexican army captain who, like Santa Anna, is missing a leg. "When he straps on Santa Anna's leg and walks it from our flag to his it will be officially returned to the Mexican people," Bobby's mother, Peggy, tells him. The captain straps on his leg and begins to walk, but before he can reach the Mexican flag the leg shatters under his weight. "Hey, wait a minute," says Bobby's friend Joseph. "That's the leg I made for the play." The episode closes with Cotton in Mexico exchanging the original leg for a driver's license.

We can read "The Final Shinsult" as exemplifying how Santa Anna's leg continues to resonate as a sign of NAFTA-induced economic anxiety, the giving away to Mexico of everything the United States feels it has rightfully earned. We can also see the leg in this episode as the objective correlative of national desire. As Cotton's body fails him, his investment in the Mexican prosthesis increases, with the result that his desire for the leg tells us more about his own feelings of inadequacy than it does about US-Mexico relations. Such insights are not novel, nor do they employ novel methods. I offer these analytic options as a call to reconsider the work of reading.

In *King of the Hill* Santa Anna's wooden leg gestures toward the collective frailty from which grounds a new political imaginary might emerge. Joseph's papier-mâché leg cannot support the political theater of international relations surrounding its return. A different kind of theater surrounds the original leg, however. Dale and Cotton's altar is a performance of devotion demanding embodied, cooperative action that remains off camera. We do not see them building it together, but the way they clink their cocktail glasses together as they look at the altar suggests that it was a joint effort. The original leg binds characters to each other, draws them into a web of historical and physical concerns. In a moment of comic relief, the leg physically unites Dale and Cotton as their bodies stumble awkwardly as one. Similarly, the idea of the leg unites Cotton with the Mexican captain at the ceremony in Arlen, and both men are connected—across time, space, and national borders—with Santa Anna. At the same time, the episode flatly refuses maudlin readings of disability by depicting the leg as a token of material exchange that allows Cotton to finally get his driver's license, thus achieving his longed-for freedom and mobility.

Desire is tricky, though, and how can we ever really be sure what Cotton longs for? "The Final Shinsult" reminds us that if we are reading to learn about the other, we are reading, most likely, to learn what we already think we know, to see what we want to see. What, then, does Santa Anna's leg mean? That, at the end of the day, is not a particularly useful question. Whether in P. T. Barnum's circus or on *King of the Hill*, representations of the leg will tell us about their representative moments, not the leg itself. And yet, there is still a leg there. An encounter with the leg produces a certain kind of affective experience with Chicanx resonance. What can we say about that experience? About the leg? Why do they matter?

These are the questions I grapple with in *Racial Immanence*. This book is a critique of representational reading and a searching out of other ways to think about the value of race and ethnicity in the arts. Within these pages, race becomes immanent and speculative, a historical node or catalyzing agent of the different trajectories my objects trace. The corporeal in *Racial Immanence* becomes transcorporeal; the human body becomes not a metaphor for subjectivity, but a way to articulate a philosophy of transformative and leveling interconnection.

1

RACE

Dagoberto Gilb's Phenomenology

Because something serious was going to happen. He knew it, knew it in his bones.
—Dagoberto Gilb, *The Last Known Residence of Mickey Acuña*

In 1790, during a project to level the zócalo in Mexico City, workers uncovered the Piedra del Sol (Sun Stone), a massive stone monument to the Aztec calendar that Alonso de Montúfar, the second archbishop of Mexico from 1551 to 1572, had ordered buried sometime around 1559. Though a few Europeans had likely seen the Sun Stone around the time of the conquest of Mexico, and Diego Durán, the Dominican friar who in the sixteenth century produced some of the best-known accounts of pre-conquest Mexico, appears to write about it in his *History of the Indies of New Spain* (1581), by 1790 it had been long forgotten. Since 1790, however, the Aztec Sun Stone has become one of the most famous archeological objects in the world, puzzled over by scholars and venerated by mystics and seekers.

The Sun Stone is everywhere and nowhere, endlessly reproduced on all manner and size of objects, yet fundamentally unknowable and mysterious. It is an irregularly shaped basalt slab weighing 24.5 tons, out of which has been carved a disk with an 11'5" diameter. The disc comprises a series of concentric circles containing an unidentifiable face in the middle surrounded by images of human hearts, glyphs representing previous suns, or worlds, and signs for the twenty days of the Aztec ritual calendar beginning with Cipactli (Alligator) and ending with Xochitl (Flower).[1] Around the outer edge of the Sun Stone are two *xihcoatls* (fire serpents), tails meeting at top, faces confronting each other at bottom (figure 1.1).

Figure 1.1. Piedra del Sol (Sun Stone), Museo Nacional de Antropología. Photo by El Comandante.

These images have long absorbed researchers, though in the years immediately following its rediscovery scholars primarily debated how the Sun Stone was used and for whom it was created. The past century of scholarship, as Khristaan Villela, Mary Ellen Miller, and Matthew Robb explain, has dwelt mostly on iconography and ideology, with scholars parsing the meaning of the stone's many glyphs and learning to sit with the impossibility of knowing for certain who or what is at the stone's center. According to Villela, Miller, and Robb, this shift of attention from use to ideology is due to the assumed transparency of Mesoamerican calendars. Ross Hassig, however, in *Time, History, and Belief in Aztec and Colonial Mexico*, argues that Aztec temporality is both more and less complicated than scholars have previously thought.

The Aztecs, like all Mesoamerican cultures, maintained two calendars: a 260-day ritual calendar (the *tonalpohualli*) and a 365-day solar one (the *xihuitl*). The Sun Stone contains glyphs associated with the former, though the two calendars were imbricated. Hassig describes the Aztec calendar as "composed of multiple, interlocking cycles of days, building into still larger cycles, until the culmination of 52 years, which itself repeated endlessly" (159). The fifty-two-year cycle was called a *xiuhmolpilli* and could be bound into the *huehuetiliztli*, or double calendar round, forming, according to Hassig, the temporal building block of Aztec historiography, which had a definite cyclical cast (8). Hassig, however, warns against granting cyclicity too much importance, arguing that there is ample evidence that the Aztecs operated with linear historical understanding and manipulated time for political gain.

The Sun Stone thus embodies a beautiful set of contradictions. It gestures toward a calendar of whose use and significance no one can be entirely sure, bearing images nobody fully understands, projecting competing notions of time. Its materiality, its impenetrability, and its politicization of time correlate in this chapter to my reading of corporeality in the work of Dagoberto Gilb, a late twentieth/early twenty-first-century US author. Across the whole of his oeuvre Gilb, as I will argue, uses the human body to narrate a durational sense of time. As the Sun Stone gestures toward the opposition of indigenous to colonial time, Gilb's temporal elasticity forces readers away from narrative time toward the time of the body that refuses to be known. The corporeal time Gilb enacts with his writing is a lingering, such as I describe in the introduction to this book, that is on par with the erratic cyclicity of the Sun Stone.

By drawing this parallel, I do not mean to invoke a mystic indigeneity that stands in contrast to the European temporality informing colonial politics. Time was just as political, and frankly just as colonial, for the Aztecs as it was for the Spanish. To call Aztec time cyclical is to call attention to the fact that, unlike the Mayan long-count calendar, the Aztec calendar lingers in the *xiuhmolpilli*. It repeats instead of progressing. To call that cyclicity erratic is to call attention to the ample documentary and monumental evidence suggesting that Aztecs understood themselves as political actors not beholden to the ideology of their calendar. Time was flexible for them, in other words, and not nearly as fatalistic as it may initially appear.

There are many things scholars do not understand about Aztec timekeeping, such as when the Aztec day began, or how the Aztecs understood hours, for example. Because the Aztecs appear to have used no clocks, sundials, or other timekeeping devices, their time, observes Hassig, "was task focused, inherently contextual, and thus necessarily elastic" (36). He grants, moreover, that many archival sources pertaining to the calendar contradict each other (35). A certain amount of temporal pliability is to be expected, then, in studies of any Mesoamerican culture, but the Aztecs appear to have directly and purposefully manipulated time.

The archives describe, as one would expect, the moving of important events such as military or trading expeditions to more providential days, but birthdays and other fixed occurrences were often changed as well, suggesting, as Hassig argues, that ordinary Aztecs saw the divinatory powers of the calendar as avoidable (36). Aztec leaders went beyond changing their relationship to the calendar; they manipulated time itself by, as Hassig describes, occasionally double counting days (38) and moving the New Fire ceremony, which marked the end of one *xiuhmolpilli* and the beginning of another (39). The Sun Stone itself stands as monumental evidence of one of the Aztecs' most significant temporal changes: the stone indicates the existence of a fifth sun, or world, in contradistinction to the four suns accepted beyond the Valley of Mexico, a change that Hassig suggests was made to both assert Aztec political authority and explain the fact that the world did not end when the *tonalpohualli* suggested it should have (65). These deliberate alterations suggest that the calendar controlled neither Aztec belief nor action, and, moreover, that they understood time as a political tool.

Calendars are inherently political. As Hassig argues, "political concerns create the calendar, manipulate it, and use it for practical purposes" (71). It is a commonplace to set Aztec cycles against the Mayan long-count, but the Aztecs bound their calendar rounds and enumerated events in chronicles that indicate linear notions of time. This suggests, as Hassig asserts, that the calendar did not necessarily condition Aztec belief so much as it served political purposes in helping to regulate tributes across the empire (123). Hassig argues further that contemporary notions of Aztec time are a legacy of Spanish friars who, concerned about the ways Aztec ritual overlapped with Catholic, placed outsized emphasis on its cyclicity at the expense of its linearity. "Modern theoretical biases have reinforced this inheritance from the colonial perspective," Hassig concludes (162).

Despite the colonial emphasis on Aztec cyclicity, I maintain that the Sun Stone presents a resistant lingering by rendering time as a fungible site of political resistance and aggression. The Aztecs engaged in both: they used their calendar to control their outlying tributaries, and indigenous timekeeping persisted well into the colonial period, with many early records indicating European and native dates (Hassig 140). The Sun Stone paves my way into Gilb as an impenetrable object that defamiliarizes and denaturalizes time. The Sun Stone makes the visceral, colonial politics of time fleetingly visible, much like Pancho Villa's death mask in one of Gilb's early short stories.

In his story "The Death Mask of Pancho Villa" (1993), an unnamed narrator is roused from bed in the middle of the night by his friend Gabe. The narrator, who has not seen Gabe for a while, is surprised by Gabe's visit and wonders at the mysterious stranger Gabe has with him. Román Ortíz, Gabe explains, possesses one of three existing death masks of Pancho Villa, whose memorabilia the narrator collects.[2] Ortíz plans to take the mask to Moscow, where the journalist John Reed, who wrote *Insurgent Mexico* (1914) about his four months traveling with Villa, is buried. Gabe wants the narrator to come see the mask, but the narrator, who must work the next day, declines. Before leaving, Gabe and Ortíz drink some beers and smoke a joint with the narrator, who, at the end of the story, is left wondering why Gabe really came to see him and why he, the narrator, refused to play along.

Like much of Gilb's fiction, "The Death Mask of Pancho Villa" is short on plot; it has no clear conflict and no resolution, circulating instead around questions concerning the relationship between the human body and historical narrative. The painfully self-conscious narrator wonders about his vulnerable, aging body in relation to Villa's mask and the history it symbolizes, while the story itself posits the corporeal trace of the mask against the textual trace of Reed's history. "Death Mask" asks us to consider whether body or text conveys greater historical truth, or whether, as Mel Chen argues, language functions as an "embodied condensation of social, cultural, and political life" (*Animacies* 13). In "Death Mask," that is, like Villa's mask, body and text operate as congruent, corporeal forms of knowledge.

The whole of Gilb's oeuvre can be read as an extended investigation of this relationship between body and text, and yet it is not common to read Gilb as making interventions in philosophical debates about meaning and ontology. He is certainly well known, and well received as a Chicanx chronicler of Mexican American lives on the border, having published two novels and several short story collections. Bridget Kevane's very favorable review in the *New York Times* of Gilb's most recent short story collection describes a narrator's "struggles with his Chicano identity." Peter Donahue, moreover, reads *The Last Known Residence of Mickey Acuña*, Gilb's 1994 novel, as the drama of Mickey Acuña's coming to terms with his own cultural identity (33). Readings of Gilb tend to follow this pattern, paying scant attention to Gilb's philosophical explorations of the body, time, language, and what it means to know.

But that is exactly what I am interested in here. In particular, I am interested in how, for Gilb, knowing is not opposed to feeling, and what that non-opposition means for reading Chicanx literature and writings by people of color more broadly. Embodied experience is a chief concern in Gilb's writing, but he does not depict it in antagonistic relation to language or cognition. Quite the contrary, the subject in this chapter's epigraph knows—he does not feel—something in his bones. Affective experiences, like those of the narrator in "Death Mask," have value for Gilb, but that value is neither ideological nor post-ideological. That is, Gilb's fiction seems to argue that physical feelings do not represent some truth about racial experience, nor do they offer a way to transcend the ideologies of race.

Feeling is not the domain of a post-racial utopia in Gilb's writing. His work foregrounds ethnic experience and is characterized by an intense, almost playful attention to language. Yet stories like "Death Mask" do not suggest that feeling exists apart from language or that race is discursive. Conversely, we might read Gilb as suggesting that race constitutes language, that words, as Mel Chen describes them in *Animacies*, "complexly pulse through bodies (live or dead), rendering their effects in feeling and active response" (54). Such a view as Gilb's and Chen's relies on an understanding of feeling far removed from theories of affect articulated by Brian Massumi and his followers, anti-intentionalists who believe that our feelings are precognitive and can thus potentially liberate political subjects from their ideological confines.[3]

Massumi's work has been roundly criticized by historians of science like Ruth Leys, who contends that humanists misunderstand and misuse scientific data, ignoring the long history of neuroscientific debates surrounding the relationship between affect and cognition. Only a very small percentage of "thinking" is entirely cognitive, Leys notes, citing one scientific school of affect studies that understands "thinking" as largely nonrepresentational practices of embodied habit (Leys 452). Similarly, Chen, emphasizing speech as a "corporeal, sensual, embodied act" (53), describes language as a series of "multimodal, conceptual directives" that happen simultaneously and constitutively in body and brain (52). Gilb's fiction, which assumes the mutual interplay of mind and body, parallels Chen's language theory and occupies the middle ground between the opposing schools of scientific thought on affect described by Leys. But Gilb is not making scientific arguments, and neither am I. What I aim to do here is use the ambiguity surrounding affect to frame my readings of Gilb and to outline a nonrepresentational way of reading race.

This poses a not insignificant methodological challenge since, as Chen notes, it is nearly impossible to read any other way. Since Western philosophy's linguistic turn in the early twentieth century, language has, Chen writes, become "bleached of its quality to be anything but referential, structural, or performative" (53). Inspired by Chen's work on the animative, vivifying, and material power of language, in what follows, I track Gilb's inscrutable yet influential bodies across three texts: Gilb's short stories "Death Mask" (1993) and "please, thank you" (2011), and his first novel, *The Last Known Residence of Mickey Acuña* (1994). Throughout these three pieces, the body maintains an ambiguous and tenuous relation to language and narrative, hovering between the poles of materiality and abstraction in the same way the Sun Stone oscillates between linear and cyclical time. The human body refutes the death mask of ethnic labels in a deconstructive critique that leans toward a redemptive, if unknowable, materiality in "Death Mask." *Last Known Residence* embraces the mysteries of the body as the protagonist, Mickey, turns away from the pursuit of knowledge to an appreciation of sense experience. Finally, in "please, thank you," the body becomes a way of being in the world, a mode of interpretation in which the protagonist, a recovering stroke victim, undergoes hours of confusing "speech therapy" that appear to him to have little to do with speech. Thus we move, in the twenty-year trajectory these texts bookend, from physical disquietude to a productive sense of "sense."[4]

To get at this sense of the imbrication of words and feelings, or text and body, I read choratically, borrowing from Rebekah Sheldon's work as I describe in the introduction to this book, in order to propose a concept of "racial immanence." With this phrase I do not mean, as Manthia Diawara does, to imply racial truths or pure racial characteristics.[5] Quite the contrary: there is no racial truth; "racial immanence" is shorthand for my argument that language, especially as Gilb deploys it, is part of an embodied, racial process. With the term I play on Kant's transcendent categories of thought to suggest race not as an abstraction but as derived from the material world. Race might elude totalizing narration, but that does not mean it is beyond our perception. Here I am influenced by Quentin Meillassoux's rejection of "finitude": the idea that absolute knowledge of any sort is impossible, that we can know the world only as it is revealed to us, through, according to Maurice Merleau-Ponty, our bodies.[6] Race might not be a transcendent category of truth, in other words, but it is, I argue, a category of physical, affective experience that catalyzes personal and political change in the world.

The Immanent Time of the Body: "The Death Mask of Pancho Villa"

Race functions as just this sort of catalyzing agent in Gilb's writing, and racial immanence is, in many ways, a strategy of disidentification. As José Muñoz defines it, "disidentification" describes "the strategies the minority subject practices in order to negotiate a phobic majoritarian public sphere that continuously elides or punishes the existence of subjects who do not conform to the phantasm of normative citizenship" (4). Gilb's deployment of the body is a disidentification with racial discourse in the majoritarian and the minoritarian contexts of ethnic studies. He privileges the body but not, as Merleau-Ponty does, as a means of achieving knowledge about the world. Gilb's approach to sensory experience more resembles that of Henri Bergson, whose theories of sense, duration, and narration, as I explicate below, illuminate Gilb's fictional project, which relies on close, at times clinical, attention to human bodies that function for him, as the Sun Stone has for centuries of archaeologists, as durational, nonreferential narrative objects.

In "Death Mask," for example, the narrator uses his physical imperfections to limn the outlines of a truth he cannot narrate. He tells the reader that he has been "getting soft" (17) from being out of work, that being barefoot makes him feel vulnerable to violence (18, 19, 21), and that he sees Gabe as "somehow being healthier than" him (19). The narrator perceives, but can neither fully understand nor articulate, his physical imperfections. Gabe's lighting a joint makes the narrator want to go back to bed, which confuses him as he usually enjoys smoking. He accepts the joint because he does not "know how to say no to this too" (21). The narrator has trouble understanding other bodies as well as his own. He takes careful note of Gabe's body language but can interpret it only as "some excess of something" that he "can't figure out" (22). Ortíz's body, too, confuses the narrator: "his gauntness . . . translates into something else [he] can't quite put a name on" (19), and his smile, which contrasts sharply with his awkward and otherwise humorless demeanor, is disturbing (19, 21).

This attention to physical health, gauntness, and inarticulable excess foregrounds the body in ways that invite analysis within a disability studies framework. Two problems arise from such an approach, however. First, while several key disability studies works share my interest in the interplay of bodily sense and social knowledge, they focus primarily on representations rather than enactments of sense experience, and I read Gilb as interested in the latter.[7] Second, while disability scholars do take careful account of disability as a function of global capital's attempts to manage the body, race is often seen as just one facet of such management.[8] Foundational works in the field tend to assume that the disabled body grounds all other physical particularities.[9] While more recent scholarship moves away from identitarian hierarchizing toward increasingly philosophical and ecumenical considerations of physical difference, such work still puts representational pressure on bodies perceived as different.[10] It is a slippery slope from representation to identity, an explanation of being that Gilb's work, with his imperfect bodies driving readers relentlessly away from meaning, is designed to resist.[11]

Just as scholars have been unable to identify the face at the center of the Sun Stone, bodies in Gilb's fiction refuse to become objects of truth; refusing knowledge of any sort, they represent neither things nor ideas. Affect theory presents itself as a welcoming home for fiction such as Gilb's that dwells on, but explicitly rejects interpreting, the body, and yet affect theory also tends to suborn race to a universal physicality. Scholars have long understood race as an ideological construct, exactly the sort of thing that affect theory might help us move "beyond." As Gregory Seigworth and Melissa Gregg explain in their introduction to *The Affect Theory Reader*, affect is "the name we give to those forces beneath, alongside, or generally other than conscious knowing" (1). If race is ideological, a function of "conscious knowing," then where do we find it in a story like "Death Mask"?

Race in "Death Mask" is wholly immanent. It manifests at the end of the story, after the narrator has definitively refused to see the mask, and he describes himself, after forcing Ortíz to justify his travel plans for the mask, as having "stolen his smile" (25). The stealing of the smile is a moment of racial immanence where history can be narrated only through bodily interaction. The men's bodies become a site of conflict that remains unwritten; the body's opacity masks interpersonal tensions that cannot emerge in narrative form because the narrator can only physically experience rather than comprehend them.

I use "race" rather than "ethnicity" to describe this sensory entanglement between the narrator and Ortíz, and it is crucial to keep the difference between the two terms in mind when thinking through racial immanence. Race, a concept developed from purportedly biological characteristics, has been used to justify all manner of state-sanctioned violence against people of color and to systematically exclude them from institutions of power and social mobility. Ethnicity, on the other hand, is seen as an index of cultural affiliation, mutable and multiply signifying.[12] Those distinctions are evident across Gilb's writing, but complicated in their analogy to body and mind respectively, or sense and language, putative oppositions whose imbrication Chen explains in their discussion of cognitive linguistics (52), and whose entanglements Gilb's writing reveals. Race, however, remains at the core of Gilb's exploration of sense experience, particularly in "Death Mask's" scene of the stolen smile.

The physicality that escapes narrative—that stealing of the smile—allows the action to remain on narrative's periphery and outside time. When the narrator returns to bed, his wife asks him what time it is, which "makes [him] smile all over again" and reply, "What's the difference?" (26). Time does not matter to the narrator, who remains in the now of physical experience. To think in terms of time and its organizing structures would vitiate the significance of the physical exchange between Ortíz and the narrator, which has something to do with Villa and the Mexican Revolution. That historical experience marks the men's bodies in ways beyond the historicity of narrative logic. The narrator cannot answer his wife's question; he can only deploy his stolen smile.

Gilb's eschewal of narrative time and logic recalls the mystery of the Sun Stone: was it meant as a connotative or denotative representation of time? His rejection of telos also puts Gilb in close conversation with Bergson's work on time, language, and experience. For both thinkers, language is a function of sense experience, not knowledge, part of the human experience of intuiting, not knowing, which unfolds over time and has no cognitive teleology (Guerlac 107). For Bergson, all beings are enmeshed in a web of dynamic matter where change and action occur via the transmission of stimuli, like words, and matter is ultimately "nothing but a path along which" the energy of change passes (*Matter and Memory* 36). Merleau-Ponty identifies Bergson's conflation of subject and object as a "mistake" that "consists in believing that the thinking subject can become fused with the object thought about, and that knowledge can swell and be incorporated into being" (*Phenomenology of Perception* 62). Unlike Merleau-Ponty, however, Bergson is interested in action, not speech—presence, not representation—a preference paralleled in Gilb's writing.

Gilb's racialized bodies do not represent knowable, ethnic selves. The Mexican Revolution and its indigenous heroes are important to the narrator of "Death Mask," but the reader never learns why, and the particularities of the narrator's life are so insignificant that the character remains nameless throughout. The narrator is simply *present*, by which term I mean to indicate both "here" and "now." The significance of presence for Gilb's work becomes clearer when read through Bergson, for whom presence is transformation, and "to be" is to be always in the process of changing. Presence, for Bergson, is impossible to narrate because subject and object interact not in sequential time but in duration. He defines duration in *Time and Free Will* (1889) as "the form taken by the succession of our inner states of consciousness when our self lets itself live, when it abstains from establishing a separation between the present state and anterior states" (100). Suzanne Guerlac clarifies, succinctly explaining the difference between duration and time when she writes that "time is the symbolic image of Pure Duration.... It is what duration becomes when we think and speak it" (69). Language, the realm of the symbolic, typically removes us from pure experience, according to Bergson—time is to duration as language is to sense, in other words—but I contend that Gilb uses language and narrative not to represent but to enact a sense of duration.

For example, we can read the narrator in "Death Mask" asking his wife what difference time makes as Gilb staking a narrative claim and articulating the terms of his fictional project. The exchange between the narrator and his wife presents the reader with two ways of conceiving time and history: the wife operates in a teleological mode in which the sequence of events gives them meaning; the narrator, on the other hand, eschews chronology and time—"What's the difference?"—to argue that the body retains a historical knowledge that resists narrative's organizing logic, just as the Sun Stone has refused to be archaeologically known. The body's resistance to text and narrative time is a core tension of Gilb's writing around which I organize my readings of *Last Known Residence* and "please, thank you." How to make sense of the fact that Gilb's temporal resistance unfolds in a form that conditions temporal existence? Narrative gives shape to duration; it puts physical, human time into historical time, contextualizes it and gives meaning to action, as Paul Ricoeur has discussed.[13] In what follows I look at how, in *Last Known Residence* and "please, thank you," Gilb has grappled with this aesthetic, philosophical, and political conundrum.

Bodies in Time: *The Last Known Residence of Mickey Acuña*

Last Known Residence opens by presenting the reader with a protagonist, Mickey, desperately trying to make narrative sense out of his sense experience. Constantly telling stories about himself, Mickey often cannot remember whether his stories are fact or fiction. He perceives his stories about Mexico as "bullshit" that "was allowed as plausible" by other characters as a way to "help pass boring time using noisy words" (44), and his own ancestry is explicitly referenced only once, early in the novel. He is an "American, a U.S. citizen of Mexican parents, one from this side of the río, one from the other" (11). Mickey understands himself as a Mexican American telling "bullshit" stories that other characters are afraid to question. In place of this "bullshit" the novel offers moments of racial immanence during which the narrator argues against Mickey's narrative cynicism. Mickey perceives his inability to tell effective stories as a failure of language. He sees language as the way to truth, but his challenge over the course of the novel is to understand language as a function of sense; Mickey must learn to value duration over time and sense experience over cognition.

Mickey's journey toward embracing sensation emerges from the tension the novel presents between form and content, as in the early scene when Mickey first meets Ema and immediately imagines that a great romance has blossomed between them. He suppresses the nagging suspicion that his love is imaginary and unrequited, but reality, in the form of physical contact with Ema and detailed descriptions of other bodies, impinges on Mickey's stories (20). As he and Ema walk through Ciudad Juárez, the corporeal materiality of Mexico's poverty and its subordination to the United States fracture Mickey's sense of self and narrative control. He intuits that his stories cannot create order out of this chaos, but the novel is not ready to give up on story altogether. Story shifts, over the course of the novel, from the past-tense, mental activity of Mickey "looking for clues" to his story's ending (40), to his future-oriented, physical certainty, "in his bones," that "something serious was going to happen" (127). By freeing Mickey from the cause-and-effect, linear patterns of scientific time, Gilb introduces the idea that causality and contingency are integral to the self, but require narrative creativity for their recounting.

The narrator's curious grammatical choices illustrate just such creativity. While Mickey throws away the western novel he's been reading because he is tired of its racist generic conventions (207), the narrator offers three grammatical workarounds for writing the things that cannot be written: the conditional tense, appositions, and double negatives. The conditional introduces contingency at the level of the word.

In sentences such as "He'd work out with weights. He'd push himself into major shape" (2), the conditional is used to indicate the future, but in other places its meaning is less clear. With apposite phrasings the narrator gestures similarly toward Mickey's need to appreciate shades of gray. Mickey wants to be prepared "for the better or the worse, mind and body" (2). He doubts the suitability of the YMCA for him because he "wanted anonymity, not publicity, privacy, not spectacle" (4). These appositions, this lexical bouncing back and forth, mirror the endless games of ping-pong Mickey plays at the YMCA and open an in-between space for the interstitial self to emerge: what is the ping-pong ball as it flies through the air? What is the middle ground between publicity and privacy, better or worse?

Gilb's use of the conditional and appositional clauses highlights Mickey's desire, implicitly subverted by our narrator, to construct a narrative world of surface. The narrator, conversely, makes consistent use of double negatives to force the point that language hides a world of meanings. Positivity lurks beneath the profusion of negative terms in double-negative constructions. For instance, the reader learns that while Mickey and his friend Butch enjoy each other's company, they both guard their private lives closely, and "that wasn't unlike anybody there at the Y" (55). Repeatedly using the negative to indicate the positive suggests that meaning lies in the difference between what is spoken and what is intended. Mickey reads this difference as an absence of meaning, but the narrator suggests that a deep significance lies in the novel's linguistic slippages, a point Butch makes when he tells Mickey, "It's not lo que dice [what you say], bro. It's how" (52).

With Butch the novel challenges Mickey to find significance in meaning's present absence. Mail, like meaning in *Last Known Residence*, is also present in its absence. Mickey waits for the mail to deliver what he describes to Fred, the YMCA desk clerk, as a "check with a bunch of zeros," an indeterminate indicator of either a lot, or very little (89). Other YMCA residents anxiously await their mail, one character is fired on suspicion of tampering with it, and another, Charles Townsend, collects mail from the trash and organizes it into dated bundles (202). Charles is unique amidst all the narrative attention to mail's absence in that he makes the mail visible in his attempts to organize it chronologically. The narrator suggests that Charles's efforts are in vain, however, when

Mickey discovers the bundles in Charles's room along with a .22-caliber pistol (202). Mr. Fuller, the YMCA manager, is later shot with a .22. Charles owns the gun, but Mickey has access to it, and the reader never learns for certain the identity of the culprit. Charles's abstract chronologies yield to the finality of the gun and death, from which no meaning can be drawn. Fuller's story has no resolution; the identity of his murderer is less significant than the fact of his death, just as the content of the mail is less significant than that it reach its destination.

The gun and the mail matter, but they do not *mean* anything. Mickey cannot tell a story about them, and so ideas about free will and sense certainty take center stage here in this moment of Mickey's narrative failure. For example, the scene of Fuller's murder is not described in the novel, but we read of Mickey's physical reaction to Fuller's death *before* we learn he has died: "It had happened. . . . And he was still alive. This he was absolutely sure of. He could hear his breath and heart beating. This was true. There was a strangeness in this sensation of life, a joy that ached like sadness" (212). Fuller's death shifts "truth" from knowing to being, from cognition to the sensual experience of the breathing, beating bodies.

Before Fuller's death, however, Mickey agonizes over what he can and cannot know, as well as whether he or some higher power is determining his actions. Mickey's anxiety is only heightened when Mária, who has been fired for allegedly tampering with the mail, tells him, "I didn't touch the mail, never," and reminds him, "Nothing is unintentional" (102). Earlier, Mária suggests that there is no intention but God's (83), but her double negative in this instance throws a shadow of doubt over such claims: if she did not never touch the mail, then perhaps she *did* touch the mail. God's intention may supersede Mária's, yet her choice of words reveals the possibility of her own, human intention. Logical puzzles such as this question about intention throw Mickey into a tailspin of doubt. But with Fuller's death, the human body emerges as will and vitiates Mickey's need to know. Mickey comes to the conclusion that his knowledge and choices do not matter: there is no such thing as a truth that stands outside the self's will to believe.

Mickey's choice of belief over knowledge is best understood in the context of philosophical debates over the nature and existence of free will. Throughout *Last Known Residence*, Mickey wonders why he is doing what he is doing, whether he is writing his own story or playing a part in a story that has already happened, whether he is, in short, acting of his own free will. Philosophy offers essentially two ways to consider Mickey's problem: his actions are predetermined or they are not; there is either order or chaos in the universe. On the side of order we have Benjamin Libet, who found that our bodies move and react to things before our brains begin processing relevant information, suggesting that the human capacity for rational thought has little bearing on what we do: our actions are predetermined through bioscience; there is no free will.[14] Libet straddles this fine line, though, arguing that free will resides in our capacity to veto undesirable actions. The more robust counter to such hard determinism points to the random catalytic action between agents. The course of particles through space and time might be predetermined but there is always that unexpected swerve, that coming together of forces producing something new that Merleau-Ponty referred to as folds in the flesh of nature.[15] This fold, or swerve, opens a space for human intention, like Mickey's belief or Mária's possibly touching the mail, and grounds the potentiality of free will.

Still the question remains: how do we exercise the will to control our actions in the moment of the fold? Can we be morally responsible actors? For Mickey this question is moot. Culpability for Fuller's death is unresolved; Mickey embraces the swerve, embraces the chances he embodies, and the novel closes with him wandering off into indeterminate border space. That conclusion reinforces the novel's larger argument that Mickey must learn to act on what he feels and not be incapacitated by his inability to know (just as the reader must forge on even though significant plot points are never resolved). For example, Mickey doubts Sarge's friend Philip's story about a local Mexican restaurant that has different menus for its Mexican and Anglo customers (67). Philip's lack of evidence, coupled with Mickey's inability to be precise about what evidence he would accept, prove to Mickey that the story is not true. But there is an element of truth in Philip's story that cannot be pinned down textually. Though Philip may have invented the story about the menus, racism is still an undeniable fact in El Paso: a force radiating from the lived experience of the brown, Mexican body. In the same way that the novel implies the insignificance or unknowability of truths such as Fuller's killer and the fate of the mail, here the novel suggests that Philip's invention of this story is more significant than its truth.

Race is immanent in the menu story: to believe Philip is to understand that race matters even if Mickey cannot know what it means. When Mickey recognizes that "you do have to decide," eventually, what will be true, he begins to perceive the experiential belief that resides in the body. Mickey eventually associates Mária's "nothing is unintentional" with the meaninglessness of the universe as he walks through the desert and comes to see the sky, the moon, and the earth as an encompassing emptiness. "Right then, he'd say, he decided" (196). This sense of emptiness, rather than evidential proof, helps him decide against hard determinism in favor of chaos. He begins to believe that he can make intentional decisions, though the reader never learns exactly what he decides.

Mickey is as in the dark as the reader as he moves into his uncertain future. He *is* certain, however, in his refusal to be tied to a past he cannot remember, to be a character in someone else's story. Ethnicity exemplifies just such a performance and so Mickey refuses this too, rejecting Chicanx identity as performed by Sarge and Omar, two fellow Chicanx residents at the YMCA. Omar, a "mixed metaphor" of defiant *chicanidad* (86), stands in opposition to Sarge's espousal of "American" values (35). Mickey is suspicious of both models of *chicanismo* as performances beholden to a higher authority of meaning. Omar and Sarge want to pin down the self, to make their racialized bodies mean something, while Mickey wants to let his sense certainty evolve into a future of its own mattering. For Mickey, identity becomes a process of historical and temporal negotiation. That is, history is significant, but the self cannot be overdetermined by it; history matters, but it doesn't mean anything. Mitchum Huehls has written on this paradox, noting that historical "content is irrelevant for producing meaning and grounding identity" in the novel while "the purely formal fact of past-ness" underlines the "foundationally temporal truth" of Mickey's life: that history is always a present absence, always past, always lost (Huehls, *Qualified Hope* 184). History is not a problem of knowledge for Gilb, according to Huehls, but rather an existential mode.

To illustrate, Mickey refers to "loop[s] in time" (2) or "location[s] in time" (74), which suggest that time is both nonlinear and spatial for him, an idea reflected in his anxiety over his story's conclusion and his feeling that he is actually reliving past events. To resolve this anxiety, he must, as the novel progresses, move away from a conception of time as space, as progression, to time as sense, toward Bergson's duration, or toward the unknowable temporality of the Sun Stone. Mickey intuits this in his argument with Sarge about Mexican politics. Sarge sees Mexico's problems as stemming from an inability to progress historically, while Mickey views history less as progress and more as process (45). When one of the imaginary commentators in Mickey's head declares, "Not everybody comes up the same way . . . there's a past you don't see or know about" (85), history is presented as one of many multiple states of consciousness Mickey might inhabit, something sensed but not known. To put this in Bergsonian terms, the past cannot be measured and narrated; it can only be sensed through the intuition of duration. This is analogous to the novel's broader theoretical assertion that the self cannot be known, but it can be believed, and belief is achieved via the body, through sense perception. Therefore, the force of history, ultimately, cannot be known via a performed ethnic identity such as Sarge's or Omar's; it can only be felt.

Mickey only comes to this understanding once he can act on his own sense perception, once he lets go of his anxiety over his inability to know. Finding significance in his own body is not enough, however. The novel suggests that in order for him to mobilize his new insights, to push himself to action, Mickey must come to terms with other troublesome bodies. He has to learn how to experience rather than understand the other, to intuit them instead of treating them as cognitive objects. "Others" for Mickey include women and queer characters, who test the limits of Mickey's narrative capacity.

Women pose the biggest challenge to Mickey, in part because he understands gender as corresponding with race. Mickey appreciates women as mystical, mysterious beings around whom he can craft elaborate fictions, but in his stories he objectifies as much as he subjectifies himself. Mickey breathlessly describes woman as "heaven and earth, the best of life itself," but he also says, "I feel how much she sees me seeing her" (46). That both Mickey and women exist as objects to be seen allows Gilb to correlate the narrative construction of femininity with equally fantastical narratives of race. When, for instance, a "cowboy" with whom Mickey has contracted for day labor refers to him continually as "mess-i-kin," Mickey retorts, "Don't call me *Mexican* again!" The narrator glosses, "It was often confusing when that Mexican word came up with people like the cowboy because sometimes it didn't mean anything and other times a lot," much like Mickey's check full of zeroes. The cowboy acquiesces, but continues, "They are the best women, though." Mickey replies that Mexican men would disagree, believing that "the light ones from this side have the pink nipples" (31). The dialogue draws a strong connection between gendered bodies and ethnic tensions, suggesting that the significance of race and gender lies less in the specific identities they reference than in their structural similarity as ways to manage human difference.

Though the novel hinges on Mickey's interpretations of his sense experience, race and gender are not abstractions for him. They matter just as much as the workings of his own body do. The novel refuses to privilege disability as a defining corporeal subtext, preferring instead to equalize all physical distinction as material with which the reader must grapple, just as Mickey must grapple with women like Isabel, the YMCA maid, who keeps Mickey from escaping into flights of narrative fancy. In his dealings with Isabel, Mickey is forced to contemplate reality, a reality signified in the novel by the disrupting presence of bodies that cannot be ignored. Mickey's conversations with Isabel are consistently punctuated by his neighbor's flatulence, and her physical activity in his room makes Mickey keenly aware of his own body (11, 45, 92).

Similarly, Lola, the waitress at the YMCA coffee shop, keeps Mickey's storytelling in check. These women signal the limits of language, where Mickey must grapple with his own status as physical object in relation to other objects. He experiences his own body as a confusing mystery, which he tries to control and order through a disciplined regime of physical exercise (100). Mickey sees that this is all for naught, however, when he is surprised by the instantaneous revelation of his body's own inner, intentional logic. When Omar teases Mickey about his excessive exercise, Mickey realizes, inspired by fantasies of physically harming Omar, that his exercise was all for a purpose: "at this moment he felt it was by design, not accident. Intentional" (190). Notably, his realizations do not unfold in space; they happen "right then" (191, 196) and "at this moment" (190) and they are sensual rather than cognitive experiences. The logic of the body unfolds in duration, in other words, in the moment of pure sensation that, for Mickey, is here figured as fantasies of bodily destruction, of kicking Omar's "fat butt," cracking his nose, and breaking his teeth (190). The intention Mickey discovers in his own body leads to his rejection of the absolute during his midnight walk (196) and a newfound faith in himself.

Physically sensing the intention of his own body pushes Mickey finally to act, to decide, to feel. Bodies are real in *Last Known Residence*; they refuse to have their differences categorized, hierarchized, or abstracted into racialized notions of the corporeal. Mickey privileges the sexed and raced body as a site of knowledge production; the novel refuses to construct those bodies as objects from which universal truths—such as the idea that disability trumps all other modes of physical difference—may be abstracted. *Last Known Residence* forces a consideration of the real: the troublesome poverty of Mexico that Mickey cannot narrate away, and the bodies broken by inexorable American values as ubiquitous as what Mickey, in conversation with Sarge, ironically refers to as "this good clean McDonald's food" (42).

Bodies All the Time: "please, thank you"

Last Known Residence fully realizes the redemption hinted at in "Death Mask": the human body is real in duration. What new idea of the self can emerge at this juncture, then, if the body is not the sign of some larger abstraction? Performances of ethnic identity like Sarge's and Omar's are moot in this case. Even the significance of history is up for grabs given Mickey and Sarge's disagreement about Mexico, and the temporal play combined with the elusive meaning of the Mexican Revolution in "Death Mask." How can the self emerge from materiality if the meaning of time and history is so unclear? Gilb's refusal of abstraction and the confusion of materiality in his fiction preclude a clear explanation of what it means to be a person in the world if personhood is rooted in the body rather than in ideas of what the body signifies. "please, thank you" (2011) unravels this puzzle.

The story, the first in Gilb's collection *Before the End, after the Beginning* (2011), features a protagonist, Mr. Sanchez, who is recovering from a stroke in a rehab facility.[16] Completely disconnected from his body, Mr. Sanchez does not recognize his own limbs. Contemplating his arm, which he had not realized he was lying on until a nurse moved him, Mr. Sanchez thinks, "a third arm and hand, not from my body. no, it is mine. or was" (5). As he struggles with his radically unfamiliar body, time loses coherence for him. We catch a glimpse of this as he observes his arm and moves from "is" to "was," "know" to "knew," shifting between present and past. More troubling to him is when his daughter reminds him that he told a doctor the year was 1994 (the year *Last Known Residence* was published), though he deflects his anxiety by asserting that the questions so annoy him he lies (6). Mr. Sanchez admits to himself, though, that he has no idea how long he has been in rehab, and he is never entirely sure what time of day or night it is. As Mr. Sanchez recovers, he finds himself reconsidering language and his patterns of speech as well as his own racial and ethnic identity.

Crucially time, not the body, is the initial index of the unfamiliar, and the story is bracketed by signs of instantaneity and the continuous unspooling of time. Attending to temporality as form, as this story demands, necessitates reading chorically for the imbrication of content and form. To illustrate, the opening sentence of the story is "at first, their people came and went" (3). The reader enters the scene in medias res, with visitors and medical personnel coming and going, but the scene remains in that instant. Gilb opens with "at first" but there is no chronological progression in the paragraph. He does not move to a "then." In fact, he switches to the present tense and describes the multitude of things that happen "at first": the visitors, the doctors' questions, and Mr. Sanchez's anger when they switch to Spanish, assuming that his lack of response is due to a lack of comprehension. The story's concluding sentences reinforce this sense of duration over scientific time: "were all moving onward. tomorrow someone else here" (24). They convey time as motion with no spatial progression. The missing apostrophe bears noting as well. This is a deliberate elision, as Mr. Sanchez has earlier described his post-stroke difficulties with spelling and punctuation. It folds being into time, conflates past with present as "we are" collapses into "were."

Mr. Sanchez's body is another site of present absence—like the missing apostrophe—where time and being are permeable. The expansive moment introduced with "at first" effectively contains all the action described in the story, but it proves initially confusing for Mr. Sanchez, who fumbles with chronological distinctions. Temporal indices lose their effectiveness as Mr. Sanchez no longer needs to keep track of time when his world has shrunk to his immediate surroundings. "i remember the era, just the other day," he says later on the same page as he thinks about "those educated lefties" of the past. In both instances, Mr. Sanchez's past bleeds into his present and the distinctions between the two are rendered moot by the continuous now of his body. In the process, the language he uses to describe his body evolves. Initially, he thinks of the difference between his body "just the other day" and his new "now." Once he begins narrating his physical therapy, however, Mr. Sanchez discusses his body in terms of "all the time." Facedown on a mat, unable to lift his leg, Mr. Sanchez thinks, "my past is past." On the one hand, this phrase emphasizes the past as distant and final, but it also indicates that Mr. Sanchez is done with the concept of past-ness. Humiliated by his inability to move, he thinks, "it is not yet time to quit." This "not yet time" evolves into the "all the time" that Mr. Sanchez then uses to describe the things he does with his body, like riding unbuckled in his wheelchair (16).

Mr. Sanchez's shift from "past" to "not yet" to "all the time" signals a shift from scientific time to duration, and it is this notion of duration that carries Mr. Sanchez outside himself to a connection with the medical staff surrounding him. As he begins to sense the contours of his new temporality, Mr. Sanchez takes note of the time the facility staff spend with him. "you work some long hours, scott," he tells one nurse (17). He notices that though another employee is slow, she works hard and arrives at the facility at six each morning (21), and one of his favorite employees, Stephanie, works "all the strangest, longest shifts." She tells Mr. Sanchez, "i only work these three days, but I have to sleep four to recover" (23). Mr. Sanchez connects to the staff (doctors are only referred to, they never appear) because he understands himself as a working man, a former Marine—"semper fi, cabrón" (3)—and an ironworker. He shares their class identity as well as the non-time of the facility. Mr. Sanchez and the medical staff coexist in duration, and that expansive moment allows Mr. Sanchez to understand his body in a new way: he cannot move himself; he is dependent upon others, enmeshed in a physical network of human care.

As time shifts from chronology to duration it demands new narrative modes, and it is through speaking and writing that Mr. Sanchez becomes fully embodied. Language and text produce Mr. Sanchez's sense of being in the world much in the same way, Merleau-Ponty argues in *Phenomenology of Perception*, that speech "does not translate ready-made thought, but accomplishes it" (178). Language, according to Merleau-Ponty, does not point to externalities but is itself constitutive of meaning insofar as language and speech are themselves physical acts. Chen, likewise, lamenting the absence of language discussions from new materialist theories, resonates with Merleau-Ponty in emphasizing language's ability to animate, or confer liveliness upon, "cognitive entities" (51). As Mr. Sanchez experiences the physical sensations of his remade temporality, therefore, language takes on entirely new dimensions of significance: his speech therapy expands into areas of his life he previously thought unrelated to language, and words become the means by which he unwittingly establishes connections with others. Words materialize shared duration as language is remade in the story from a sign of difference to a thing in itself.

Word literally becomes flesh in "please, thank you" when Mr. Sanchez describes his typing difficulties, which offer the reader another opportunity for choratic analysis. "i hate the mistakes i have to fix, the waste of time, the enthusiasm they drain," he types, and then goes on to describe the various mistakes he repeatedly makes (18). When he refuses to correct himself—"see those mistakes? im noy fixing them to show my point"—language becomes the material index of his physical struggle. It is not a sign; it is the struggle itself, the physical act he is plodding through, however clumsily.[17]

Mr. Sanchez's frustration with himself is not nearly as powerful as his ire over his speech therapy, which enfolds all aspects of his existence. "youd think speech therapyd be about speech," he complains (12). Instead, Mr. Sanchez finds himself organizing pills and balancing a pretend checkbook whose checks, dated 1981, are even more off the mark than Mr. Sanchez's earlier guess that it was 1994. He angrily resists his therapist's rigidity and structure: "she times things i do. I hate this. I hate this speech therapy," he fumes (12). Significantly here, in the image of the stopwatch-wielding speech therapist, chronological time is imbricated with confusingly abstract linguistic structures. Just as the story tweaks Mr. Sanchez's temporal sense, it playfully manipulates words and reimagines speech. Language still conditions experience, as the expansive speech therapy shows, but the story, through Mr. Sanchez's experience of language, reimagines the significance of speech.

As Mr. Sanchez recovers, speech becomes not a means of imperfect communication but an innovative means of interpersonal connection. An obvious example of this is his attempt to get his children to do his speech homework for him (18). More interesting is when he begins to adopt the speech patterns of others. He says "thank you," for example, to Scott, a nurse whose use of the phrase "thank you" Mr. Sanchez has previously found confusing (10), and when he thinks—he does not say this; he thinks it—that speech therapy feels "like Sunday school with mormons," his therapist asks how he knew she was Mormon (13). In both instances the lines between thought and speech, and even the distinction between characters, are blurred. Shared thought, shared language is the flesh that unites everyone at the facility, and it is how Mr. Sanchez ultimately, through his interactions with Erlinda, reimagines his ethnic identity.

"my typing is interrupted by erlinda, the custodian," Mr. Sanchez relates toward the end of the story (20). Typing, Mr. Sanchez's complicated physio-linguistic engagement with his post-stroke world, is halted here by Erlinda, a Spanish-speaking janitor from the suburbs of Mexico City who likes to talk to Mr. Sanchez because, according to him, "the only other person she gets to talk spanish to all day is the other janitor" (20). Erlinda can speak English, but she prefers not to if she does not have to, and in this scene she tells Mr. Sanchez about a fight she had at Walmart when a woman in line behind her complained about Erlinda's speaking Spanish. "so, she says, she told that woman in english that it was none of her business. that, see, she could talk in english" (20). This conversation results in a physical altercation, broken up by store guards, and Erlinda wants to know whether Mr. Sanchez thinks she did the right thing.

"but i don't know why she asks me. probably because theres no one else, besides beatriz, to tell?" Mr. Sanchez thinks (21). The only connection between Erlinda and Mr. Sanchez, he thinks, is that they speak the same language, and he doubts that is enough to justify her faith in him. When he asks Erlinda whether she really wants his opinion, "she says please. that makes it harder" (21). "Please" emphasizes to Mr. Sanchez how much Erlinda wants something from him that he is not sure he can give. As he struggles to formulate a response, he thinks, "i sit in the wheelchair much of the time now," a point of physical fact that Mr. Sanchez thinks devalues his opinion.

His response to Erlinda evolves from his feelings about the time of his body, the "much of the time" that is closely related to the "all the time" he experiences in physical therapy. Erlinda is part of the temporal fabric of the facility, the "all the time" Mr. Sanchez shares with the staff. Their connection is more acute because of their shared language, which Mr. Sanchez resents at the beginning of the story when doctors try to ask him questions in Spanish, but here is the means by which he is able to comfort and empathize with another. "stupid, mean people, they're just like that . . . its not everybody, its not all the time," he tells Erlinda (22). Mean people are *not* "all the time," but Mr. Sanchez's body and the relationships he forms at the facility are experienced in duration.

The advice he ultimately gives Erlinda is similarly temporal. "you just . . . move forward. why dwell on that ugliness? youre fine now," he says (23). He tells Erlinda to move forward, not to dwell on hatred, and the story ends with his observation that "were all moving onward. tomorrow someone else here," an implication of cyclical over progressive time that recalls the Sun Stone's cryptic duration. Throughout the story, but particularly in this scene with Erlinda, time and language are ways Mr. Sanchez can connect with some at the expense of others; they help him stand in solidarity with Erlinda against the mean people who are "not all the time." All the action in the story leads up to this conversation. The title comes from the close of their exchange, when Erlinda says "thank you" and Mr. Sanchez says, "please, no reason to say that" (22). He uses the "please" that Erlinda utters previously and which compelled him to answer her honestly; the "thank you" of the title references Erlinda's gratitude here but also Scott's "thank you" that Mr. Sanchez borrows despite finding it puzzling. "Please" and "thank you" are niceties that reference manners and politesse, but they are also, in this story, physical and material points of overlap between characters that connect them in a meaningful way. The words, that is, reference ideas outside themselves, but as things in themselves they are the choratic objects that connect Mr. Sanchez to the people who surround him.

These connections are cross-racial, but Mr. Sanchez also observes a value in particularity. He can borrow Scott's words, but he also sees his own similarity to Erlinda. That recognition lies at the heart of "please, thank you." Mr. Sanchez initially understands an ethnic identification as Mexican as a kind of handicap. He resists being spoken to in Spanish "like im from mexico and just crossed, not American like them" (3). He is racially conscious, but only in relatively facile ways: he jokes that he is being given pills "to keep my people down" (10), he tells his son that "white people work all the crazy shifts," and to himself he observes that Anglos "rule the world, even if they don't have any players of importance on any playoff team" (11). Such scattered observations about race isolate Mr. Sanchez. His challenge is to find value in his *mexicanidad* and to foster solidarity across racial lines. As he develops affection for Scott, who is white, Janette, a Haitian nurse, Deena, his Korean occupational therapist, and Nancy, his physical therapist about whose sexuality he is unsure (14), their categorical singularities diminish as he begins to see their unity in difference. Mr. Sanchez learns to connect with others in the web of care that fills the "all the time" of his recovery, and in formulating a response to Erlinda, he learns to value their shared heritage. "please, thank you" documents the emergence of Mr. Sanchez's relational self as the artificial borders of his body disintegrate.

Final Feelings

As his body rebuilds and recovers, Mr. Sanchez's race becomes a condition of his sense experience, from which he develops an ethnic identity predicated on positive attachments to other people. In this scenario race and ethnicity are modes of being in the world, not means of subjection. That is, there are no pills keeping Mr. Sanchez's people down in "please, thank you." There is only shared time, shared language, and shared—if differentiated—experience. To think of race in this way, as a mode rather than a knowable object, does not mean, however, that it is unreal, fictional, or imaginary.

But if we cannot know something, then how can it be real? What are things, like race, if not objects of cogitation? Philosophers have long argued about what it means to be and to know. Empiricists like Locke and Hume worried about getting to the truth of objects, whereas Kant stipulated that we could never know the truth of objects and should therefore focus on subjects. We cannot know things as they are, Kant argued, only as they appear to us; we can only know phenomena, not noumena. This is, essentially, Merleau-Ponty's position when he defines language as the culmination of thought. For all the emphasis he places on sense experience, Merleau-Ponty believed that we could only know things about which we could speak (*Phenomenology of Perception* 178).

If the only reality we can know is reality as it presents itself to us, do we then have no access to things as they are, to things that lie beyond our comprehension? Such a belief privileges the human in ways that seem unreasonable to more contemporary thinkers like Graham Harman, Levi Bryant, and other object-oriented ontologists, philosophers who see all entities (animate and inanimate) as objects of equal status in constantly shifting relation to each other.[18] Their decentering of human subjectivity grounds my own reading of Gilb's work as an argument, extended over several texts, that though race might be unquantifiable and inarticulable, it is nevertheless real. It exists beyond our comprehension, and our sense experience gives us limited access to it. In "please, thank you," for example, what Mr. Sanchez thinks he knows about race, correlating it to pills and shift work, is mere surface distraction. In "Death Mask," the narrator cannot narrate the significance of the Mexican Revolution, but the story reveals its profound physical influence on its racialized characters. Finally, Mickey refuses to be called "Mexican" and throws away the western novel whose stereotypes condition his lived experience, but the nagging materiality of Mexico's poverty and Mickey's irrational body remain just out of narrative's reach.

In each of the above examples, sense appears to triumph over epistemology. There are things that cannot be known, but in each instance characters' feelings are more important than any kind of objective truth, as, for example, when Philip invents the story about the two menus in *Last Known Residence* (67). Linda Alcoff reads the accretion of such feelings as the building blocks of racial identity. She argues that racialization occurs in microprocesses of everyday life predicated on visibility and our perception of the real. Taking a subjectivist approach to the study of race, Alcoff sees race as "constitutive of bodily experience, subjectivity, judgment, and epistemic relationships," a fundamental part of "everyday embodied existence, psychic life, and social interaction" (183). Though Alcoff follows a phenomenological method and is explicitly influenced by Merleau-Ponty (184), her readings of the body differ substantially from the approach of affect theorists also inspired by Merleau-Ponty's work.

While Alcoff sees racial feelings like those described above as responses to microaggressions, they can also be read not so much as responding to as beginning to operate outside their ideological confines. Free from the controlling rhetorics of history, the novel, and menus, Gilb's bodies might be charting their own affective paths. From this perspective, the characters' feelings can be read as pre-predicative, to borrow Merleau-Ponty's term, or "autonomic," to borrow the word Brian Massumi uses in *Parables for the Virtual* (28). Drawing on the work of Silvan Tomkins and Paul Ekman, Massumi takes affect to be independent of, or only contingently dependent upon, objects in the world.

Both options are limited, however. Whether we see Gilb's characters' feelings as reactive or proactive, following Alcoff or Massumi respectively, we are still not attending fully to the confluence of body and brain in human behavior.[19] As Leys describes Tomkins's and Ekman's work, they "posit a constitutive disjunction between our emotions on the one hand and our knowledge of what causes and maintains them on the other" (437). Daniel Stern makes a similar argument in his work on infant attunement, which has been as influential as Tomkins's and Ekman's, but which is also, as Constantina Papoulias and Felicity Callard note in their overview of humanities-based affect theory, quite old and hotly debated. Stern's *The Interpersonal World of the Infant* (1985) is part of a rich dialogue in neuroscience research on the role and nature of affect in human behavior. Leys glosses the conversation, discussing research by Richard Lazarus (470), Alan Fridlund (439), Lisa Barrett (439), and others who have been highly critical of Tomkins's work and its implications. Like Leys, Papoulias and Callard note that affect theory takes no notice of studies like these that postulate the body's inability to circumvent mind, the fundamentally cognitive nature of attunement, or the shifting patterns of body and brain dominance in the development of human cognition (47).

Much as Chen argues in their linguistic study, Leys, Papoulias, and Callard emphasize that corporeal does not necessarily mean precognitive, and, moreover, that these are matters of energetic debate in contemporary neuroscience. Where Leys doubts the possibility of fruitful interdisciplinary work in affect, Papoulias and Callard issue a call for more rigorous cross-talk. They "seek not to argue that to focus on the role of affect in social life is misguided, but rather to interrogate the prioritization and translation—and mistranslation—of particular scientific knowledge" (48). They would like, in other words, for scientists and humanists to be better readers of each other's work.

Such encounters could begin with Dagoberto Gilb's writing, where body and mind are mutually constitutive. Feeling, sense experience, and the failures of language are of supreme importance in Gilb's fiction, but affect and cognition do not appear in his work as separate systems. His characters reject the ideological constraints of racial narratives, but they do not reject story altogether. Mickey, in *Last Known Residence*, throws away his western novel, for example, and balks when his employer calls him "Mexican," but he still wants a story. It is, however, a story he cannot write; he can only perform and experience it. Likewise, John Reed's history of Pancho Villa lingers at the margins of "Death Mask," and the unnamed narrator feels the meaning of history in his body as he decides not to tell his wife what has happened with Gabe. Lastly, Mr. Sanchez will not participate in his doctors' textual meaning making. He will not answer their questions, or he answers them with nonsense. "this is how they beat you down, and they make money," he thinks of his doctors. He will not play what he perceives to be their game, but he also thinks, "im not going to do nothing. im not not saying something" (6). Mr. Sanchez will not let his doctors beat him down with words, but he struggles to write, and those struggles are materially manifest on the page in misspellings, lack of capitalization, and chaotic or absent punctuation. Mr. Sanchez will not let his doctors write his body; he will forge a new relationship between body and text, a relationship that must be read choratically rather than representationally, taking the materiality of language into full account.

Mr. Sanchez's insistence on the majority language to do the work of this forging marks his writing as resistant and minor in the tradition Gilles Deleuze and Félix Guattari describe in their work on Franz Kafka. "Minor literature," as Deleuze and Guattari understand it, "is affected with a high coefficient of deterritorialization"; it conveys a sense of being literally and figuratively out of place, using language to perform new modes of speaking and being. Minor literature, crucially, "doesn't come from a minor language; it is rather that which a minority constructs within a major language" (16). It is how a subordinate community stakes a claim for itself. Despite Renato Rosaldo's famous discounting of

Deleuze and Guattari's use value for Chicanx studies, their concept of a minor literature, a kind of disidentification *avant la lettre*, does offer a way to appreciate Gilb's attempts to bridge bodily sense and language.

Rosaldo called Deleuze and Guattari "Eurocentric and elitist" for attempting to extrapolate a philosophical concept from canonical writers whose experience of migration, moreover, bore little resemblance to that of writers like Ernesto Galarza or Américo Paredes. Paredes and Galarza, Rosaldo notes, did not cross borders but rather had borders cross them in the nineteenth-century shift from Mexican to US rule in the southwestern United States, and so Rosaldo doubts "to what extent [Deleuze and Guattari's] analysis holds when applied to less recognized voices among American minorities" (66). Gilb's consistent foregrounding of the body, however, resists simultaneously Rosaldo's ethnic labels as well as the kind of deracinating abstraction Rosaldo fears. Gilb's bodies insist on the specificity of Chicanx experience while also subverting received narratives of the same, just as the Sun Stone preserves Aztec iconography while remaining fundamentally illegible to scholars. Gilb uses language to mark an ephemeral otherness, but he refuses to allow that otherness as beyond the reach of language; it is accessible, powerful, and rooted in the body. Gilb does not privilege an emancipatory, ethnic self who stands outside the subjecting and restrictive confines of oppressive language. The self feels, but that feeling is for Gilb a function of language. Language and narrative do not represent the self, they *are* the self; they are part of the self's unfolding into the world, and the writer's challenge is to craft words that enable that process. Language is not an imperfect reflection of the body, in other words; self and story, affect and cognition, are mutually constitutive, and Gilb's writing challenges us to rethink our understanding of language and experience.

On this Gilb echoes Bergson in *The Creative Mind* (1934). Bergson says that a novelist's description may paint a full picture of a character, but that description cannot be the same as an encounter with an actual person; the words reflect a form, but deflect from the sense of interpersonal connection. Similarly, photographs of a city are not the same as the "dimensional" experience of walking through a city (134). Words and pictures are, for Bergson, symbols that delineate a thing by comparison with other things already known to the viewer. Any knowledge we might derive from words and pictures is deceptive and incomplete, according to Bergson, and we might apply his critique to ways of appreciating ethnic fiction as reflections of ethnic experience and identity.

Cecile Pineda, whom I discuss in the following chapter, articulates Bergson's point perhaps even more powerfully than Gilb. Building on the Bergsonian themes of this first chapter, I read Pineda alongside contemporary photographers in order to draw out the idea that the term "Chicanx literature" describes, to a certain extent, things we already think we know. Neither Pineda nor Gilb tells readers what they expect to hear, nor do they show readers what they expect to see. They challenge the readerly desire to be passively shown in the first place. Gilb and Pineda do not depict experiences so much as they create physical experiences with their words.

Such experiences happen in alternate temporalities like the "what's the difference" of "Death Mask," Mickey's uncertain future in *Last Known Residence*, and the expansive "all the time" of Mr. Sanchez's recovery, alternative, lingering temporalities that recall the Aztec politicization of time and that resonate across the chapters of this book. The web of fleshly, durational interconnection that builds throughout Gilb's work expands and shifts when we turn to Pineda, whose theater and fiction help crystallize the stakes of the racial immanence that Gilb has brought into focus, those moments where language fails and text struggles to embody, not just to represent, the experience of race.

2

FACE

Cecile Pineda's Spectacular Blank Slate

In Cecile Pineda's novel *Face* (1985), the protagonist, Helio Cara, loses his face in a tragic accident. The novel documents the aftermath of his misfortune, as Helio grapples with his changing social world and strives to remake himself, piecing together both his face and the story of his life bit by painstaking bit. Having grown up in the poverty-stricken "hinterland" (105), Helio has remained on the margins of the unspecified metropolis in whose slums he lives at the time of his accident. Barely literate and struggling to make a living as a barber's assistant, Helio nevertheless has a girlfriend, Lula, and a place in his community. That place is upended, however, by his accident, which snaps the fragile communal bonds that held him in place.

Helio is first isolated in the hospital, then violently rejected by his neighbors upon his release; his story, like Dagoberto Gilb's "please, thank you" in chapter 1, provokes an exploration of the relationship between the human body, community, and belonging. Mr. Sanchez, the protagonist of Gilb's story, suffers a stroke that forces him to become part of a community that the story builds from the inside out, working from Mr. Sanchez's physical and emotional feelings about his own body and the people around him. Helio's accident, by contrast, removes him from his community, which the story depicts from the outside in, relying less on Helio as focalizer and more on how he is seen by other characters. *Face* emphasizes sight as key to community building, while "please, thank you" dwells on sensation, but in both, text is a constitutive element of the circuit of feeling upon which political belonging depends. Textual experimentation, that is, in both *Face* and "please, thank you," are how each argues for the body as a conduit for racialized communal connections rather than as an index of subjectivity.

Helio's face anchored him in social space. In its absence, Helio becomes foreign because, for his neighbors, Helio's face signaled a transcendental truth about his subjectivity, recognition predicated on the assumption that the body references something external to itself. Both Helio and Mr. Sanchez reject this referential reading of the body: at one point Helio wonders where his hands have come from and is confused about whether they are even attached to him (30), and after his stroke Mr. Sanchez cannot understand his numb limbs as parts of himself. In both, the body becomes an interactional means of establishing community rather than a symbol of the self.[1] In the previous chapter I explored the politics of feeling; here I attend to the politics of sight. What, *Face* asks, does it mean to look and see? How does a person physically respond to these things and how are they community-building actions both of and about the human body? Informed by Pineda's background in theater, *Face* pulls together instances of looking in three distinct modes: looking as an element of performance, viewing images, and reading text. Reading *Face* alongside the works of two contemporary photographers—Stefan Ruiz and Ken Gonzales-Day—I argue that the novel both undermines assumptions about and builds a politics around reading, writing, and looking.

Pineda was similarly iconoclastic in her work with Theatre of Man, a company she founded in 1969 and ran until 1981 as Cecile Leneman, her married name. It was toward the end of her time in theater that *Face* began to take shape. In 1977 Pineda read a newspaper article about a man named Walter Alves Pereira, who had been left with a severe facial deformity after falling down a flight of stairs in Brazil. His story came to international attention when Agence France-Presse reported that Pereira had "stupefied the Brazilian medical world by carrying out 15 plastic surgery operations on himself." The article described Pereira's use of local anesthetic and household items as surgical tools, how he lost feeling around his mouth after his first surgery, and how he used builder's plaster to stop the bleeding from his skin grafts. "I started operating on myself because I was desperate," he is quoted as explaining. "I did it solely to survive, so that people would stop calling me names, leave me in peace and stop throwing stones at me" (Agence France-Presse). Pineda was so moved by Pereira's story, which she saw in the *San Francisco Chronicle,* that she clipped and kept the article tucked in her personal files, which were then largely consumed with the running of her theater troupe.

Two years later, in 1979, Pineda was divorced and looking to move on from Theatre of Man, which she hoped to oversee part-time with the help of a newly hired permanent staff (Letter to Yaffa Corteen). Though by September 1981 Pineda had sold the theater and was working on *Face* (Letter to Andrzej Ekwinski), both her writing process and the content of the novel were heavily influenced by her theatrical work. In its press release for the novel, referring to Pereira's story, Viking described Pineda as "using the bare facts of this bizarre and incredible incident" (Viking). Crafting art from life was integral to Theatre of Man's experimental, developmental work, where performance text emerged collaboratively from action and dialogue improvised during intense, meditative rehearsals.[2] Over the years, however, audiences and theater itself grew less adventurous, in Pineda's estimation, and certainly less willing to support Theatre of Man's challenging work, developments that inspired, in part, her turn to fiction (Letter to Andrzej Ekwinski).

Pineda took up fiction the same way she approached theater and met, initially, with a similar lack of support before *Face* was picked up by Viking.[3] She researched her topic rigorously, incorporating details from Pereira's story such as the loss of sensation after the first surgery (135) and the use of builder's plaster (142) into her own ethereal prose that, in some cases, is lifted directly from her diaries and dream journals.[4] This writing process mirrors the developmental rehearsal process that gave birth to Theatre of Man's *Threesomes*, which featured three actors on a stage, inhabiting large sculptures that "represented the psychic skins of the actors" (figure 2.1). From here they delivered lines that "asked an audience to find itself directly in their experiences, dreams, and games" (Theatre of Man). Theatre of Man understood itself as "renewing both actors and audience through shared experience which transcends individual lives," but reviewers called *Threesomes* "improvised drivel" ("Experimental, Improvised Drivel"), "tedious," and a "non-play" that drove audiences to leave at intermission (Rowe). *Face*, by contrast, was well received, though it challenges readers similarly and is as intensely experimental and developmental as any Theatre of Man performance.

Pineda expects of her readers the same things she expects of her audience. Just as Theatre of Man staged interactive, meaning-making

Figure 2.1. Greg Wagers (*right*) and Mary Tepper (*left*) in Theatre of Man's *Threesomes*. Cecile Pineda Papers, M1176, Department of Special Collections, Stanford University Libraries.

events, *Face* is less concerned with representing Helio's experience than in creating an event for the reader. The novel does this by positing the human body as a conduit between text and image. As various pictures and words circulate around Helio, *Face* argues that text, image, and body mediate experience similarly; neither gives us more or less access to the real. Photographs can lie; they are not as documentary as viewers might assume. Conversely, text can be true, less empty and purely referential than readers might think. The body shares interpretive difficulty with text and image: assumed to reference things outside themselves, all three are, in fact, things in themselves. From this shared status *Face* begins to build a theory of political community and belonging.

The cover art to the 2003 reissue of *Face* enacts the interplay of text, image, and body as well as the imbrication of presence with absence from which *Face*'s political ideas evolve (figure 2.2). It features *JBN*, a photograph from Kathy Vargas's series *The Living Move* (2000). Taking up most of the frame is an over-exposed, hand-colored, black-and-white image of a man's face, over which Vargas has imposed small, brown, thorny branches. The branches echo the color of the faint, illegible handwriting that also covers the face. The sharp, rightwards slant of the handwriting conveys a sense of motion and resistance as it pushes toward the edge of the frame and against the branches, its liveliness a stark

Figure 2.2. *Face*, by Cecile Pineda (Wings Press, 2003). Cover art by Kathy Vargas. Design by Bryce Milligan.

contrast with the surreal, ghostly glow of the face lying beneath. Face, thorn, and text seem to be working with, not against, each other to convey a general sense of illegibility. The face is blurry, the text unreadable, suggesting both as indices of relation, not reference: they mean nothing, except insofar as they interact with each other in the moment, or within the frame, of the image.

Such refusal of meaning is characteristic of Vargas's work. "I don't use a *lot* of 'reality' in my photos. But I refer to a lot of events in the world," writes Vargas in a personal letter to curator Lucy Lippard (in Lippard 23). Pineda describes herself similarly as "not interested in producing narrative" but in writing "something in contrast to writing about something." Pineda understands this as "the difference between event and story," where her writing becomes the event itself. Her novels *are* things, in other words; they are not *about* things (in Biggers 3). Both Vargas and Pineda see their creations as tracing the outlines of a present absence, where, as Vargas explains it, "what isn't there becomes the 'weight' for what is there, the anchor" (in Lippard 22). Pineda, likewise, describes herself as a "novelist of image" for whom the visual opens the door to a range of senses and sensibilities, and, as with Vargas's work, the seen simultaneously masks and gestures toward the unseen (in Biggers 3).

Theatre of Man might have presented drivel, but its performances gesture toward the unseen world of personal consciousness, not in the service of representation but in order to create shared time and space with its audience. This is evident in *Threesomes* as well as in *TIME/PIECE*, the one production in which Pineda appeared, which, like most of the group's productions, grew from an intense rehearsal process during which action and dialogue were developed from actors' personal histories (figure 2.3).[5] Theater, for Pineda and her performers, was "a transfiguration of apparently staged events into moments during which something real occurred" ("Organizational History"), which formulation echoes Pineda's struggle to write things, not *about* things. Pineda's novels and plays, in other words, enact a choratic tension and should be considered events in and of themselves, not simply representations or stagings of things that have happened.

Face embodies this quality especially; the first page of the composition book in which Pineda began writing the novel has a note about

Figure 2.3. *From left to right*: Cecile Pineda, Greg Wagers, Tom Macaulay, and Mary Tepper in Theatre of Man's *TIME/PIECE*. Cecile Pineda Papers, M1176, Department of Special Collections, Stanford University Libraries.

her trip to Mexico, then a seemingly random observation: "Realization that something—TIME perhaps—was out of joint. Or my need to leave time as I know it" (Composition Book). Time is definitely not as the reader knows it in *Face*; it elongates, unfolds endlessly, and is intimately connected to physical sense and emotion. *Face*, like "please, thank you," is invested in writing the durational time of the body. Pineda understands this connection between body, time, and text in explicitly phenomenological terms, taking her epigraph from Maurice Merleau-Ponty: "Like a novel, the face is a web of living meanings, an inter-human event, in which the thing and its expression are inexplicably joined."[6] The human body, says Merleau-Ponty, is "accessible only through direct contact" (*Phenomenology* 151), like a novel, he argues, much as Henri Bergson argues for spaces and persons, as I explain in the previous chapter. For Merleau-Ponty, the novel is a "nexus of living meanings" (151) that, like all works of art, acquires significance through human touch, human sight, and human feeling.

Merleau-Ponty's formulation echoes Roland Barthes's meditations on photography in *Camera Lucida*. A photograph can infinitely repeat that which "has occurred only once" (4), but that event is singular, unique, and eternally connected to the photograph. A photograph is always a response, "an antiphon of 'Look,'" and that event of looking is manifest in the material photograph (5). A very good photograph makes the viewer aware of the event of the look; it has an element of incongruity, what Barthes calls a "punctum" that punctuates the "studium" of general interest in the photographic scene (26). These ideas allow Barthes to "discover the truth of the face [he] had loved" when looking through old pictures shortly after his mother's death. In a photograph of her and her brother as children Barthes finds his punctum in the particular angle of his mother's body and set of her face that connects him to her across time, space, and death (67).

The face is an antiphon of feeling as much as the photo, in Barthes's analysis, is "an antiphon of 'Look'" (5), recording an object as well as the trace of the photographic event itself. Photography inhabits the liminal zone between thing and event. It serves as the textual emblem of expression in *Face*, which pulls these bodily, textual, performance, and imagistic events together in parallel series of scenes juxtaposing mirrors and photos. Helio encounters broken mirrors, whole mirrors, and missing mirrors that destabilize his sense of self. At the same time, he builds a visual sense of self through newspaper photographs and the one photo he has of himself and Lula, a description of which is repeated throughout the novel before it becomes clear that the canoe outing it depicts is a staged, studio portrait and not an experienced event.

Helio's photograph captures some of the foundational debates in the history of photography, debates central to the narrative experimentation around which *Face*'s politics emerge. Lula and Helio are both there and not there in Helio's photo: present in the picture, but absent from the real scene it depicts. At its core, photography is about this ambiguous presence and absence, about whether it documents or invents, about, in short, whether or not it is art. Photographs can be endlessly reproduced, and they are themselves reproductions of things in the world rather than creations, except when they are not. Except when, as with the work of

Stefan Ruiz and Ken Gonzales-Day, two contemporary photographers whose work I consider here along with *Face* in order to draw out its theories of political belonging, a photograph is able to render the invisible visible, to invite the viewer to see the unseen.

Ruiz and Gonzales-Day are widely recognized as artists, but their work exploits the play of photographic presence and absence that fueled early debates over the medium. Practitioners responded one of two ways to late nineteenth-century criticisms that photography relied more on technical skill than artistic invention: they either ceded photography's difference and worked to exploit the technical capacity of the form, as did Jacob Riis and, later in the century, Walker Evans; or, like Edward Weston, they emphasized the role of the photographer in crafting artistic images.[7] Uniting both these approaches is a shared understanding that a photograph bears some direct relation to the world outside itself. To Fredric Jameson's characterization of contemporary photography as "renouncing reference" (179), one might, as Liz Wells does, posit Barthes's observation that a photograph is always *of* something (*Barthes* 28). A photograph might not be a direct and unmediated representation; in fact, Wells concedes, "analogical theories of the photograph have been abandoned; we no longer believe that the photograph directly reflects circumstances" (18). But, she continues, it is the material trace of something, the physical effect of light recorded with chemical on paper or in binary code on silicone.

A photograph, in its near-perfect embodiment of chora, represents the anxiety of not knowing. It is simultaneously itself as well as a reflection of something else, repetition with a difference, itself and something more. As Ossip Brik notes, the job of the camera is "to see and record what the human eye normally does not see" (90). At the same time, as Martha Rosler argues, "Any familiarity with photographic history shows that manipulation is integral to photography." In other words, a photograph can show us what is both present and absent. The history of photography underscores the fragility, not the primacy, of vision with its potential to undermine our assumption that it documents only presence, not absence.

Ruiz and Gonzales-Day put pressure on this assumption by exploiting the tension between seeing and being seen captured in *Face* and represented visually in Vargas's work. Ruiz is a well-known commercial photographer whose work has been incredibly influential in forming one of the "key looks" of early twenty-first-century photography. His photos share the social concerns of documentary photography, but Ruiz presents them with commercial photographic values and gives them "a loose, conceptual art-world wrap" (Bainbridge 25).[8] His second book, *The Factory of Dreams*, which documents the acting school at Televisa Studios in Mexico City, showcases his iconic, large-format work. Gonzales-Day, conversely, does not work in commercial photography as Ruiz often does. An art photographer and professor at Claremont College in southern California, Gonzales-Day is known for his photo series, including *Erased Lynchings* and *Searching for California's Hang Trees*, that illuminate California's history of racial violence.

Whereas Gonzales-Day's photos present absence, Ruiz's photos in *The Factory of Dreams* strongly assert the presence of the brown body in painfully bright and startlingly clear shots. The portraits are visually crisp but fundamentally ambiguous as the viewer is never really sure whether they are seeing an actor or a character. Gonzales-Day similarly undermines any idea of the photo as documentary evidence. In the *Erased Lynchings* series he digitally removes the lynched body from archival images, thus demonstrating how this history has been rendered invisible. *The Factory of Dreams* disconcertingly asserts the presence of Mexicans, while Gonzales-Day playfully enacts their absence. The brown bodies in the works of both photographers are, like Helio, both here and not here.

In *Face*, Pineda works through the complex nexus of visible and invisible, focusing on the present absence of the human body and how Helio is variously seen and obscured as he moves through the city after his accident. To fully appreciate the novel's complexity, one must read choratically, paying equal attention to the materiality of language and to the things toward which it gestures. Performing her own dictum to write things, not about things, Pineda's novel embodies the central questions of its content: Does the human face trace the real self, or is it an accretion of interactions with no real referent? Helio's face emerges textually from a series of interactions and repetitions. Key events and conversations are narrated more than once, each time with a slight difference, demonstrating the temporality, spatiality, and textuality of the body. Pineda rejects novelistic conventions of ideality and individual subjectivity in her depiction of a mutable protagonist and plot of shifting, uneven clarity. Helio's face is iterative in its utility yet singularly his, and Helio is the focal point of a novel that enacts photography's existential angst.

Face is the process of rebuilding, of literally re-membering, Helio's body, of rendering his invisibility visible. This, however, is in the service of asserting the value of community, not of abject subjects. *Face*'s second epigraph illustrates this nicely; it comes from the nuclear disarmament activist Jonathan Schell's *The Fate of the Earth*: "The meaning of extinction is . . . to be sought first not in what each person's own life means to him but in what the world and the people in it mean to him." Somewhat conversely, Pineda has written, "the most satisfying reaction to *Face* came from a struggling third-world student" who identified deeply with the novel because he saw it as "about being invisible," but *Face* does not articulate anything like a Third World subjectivity (*Face* xvi). In tracing Helio's path from seen to unseen and back again, *Face* documents how community gathers around and through the human body, how Helio's face galvanizes different groups into action, just as Theatre of Man hoped to galvanize audiences. Ruiz and Gonzales-Day deploy the body similarly to emphasize not the unique histories attached to individual bodies but rather the communal networks gathered around the bodies featured in their photographs. Like *Face*, the two photographers' work can be seen as an extended project of reintegrating the brown body into historical memory and rescripting its political future away from subjectivity and rights and toward networks, institutions, and issues.

Ruiz's Abundant Presence

In *The Factory of Dreams*, Ruiz is concerned to present his actors in the thick context both of the dramas in which they perform and of Televisa, the studio that produces their shows. The resulting portraits are exemplary of Ruiz's distinctive style, blending the high concept of art with advertising's clean and crisp images. Ruiz's signature look permeates commercial photography of the 2000s and 2010s to the extent that it is easy to forget that it had a progenitor, though Ruiz's innovative campaigns for iD and Caterpillar are widely recognized as their genesis (Bainbridge 25). Working in both the art and commercial worlds, Ruiz has found himself in "so many different situations all over the world—from prisons to insane asylums, emergency rooms, refugee camps, celebrities' houses, police raids, travel stories, advertising shoots" that he consistently feels like an observant outsider who, as he has noted often in interviews, negotiates his own shyness with his camera (in Ibarra 56). Ruiz's persistent sense of low-grade discomfort resonates throughout his work, and in thinking of Ruiz alongside Pineda I want to focus on two elements of his practice in particular: his use of a large-format camera and his explicit, visual references to the artificiality of the photographic image. Pineda calls attention to the craft and temporality of writing in the same way Ruiz calls attention to the made quality of the photograph; these aspects of Ruiz's work thus pave the way for a discussion of Pineda's experiments with form and the event of writing.

Like writing, large-format photography is an event in and of itself. Primarily "large format" refers to the size of the film, but it also refers to the type of camera Ruiz uses, though there are SLR (single-lens reflex) cameras that use larger film. The difference is this: SLR cameras use a lens and mirror to reflect the exact image captured through the viewfinder. They are "fixed plate," which means that the photographer cannot adjust the alignment of lens, mirror, and film. By contrast, large-format cameras have front and back "standards" that can be shifted and tilted out of alignment with each other, allowing for better depth of field and clarity of image. More so than SLR images, large-format shots are, as Barthes describes photographs in *Camera Lucida*, "an antiphon of 'Look,'" a recording of an event of looking as much as they record the object seen (5).

Ruiz's turn to large-format photography reflects his classical art training. He studied drawing and painting at college and in Florence, where he describes himself as being "totally immersed in Pre-Renaissance and Renaissance painting, sculpture, and drawing," training that attuned him to "colours, shapes, subject, composition, intensity, lighting" (Ibarrra 56). Large format makes it impossible to point and shoot as one does with SLR; it allows Ruiz to compose his shots the way he would compose a painting.

For example, the cover photo of Ruiz's *The Factory of Dreams* features Daniel Cortés of the Televisa Acting School (figure 2.4). Cortés is topless, sprawled across a bed and gazing confidently at the camera, his lips curled in a seductive half smile. The bed is placed in front of a window,

Figure 2.4. Stefan Ruiz, *Daniel Cortés, CEA, Televisa Acting School*, 2004, from *The Factory of Dreams* (Aperture, 2012). © Stefan Ruiz.

through whose open venetian blinds is visible a cityscape at dusk. The shot employs pyramidal composition, anchored by a series of triangular relations: at the center is the triangle formed by Cortés's nipples and belly button, drawing the viewer's attention to Cortés's belt buckle and crotch, cradled gently by his right hand; the roofs of the visible buildings form an inverted triangle reflected in the curve of Cortés's hip framed by his right arm and leg; the bends of his shoulder and knee are emphasized by two lamps on either side, whose triangular shades echo the curve of both the skyline and Cortés's body; those lamps form a triangle with the folds of the bedspread, which form a curve at the center of the bed, falling just below Cortés's belt buckle and crotch, the gravitational center

Figure 2.5. Stefan Ruiz, *Rubí, Televisa Acting School*, 2004, from *The Factory of Dreams* (Aperture, 2012). © Stefan Ruiz.

of the image. Everything about the image is clean and crisp in both the foreground and background. The sharpness of detail—from the numbers on the bedside clock to the pattern on the rug to the cloisonné box on the bedside table—calls to mind Pineda's naturalistic description. "One stair, at the top, is etched with a crack now," she writes on the first page of *Face*, continuing, "The concrete in the vein has crumbled. Little pebbles, aggregates of dust, perhaps, have settled in the interstices" (7). The words paint a vivid picture of the dilapidated stairs.

That "perhaps," however, gives the reader pause. Pineda throws an element of doubt into her precise description, suggesting that the visible is not entirely knowable. Ruiz does the same in his portrait of Cortés.

Though the folds of the bedspread frame Cortés perfectly, the viewer notices a disheveled air to their arrangement; and the lampshades that accentuate the angles of his body are askew. The viewer's eye moves up the portrait, taking in these slight imperfections, to the ceiling of the room, which, it turns out, is not a room but a set: where the ceiling should be, the viewer sees lights, cameras, and wires. Ruiz achieves a similar disorientation with *Rubí* and *Amorcito Corazón* (figures 2.5 and 2.6), photos of set backdrops leaning against sound stage walls, which foreground background, creating a confusion of depth and perspective. Ruiz's tight composition emphasizes the presence of an

Figure 2.6. Stefan Ruiz, *Amorcito Corazón (Darling Sweetheart), Televisa Acting School*, 2011, from *The Factory of Dreams* (Aperture, 2012). © Stefan Ruiz.

arranger or creator, but that presence is not determinate. The slightly off elements and the deliberate perspectival play emphasize chance and lack of total artistic control in ways that evoke Pineda's play with narrative convention.

As Ruiz does with his photographs, Pineda makes apparent that an ambiguous and fallible hand renders her text. She opens *Face*, for example, with a prologue that purports to be from a speech "by T.G., doctor of plastic and reconstructive surgery," at an annual convention of plastic surgeons in Rio de Janeiro. This entirely fictional prologue trades in the convention of the frame tale, lending an air of authenticity to an invented story. As Juan Bruce-Novoa notes, however, Pineda upends readerly expectations when this apparently omniscient narrator turns out to be imperfect (Bruce-Novoa 73).

Later in the novel the name of Helio's plastic surgeon is revealed as Teofilho Godoy, presumably the T.G. of the prologue. The prologue sets up T.G. as the narrator of the tale of Helio's facial reconstruction, but Helio rejects Godoy's offer of surgical charity. He leaves the city for the hinterland, where he begins a series of surgeries on his own face. When Godoy reaches Helio by mail toward the end of the novel to extend his offer once again, Helio does not reject it out of hand. "Godoy would wait," Helio thinks after reading the letter. Too tired to decide, he blows out his candle and goes to sleep (168). In the novel's concluding scene, Helio boards a tram in the city and notices his former girlfriend, Lula, who "sees him clearly, looks right at him. But there is no recognition" (170). The reader assumes that Helio has a new, perfectly normal face that is both unremarkable and very different from his pre-accident visage. But is this the face Helio made himself, or did he accept Godoy's offer, return to the capital, and have Godoy make over Helio's earlier efforts? The reader remains uncertain.

The unknown maker of Helio's face corresponds to the ambiguous narrator of the novel. Helio usurps Godoy's narrative authority, but his departure for the hinterland effects no apparent shift in focalization. The narration remains omniscient and in the third person, but that omniscience is occasionally called into question. For instance, the scene of Helio's first auto-surgery attempt is narrated in precise detail as Helio carefully balances his mirror and angles his body to get a clear view into the "thick" glass. "He passes his right hand in front of it, checking for distortion perhaps, or to remove a speck of dirt from its surface" (132). The "perhaps" here recalls the "perhaps" of the first page, suggesting in both places that seeing is not necessarily believing, and it is most certainly not knowing whether the narrator cannot explain Helio's actions. "Perhaps" also makes the reader aware that text is not a transparent window onto the real. "Thick" like Helio's mirror, text has a potentially fallible agent who does not know everything.

Pineda uses repetition to make this same argument at the level of form when, for example, she connects a memory Helio has of Lula to a conversation with her in the hospital using repeated images of paper stars. In the memory, the stars "revolve lazily in the warm air currents" (25), while in the hospital, her questions hang "unanswered like paper stars . . . dangling in the night hum of the electric fans" (26). Recycling the image invokes an authorial presence who recognizes that the paper stars reflect natural stars in the same way that text is a pale reflection of the real. Pineda repeats text to invoke connection as well as distance, however, as when early in the novel the reader first sees Helio remembering his accident. A child catches sight of his disfigured face and runs away crying, "Mamae, Mamae" (9). This provokes Helio's memory of calling out for his own mother as he falls, being dimly aware of a child witnessing the accident calling out to his mother, and thinking that his now wordless scream is being made by his own mother (12–13). The word "mamae" connects Helio to the idea of his mother as well as to the two boys, one who witnesses Helio's fall and the other who witnesses Helio's remembering.

In *Face*'s opening pages, with her errant narrator and the intricate description of Helio's fall and memory, Pineda weaves a lexical web that lays the foundation for the novel's arguments about repetition, creation, connection, and distance: words bring people closer together at the same time they drive them apart; words represent the world around us at the same time they emphasize the impossibility of true reflection. Words, and the ability to read them, are nevertheless supremely important in the world of *Face*. Helio's literacy, for example, allows him to study his stolen textbook of plastic surgery and reconstruct himself. That is the primary plot arc of the novel, and yet smaller, parallel arcs run alongside this one, arguing that agency in the world is not activated through text, but built through physical, sensory experience.

The parallels Pineda draws between text and the body are ways of exploring what it means to be human. In her introduction she writes that part of her project in *Face* was to explore how much "of the body can be lost or destroyed before a person loses all claim to inclusion in the human race?" (xiv), meaning both how much of a body does a person need to be recognized as human, and also how much of our self resides in our physical, sensual experience of the world? Recognizing others as human relies on patterns of repetition: "they" look like "us." *Face* builds on this truism by asserting, through Helio's sensual experience of his face "unfolding like a map" (157), that recognizing ourselves as human also relies on patterns of repetition, but of sensual, not visual, experience.[9] Writing links these repetitions: Pineda's paper stars repeat the stars in the sky at the same time they anchor Helio's memory. Throughout *Face*, Pineda's writing explores the overlap of knowing the other and feeling the self, the choratic overlap of body as object and subject.

Visual experiences are the primary mode through which *Face* explores this overlap. "I want to invite each reader to look beyond surfaces, and look again. And again," she writes in the introduction to *Face*, throughout which she explicitly, repeatedly references the linked events of seeing and being seen (xvi). On the first page, for example, Helio gazes at the waves, "looking away, then rapidly looking again" to catch a sense of the ocean's movement (7). Likewise, on the tram, after his accident, passengers look at Helio, avert their gaze, and look again. "Now looking, now turning away. The gesture repeats itself. It has become the coin of his personal marketplace" (73). Finally, the novel concludes with Lula and her friend looking at Helio, then looking away, and finally, in *Face*'s concluding sentence, "Then they both look up at him" (170). The repeated physical movements of looking, turning, and returning mirror how Pineda wants readers to engage her work, and they perform the sensual and cognitive work of knowing the body. The repetitive looking constitutes not a knowable object, but a collection of experiences that gather around Helio's body. These experiences are accessible only though text, however, despite its inability to access the real, and despite *Face*'s fallible narrator. Helio comes to know his body through repeated experiences, but the body is also, *Face* argues, built through text and sound.

Text and sound, *Face* reminds readers, are also physical experiences. Helio's fall is precipitated by a telegram about his mother's failing health, and later his mother's neighbor tells him, "She called for you. When you didn't come . . ." (112). His mother's call brings Helio back to his birthplace, known as "The Street of The Scream," after a story about a woman who gave birth there for fourteen days "screaming without cease" to multiple children representing all the races of the world (101). The legend conjures the difference between speech and voice, between the laboring cry and the name of the street, that is analogous to the difference between the street and the hospital, another place where Pineda clearly shows speech structuring space and experience.

At the hospital, Helio regularly hears "the approaching march of the medical students" and "the commanding tone of the chief surgeon," whose "mapping" evokes the human body as both a thing and a place to be linguistically explored. The surgeon speaks in spatial terms—"here," "to the right," "in the next bed"—as he announces disarticulated body parts: "the hand, the knee, the eardrum" until finally it is Helio's turn and he is called into being as the surgeon announces, *"And the face"* (23). The surgeon's speech pulls the body parts together into a recognizable whole, a fusion symbolized in the "terrazzo corridors" muting the students' words (22).[10] Their remarks are "muted" but the sounds of their moving through space are sharp.

While the phenomenology of speech and sound are central to *Face*, so is written language. Writing—both the action and the object—does real work in the world, Pineda argues. Describing the literary project of *Face* in her introduction, Pineda wonders, "How can the writer emblemize the slow, minute increments that accompany cellular change?" (xiv). Pineda sees her writing as, like the human body, an event unfolding over time, a search for, and an attempt to make visible, moments of change in a web of meaningful moments. "Where and how does a transformative moment come about?" (xv), she asks. She wants to make visible that slow change, but most importantly she wants to *write* it. In *Face*, then, textual objects are just as significant as sense experience.

Face is organized around Helio's engagement with several key texts. There is the telegram that calls Helio to his mother's deathbed. There is also Helio's memory about learning to read from a tabloid article about a man born with a facial disfigurement and his confusion over how letters correlated to words and then to things in the world (53). These first two texts, the telegram and the tabloid, set up the novel's crisis, while the final two enact its resolution. Waiting in Godoy's office for their first meeting, Helio sees "the solid bank of journals, bound identically, lining the wall.... They are called simply, *Face*" (85). From this he deduces that surgical talent and skill are tied to a natural facility with text and its production. Finally, though, Helio decides that textual talent can be cultivated when he steals *Basics of Dermatologic Surgery* from his local library and proceeds to study it.[11] "Carefully he reads the captions while pointing to each word, forming the syllables with his lips" (139). Text and the body are not discrete in this description of Helio's academic labor. He engages physically with the words on the page as much as he absorbs and enacts their instruction when he operates on himself.

The face is a written text Helio can study, but it is also a phenomenon that cannot truly be written. The novel does not describe the surgery in which Helio builds himself a new nose, for instance. A paragraph ends with him buying lidocaine, and the next begins with him lifting his stitches post-recovery (153). "What is there to say about a man without a face?" the narrator asks a few pages earlier, proleptically explaining the decision not to narrate this surgery (145). Helio's status as human depends on his access to language and text. In the hospital he's dependent upon the surgeon's words to make him visible, but once he leaves the city he must rely on his own literacy to bring himself back to life.

The hospital surgeon, Godoy, and Helio are all authors, text makers from whom Pineda nevertheless distinguishes herself when she asserts, "I do not think anymore that writing—mine or another's—can change the world." Writing can give voice to the voiceless, Pineda cedes; but, she counters, "at best, in the very smallest scheme, writing can provide a moment of grace" (in Biggers 24). Pineda offers moments, not things, sense experience instead of objects, form over content. Her project is to emblemize change, an effort that resonates with Henri Bergson's distinction between duration and scientific time. As explained in the previous chapter, Bergson sees narrative as commensurate with the latter and incompatible with the former. In her desire to "emblemize" change, however, Pineda, like Dagoberto Gilb, is clearly narrating Bergson's duration. This becomes a feature of content—the novel contains no description of Helio's mangled face, for example—as well as of form: the novel is narrated in present tense but makes liberal and confusing use of the conditional mood. The consistent use of the present tense creates confusion about when events are happening, and the conditional creates confusion over whether they are happening at all. Pineda's focus is less on the events described and more on the feelings that gather around the events.

To illustrate, Pineda does not narrate Helio building his nose; she only describes that which gathers around the nose. The implication here is that text can only ever scratch the surface of the real, can only ever give readers "perhaps," not certainty, and yet it conditions human lives, like the recurring image of a newspaper in Helio's dreams. Helio cannot read the writing, but it is "as familiar as the inside of his eyelids shut against the noonday sun." The text is part of him, in other words, written on the inside of his body, in fact, and yet "it resisted decipherment" (70). The dreams make explicit what is implicit elsewhere: text can be simultaneously significant and nonreferential. Literacy is central to Helio's surviving and thriving, but text is also a choratic object in the world whose significance goes beyond its meaning.

Put another way, text for Helio is an emblem, as Pineda describes her own writing. Text is also, for Helio, an image and an object, as illustrated by his first visit to the general hospital to apply for government assistance. He takes along a photograph of his pre-accident self, which he carefully wraps in newspaper. In a moment of crisis Helio realizes he has misplaced his package, which he ultimately finds just as a janitor is about to incinerate it with other "scraps of crumpled paper" (77). Text and image, here entwined with each other, are both just plays of surface whose significance is purely relative. Like the paper crumpled around nothing, with which Helio finds his photograph, his texts and his image have nothing stable at their center. They are not *of* anything, but they are in and of themselves important things.

The content of a photograph is always subordinate to context, as both Walter Benjamin and Martha Rosler argue. Photography gestures rather than explains; it "extends our comprehension of the necessities which rule our lives," writes Benjamin (50). Rosler, working from Benjamin's observations, argues that photography has never been an index of visual truth. Photographic manipulation, whose long history she traces, is simply endemic to the medium, she asserts, and is "in the service of a truer truth, one closer to conceptual adequacy, not to mention experience." The assumption, then, of a priori distance from the real is central to reading photography, Rosler says. It is also central to understanding the significance of Helio's photo, which becomes a political object when read in the context of Stefan Ruiz's portraits of people pretending to be other people in *The Factory of Dreams*.

The significance of Ruiz's book is difficult to overstate. Its publication by Aperture, the prestigious, nonprofit photography foundation, signals both Ruiz's stature in the field and the importance of his subject matter. Aperture's recognition of the *telenovela* as a significant, international cultural form indicates the growing importance of Spanish-language media in US markets.[12] Televisa, whose studios Ruiz visited, is the undisputed leader in producing and distributing telenovelas worldwide. Telenovelas in Latin America follow a similar business trajectory as the US soap opera, beginning production first as radio dramas, then migrating to television in the 1950s and 1960s. By 1985 telenovelas had made possible a significant decrease of US television imports into Latin America, displacing US products altogether in some markets (Rogers and Antola 24), and today telenovelas routinely outperform US TV in many international markets (Martínez 65). In Latin America telenovelas are marketed to and consumed by all demographics and air in prime time. Their popularity has only grown since the 1980s as Televisa in Mexico and TV Globo in Brazil have extended themselves internationally and, increasingly in Televisa's case, into the United States.

In the early part of the twenty-first century, however, the dominant Anglo majority in the United States remains largely unaware of these enormously popular shows. They look, if they look at all, and then look away, as the passengers on the tram do to Helio Cara, whose name means "sun face" in Portuguese, and who burns so brightly he is impossible to see. Pineda and Ruiz both play with this idea of willful blindness by emphasizing the instability of the seen. What one sees is not necessarily what one gets, their work suggests. What, then, is one getting that one is not seeing? And what to make of the difference between the unseen and seen; how to chart the increasing visibility of the invisible?

Helio's leisure reading offers one strategy. Perusing a magazine for new faces he might like to have, Helio thinks of the men featured, "Who are they, these men? He reads their names. But who are they really?" He wonders whether they always dress the way they are pictured, whether they ever had to work or "beg for bread." Helio imagines them as "mannequins" trapped in an unreal, ideal world. As with a Ruiz portrait, something feels off to Helio. He describes the men in the magazine not as "perfect" but as "trained to look perfect" (50). Through Helio's perception of their forced perfection we sense the class disparities that condition Helio's life. He reads the words and sees the pictures, but neither tells him anything beyond what he already senses from the "trained" quality of the photo spread. The gold chains he does not have and the begging the models will never have to do emblematize Helio's lack of resources and social capital, a distance he might not be able to traverse.

Similarly, Ruiz's photos make visible a host of things in their self-conscious performativity. "I didn't want to make fun of it," Ruiz says of the telenovela industry. "I treated it as documentary." Even though the emphasis in Ruiz's photos is on the manufacturing of televised fantasy, the images do reflect reality, depicting a decade of social and political upheaval in Mexico. Ruiz spent eight years off and on shooting at Televisa. At the start Ruiz found himself on fancy apartment or hacienda sets, while toward the end he reports shooting "a set for a kidnapping room, as well as lots of jails. You didn't used to see that at all" (in Miranda 31). Beyond that sort of decorative content, however, the photos reveal Ruiz's concern with "how we live: race, class, politics, art, creativity and humour," which he says "are all important themes" in his work (in Ibarra 56). In *The Factory of Dreams* we see maids and cooks, and while it's true they are actors, their appearance as performers in these roles points to the artificiality and inequity of class distinctions. One photo makes this case very eloquently (figure 2.7). On the set of *Amarte es mi pecado*, the characters Arturo and Nora embrace by a window in the center of the shot. The edges of the frame are dark, but wires and other hardware are visible. Along the right side of the shot a person, cloaked in shadow, operates a camera, their form just discernible in front of the bright close-up in the viewfinder of Arturo and Nora almost kissing. Like all the photos in the collection, this one destabilizes the idea of photographic truth, but unlike the others, this photo makes visible the human labor upon which that delusion depends.

The shadowy camera operator recalls Helio studying his magazines, absorbing the strained performance of the leisure class. Pineda places Helio in similarly strained images throughout *Face* as Helio repeatedly remembers an afternoon boating with Lula. The scene is described

Figure 2.7. Stefan Ruiz, *Sergio Sendel and Yadhira Carrillo as Arturo and Nora, "Amarte es mi pecado" (Loving You Is My Sin)*, 2003, from *The Factory of Dreams* (Aperture, 2012). © Stefan Ruiz.

three times. In the first, "He is rowing" (18). Then, "They are rowing in a boat on the lake" (31). Finally, "He was rowing in a lake which seemed endless, he was rowing very hard, with all his might" (70). From first to last the scenes increase in their physical descriptions. As indices of Helio's emotional state in the scenes immediately preceding the boating scenes, they become more intense, mirroring and foreshadowing the scene where Helio, distraught over Lula's emotional distance after the accident, rapes her (69). The repetition with a difference of this boating episode suggests that human emotional response to the same memories and events varies over time, and in that variation lies a truer and more immediate truth than any documentary evidence that may exist pertaining to said event. For, the reader discovers eventually, the photograph that Helio almost loses at the hospital, the only photograph he has of himself, is of him and Lula posed in a boat, "Sunday rowers painted behind them, paddling in an idealized lagoon, sky blue, clean of debris and floating orange peels" (78). The memories of rowing that never happened are built around this single image that reveals, through Helio's memories, more than it displays.

When Helio's fiction belies and blends with documentary evidence, and as Ruiz's models' performances of character blend into the sociopolitical realities of contemporary Mexico, we see that the photograph does not always document what we think we see. Put differently, there is an excess of presence in Ruiz's Televisa portraits. In *The Factory of Dreams* we see actors and characters overlapping in one shot; we see lavish settings at the same time that we see evidence of their artificiality: the wires, frames, lights, and cameras at their edges. In their emphasis on artifice and performance, these images also emphasize the event of the photograph, the labor that went into composing each shot as well as the relationship between photographer and subject upon which the frank and open facial expressions of Ruiz's models relies, both of which Ruiz slyly hints at in his shot of the camera operator on set at *Amarte es mi pecado*. In their excess, Ruiz's photos open up kaleidoscopically, just as Pineda's prose makes *Face*'s narrative arcs simultaneously rich and difficult to parse.

Gonzales-Day's Weighty Absence

By contrast, just as Pineda often achieves narrative effect through omission, Ken Gonzales-Day's photographs are marked by their reliance on conceptual and physical absence. His *Erased Lynchings* series features archival, souvenir postcards of lynchings in California from which he has digitally removed the dead bodies, as in *Disguised Bandit* (figure 2.8).[13] A related series, *Searching for California's Hang Trees*, consists of photographs of lynching sites in California, in particular the trees from which bodies were hanged. Where the trees are no longer present, Gonzales-Day installed them on existing advertising billboards, as in *Nightfall II* (figure 2.9). Both these series document the absence of these lynchings from the history of racial violence in the United States, and in California especially. In his scholarly study, *Lynching in the West, 1850–1935*, Gonzales-Day explains lynching as a core feature of Anglo-American governance in early California, with meticulous archival research revealing that Latinxs

Figure 2.8. Ken Gonzales-Day, *Disguised Bandit*. Photo courtesy of Luis De Jesus Los Angeles.

were lynched more frequently than persons of any other race or ethnicity in California (206). Vigilante and institutional violence against people of color increased exponentially in direct relation to Anglo immigration to California and the economic transformation of the region, Gonzales-Day argues. It is, he writes, "deeply linked to the formation of our young nation" (6).

It is deeply linked, but largely absent from most discussions of lynching in the United States, the majority of which, Gonzales-Day notes, give little thought to the West. Native Americans, Chinese, and above all Mexicans and other Latinxs were executed just as African Americans were, however, in public killings motivated by "anti-immigration sentiments, the fear of miscegenation, a deep frustration with the judicial system, or in combination with white supremacy" (Gonzales-Day 3). Through his art, by satirically removing the battered bodies from souvenir lynching postcards, Gonzales-Day aims to make visible both the violent removal of people of color from California and the removal of their removal from California history. With Stefan Ruiz's photographs I am interested in what is hidden by spectacle. With Ken Gonzales-Day, conversely, I explore what is made visible by hiding.

Gonzales-Day's work unmasks the racial violence of modernity, which I define here, not uniquely, as the rapid industrialization and the accelerated pace of technological and social change at the turn of the last century in Europe and North America. The spectacle of modernity occludes people of color just as modernism, as a literary phenomenon associated with these developments, renders voices of color inaudible except insofar as they reflect recognizably modernist qualities. In using Gonzales-Day's photographs as a lens through which to read *Face*, I am

Figure 2.9. Ken Gonzales-Day, *Nightfall II*. This was displayed on a billboard along La Cienega Boulevard in Los Angeles during February 2007. Photo courtesy of Luis De Jesus Los Angeles.

interested in thinking through the links between modernity, modernism, and race. I am interested, that is, in what is both hidden and revealed when we identify *Face*, as some critics do, as a modernist novel.

Stefan Ruiz's photos make the case that the more visible something is, the less apt a viewer is to *really* see it. To make racism *really* visible, Gonzales-Day removes the seen object of racial hatred, the mutilated body at the core of the souvenir postcards. In *Face*, the dolls Helio encounters in a plantation owner's living room make a similar argument. Each doll is "dressed in the way of the countryside: gentry, children, farmers, all untouched and shiny, their cheeks rosy, all with the same smiles, their eyes wide, expressionless" (124). Like Ruiz's telenovela actors, these dolls are social objects whose display renders visible the artificiality of class and social position, both of which are predicated on racial ideologies that foreground the visible at the expense of invisible truths.

The reality of race lies less in spectacle than in invisibility, that is. It lies less in the market saturation of Televisa's telenovelas than in the forgotten history of racial violence Gonzales-Day documents, less in the owner's dolls than in Brazil's politics of class and race that condition Helio's life and recovery. Pineda thus resists racial identification. Both Helio and the dolls remain racially unmarked, an ambiguity that is both a nod to the permeability of race in a Brazilian context and an argument against racial spectacle.[14] The reader gets some clues as to Helio's race, however. Thinking about his fall, Helio remembers hearing someone call out for their mother. "Had it come from him?" he wonders. "Was it his own black cry?" (12). Less cryptically, thinking about his future face, Helio imagines a time when he returns to social life, walking down a crowded street, appreciating beautiful women who in turn shower him with "inviting" looks, "appraising his dark body" (140). Pineda gives enough evidence to ground a well-supported guess that Helio might be black, but she does not make his race explicit.[15]

Race is more important in *Face* at the level of form than content because the novel is more interested in the structural significance of race over the performative. Helio does not perform a racial identity, but he is a character in a novel that, by virtue of its form, embodies the paradoxes and inequities of race. After his accident, Helio has to struggle to carve out a new face as well as a new place for himself in his community.

That struggle is mirrored in his earlier fight for literacy and consequent struggle against a world that wants to tell his story for him. Godoy wants to remake Helio's face but Helio does it first, and Godoy's speech frames the novel, but *Face* rejects an omniscient narrator. That legitimizing frame tale also invokes the slave narrative, formally evoking a racialized genre of US literature that Pineda promptly rejects.

These are coquettish racial allusions, however, and Pineda's attention to form over content, her avoidance of explicit racial pronouncements or ethnic identification may, as Juan Bruce-Novoa suggests, account for critics' silence regarding her novels (72). It also accounts for why the few critics who are concerned with Pineda's novels, especially *Face*, read them as being unconcerned with race or ethnicity. Astrid Fellner, for example, reads *Face* as being "about the dismemberment of an ideal masculine stability" (64) and sees Pineda as part of a group of authors who "have shifted the focus to larger concerns and preoccupations of the human condition" (62). Along those same lines, Bruce-Novoa thinks that Pineda "exemplifies a trend towards a less regional and ethnically specific, more international and universal approach" (80); and David Johnson, working from the assumption, shared by Fellner and Bruce-Novoa, of the body as a universalizing, if fictive, construct, reads *Face* as being about "the essential facelessness of the social or human face" (80).

Marcial González is a notable exception to this trend of erasing the race of *Face*. Responding to John Christie's reading of *Face* as exemplary high modernism, González argues that the modernist designation makes sense only if we think in terms of José Limón's "critical modernism," in which formal experimentation is deployed in the service of provoking social change (González 154). Christie celebrates *Face*'s "interlingual play" and the ways it "deflates authority" (147). González, by contrast, reads *Face* as a "philosophical investigation into the limits and possibilities of social identities in late capitalism" (159). With this, González argues against visible markers of social identity that he says "provide subjects with epistemological focal points" at the same time that they "limit an individual's capacity to comprehend social relations and history" (160). Explicit pronouncements of race and ethnicity are, in other words, a distraction from the real consequences of race, in which, González asserts, Pineda is interested.

González equates modernity with the rise of the "modern capitalist state," of which he reads Godoy as a scientific representative. González limits his engagement with modernism to noting Pineda's allusions to Sartre and Beckett. The question of whether or not we can call *Face* "modernist," however, can extend beyond a discussion of her influences and her anti-representational narrative strategies, and even beyond capitalism. Granting that Pineda's narrative experimentation echoes Gonzales-Day's photographic engagements with racial violence, making a case for *Face* as a modernist novel pushes modernist studies to novel considerations of race and geopolitics. For, though the field began a period of self-reflection and reorganization in the early twenty-first century, that sea change extended meaningfully to neither a discussion of non-Anglophone works nor works by American, broadly defined, writers.

Douglas Mao and Rebecca Walkowitz, to illustrate, describe in their introduction to *Bad Modernisms* and their article "The New Modernist Studies" how, at the dawn of the twenty-first century, modernist studies expanded along three axes: the temporal, the spatial, and the vertical. Mark Wollaeger rehearses this trajectory as well in his introduction to *The Oxford Handbook of Global Modernisms* (9). This expansion entailed the blurring of traditional distinctions between high and low culture (vertical), a questioning of easy periodization (temporal), and a "transnational turn" (spatial) in which scholars "attend to works produced in, say, Asia and Australia" at the same time that they account for sociopolitical exchange between "for example, Europe, Africa, the United States, and the Caribbean" (738). Crucially, Walkowitz and Mao note the United States, and not the Americas. Even though they go on to say that "scholars of British or United States modernism can no longer exclude nonanglophone works from our teaching and research" (742), their examples and the essays they include in their edited collection adhere for the most part to the British Commonwealth, and their easy assumption that US modernism would necessarily "exclude" non-Anglophone work betrays a disregard for Latinx literature and literature of the Americas.[16] In their introduction, Walkowtiz and Mao do briefly discuss Rubén Darío's *modernismo* and the "vigorous debate" (9) around its relation to modernism. The conversation leaves unconsidered *modernismo* as homage to French symbolism, and does not acknowledge that what Walkowitz and Mao refer to as "modernism" was known in Latin America as *vanguardismo*, and came significantly later in the century.

Laura Lomas does parse these distinctions, though, in her introduction to *Translating Empire*, her study of the Cuban writer and revolutionary José Martí. She and Ramón Saldívar bring Walkowitz and Mao's oversight into a critical field of vision and provide context for thinking through *Face* as a modernist novel. In *The Borderlands of Culture: Américo Paredes and the Transnational Imaginary*, Saldívar argues for "modernism as social movement" (248) whose European resonances fall flat in an American context. Writers like Paredes, he argues, employ modernist strategies, but "commonly held characterizations of modernist ideologies as ahistorical and apolitical are not adequate for explaining the cultural productions of writers actively engaged in decolonization struggles" (197). Building on Saldívar's work, Lomas uses "the term imperial modernity," she explains, "to define a political and cultural project in pursuit of political and economic expansion" (5). Lomas sees Martí imagining "an 'alternative modernity' that acknowledges different cultural locations in the Americas, and rejects the idea that modernity is of strictly European origins" (9). Rejecting modernity as a solely European product requires Lomas to prove the centrality of Latinx literary life to US culture at the turn of the century and to "recast . . . the history of transnational literary modernism and imperial politics in the humbling light of their planetary smallness," to show it, in other words, as part and parcel of a longer, broader colonial and postcolonial process.

To call *Face* a modernist novel, then, requires more than just identifying Pineda's affinities with the high modernist canon. It means building on Lomas's work to bring Latinx texts into conversations about modernism, colonialism, and their post-isms that typically exclude the United States save for considerations of African America such as those pioneered by Brent Edwards in *The Practice of Diaspora* or Michelle Stephens in *Black Empire*. Calling *Face* modernist means pushing modernist studies to grapple seriously with the Americas and to consider the violence against people of color upon which imperial modernity depends.

Face makes this violence visible by rejecting the visibility that comes through commodified and easily articulable identities. The novel rejects the unifying fictions of the body and the identity it putatively represents at the same time that it insists on flesh as an index of the self. That insistence keeps the novel from sliding into the decentered, relative subjectivity of the postmodern. In its insistence on the fundamental disunity of the body, *Face* deploys what I have elsewhere referred to as the "Latino dismodern."[17] As an aesthetics of resistance, the Latinx dismodern rejects a performative identity politics in favor of engaging deep structural inequality and using the body to assert the fundamental interconnection of a collective body politic.

Face, in other words, refuses to let the body be an index of individuality. Helio's accident is not just Helio's misfortune; it reverberates throughout his community. The most disturbing example of this is in his interactions with Lula after his accident. When she first sees Helio without his bandages, Lula cries, and Helio, offering her a handkerchief, feels disconnected from his own body. "It is his hand," he thinks as he watches himself. "And yet, for the first time, this hand. From where does it come?" (30). This dissociation meets its violent culmination when Helio, distraught at Lula's rejection, rapes then beats her, feeling "nothing as the small white teeth shatter against his knuckles" (69). Pineda says in her introduction that she wants to explore how much of the body "can be lost or destroyed before a person loses all claim to inclusion in the human race" (xiv); *inclusion*, not *identification*. Our bodies connect us to a web of humanity, Pineda asserts, and while Helio's accident makes him see this connection, how his hand is, for example, part of a larger network of meaning, he also must take responsibility for other bodies.

The novel lays the groundwork for this notion of connection and responsibility in the hospital scenes, where Helio hears the surgeon narrating discrete body parts as he performs rounds with the medical students. All those fleshy pieces belong to one abstract human body set apart from the body politic by the artificial constructs of the hospital and injury. The body politic itself is a fiction, of course, but in as much as *Face* might be read as a narrative of Third World struggle, it can be read as a struggle to integrate the hospital's body into the world surrounding it. Hospital and government bureaucracies mark these bodies as eternally different and separate, narrated by the doctor, charted, organized, and funneled through civic space by the endless forms, lines, and waiting rooms that Helio encounters after his release. He rejects those distinctions, however, when he throws his facemask away (42). It is uncomfortable, but, as a civil servant tells him, "It's not supposed to make you comfortable." The mask standardizes him as different; it "lets everyone know right away there's nothing wrong with" him (63).

There is "nothing wrong with" anyone in this novel. Thus Helio rejects the notion that he must mark himself. He will move through social spaces as he wishes with the "hat and the handkerchief" that toward the end of the novel are "his skin" (140). These objects take on human qualities that weave him back into himself and the world, like the "tufts of hair" he sweeps at the barber shop that float and drift around everyone's feet, "with a life of their own" (52). Helio's injury brings the fragility of social institutions into focus, and his resistance to institutional narratives of his accident form the foundations for a new politics that eschews individual rights in favor of connection and collectivity.

Face, though, stops short at a total resignation of the individual. Helio wants a "utility face . . . free of distinguishing marks, a slate wiped clean" (146), which Marcial González reads as the desire for a reified identity removed from social conditions. Helio's wish to merge seamlessly into the world around him indicates, according to González, an absence of class consciousness and an unconcern for the inequities that have shaped his life. Helio's desire to blend in also signals, as I've argued, a move on the novel's part to refashion politics by dismantling distinctions of class, race, self and other, human and nonhuman. Helio wants a face free from the "black particles" (146) of earth still embedded in it, but he fashions his new nose from a child's ball (149). That is to say, Helio does get an "unremarkable" face, "But no. Not like anyone." His face is "his, his alone. He has built it, alone, sewn it stitch by stitch. . . . It has not been given casually by birth, but made by him, by the wearer of it" (168). *Face* presents readers with an irresolvable contradiction: Is Helio remarkable or not, a unique individual or an indistinct node in an interconnected web of matter?

Face does not offer answers, just moments of clarity, moving easily between the individual and the collective. The face repeats throughout the novel: there are pictures of faces, memories of faces, books about faces, Godoy's journal about the face. There are many faces on display in this novel about the drama of seeing and being seen, about technologies and angles of vision. In his facelessness, Helio is both radically present and radically absent. He asserts the significance of the ambiguously brown body as Stefan Ruiz's portraits do in *The Factory of Dreams*. Helio also embodies the violent and incomplete erasure of histories of racial violence as do Ken Gonzales-Day's *Erased Lynchings* photos. Like those photos, and like the novel's facial iterations, Helio is one face among many. He understands his face, however, as "his alone." Though he asserts himself as its maker, moreover, it is unclear at novel's end whether Helio or Godoy has made Helio's final face.

Face will not solve that mystery because ultimately the novel is less about Helio's face than the web of meaning that gathers around it, in particular the moment when "he finds his own eyes in the mirror" (169). This moment when Helio connects with his own reflection marks a decisive break with previous instances of looking and looking away, of not seeing. That reflection, those eyes, are not an index of anything; they represent nothing. Helio, in that moment, simply exists. His body interacts, reflecting nothing other than itself, functioning the way Pineda would like her writing to: choratically, as a thing in the world, not as an abstract reflection of things. Both writing and the body here refuse to represent. Writing in this instance enacts a certain kind of physical experience in the world. It threads its way through the world like Helio's gossamer, like the key he "threads" in the lock (145), like himself "threading a pathway" through town (167) after hearing from Godoy. Words connect the disparate world and things of *Face* just as they connect bodies and places in the next chapter of this book and just as surely as Helio's thread pulls together the disparate parts of his face into a unified whole whose representative capacity is as fictive as the novel it lives within.

3

PLACE

Authenticity, Metaphor, and AIDS in Gil Cuadros and Sheila Ortiz Taylor

Language and writing, in the previous chapter, create the materiality of the body and the physical world it inhabits. Such ideas, as I trace them there, emerge from the rarefied and relatively abstract worlds of experimental theater and art photography. Here I explore their material consequences by considering two works that engage the relationship between words, bodies, and the real in the context of AIDS, a pandemic with life-or-death stakes. Such stakes are, as Paula Treichler argues, precisely what make language's imbrication with the real visible. AIDS, she says, helps us understand that "language is not a substitute for reality; it is one of the most significant ways we know reality, experience it, and articulate it" (4). We see this world-making power of language in Gil Cuadros's *City of God* and Sheila Ortiz Taylor's *Coachella*, two Chicanx works explicitly about AIDS that nevertheless resist being about the Chicanx experience of AIDS, instead leveraging the pandemic as a crisis of signification that makes apparent the interconnection of all being.

A guiding question in this chapter, then, is what it means to tell stories about AIDS. Treichler maintains that there is a "machinery by which scientific discourse is produced and accepted" (166), that there is, to a certain extent, little difference between novels and scientific narratives. Of course, she understands that AIDS is an actual disease whose reality lies at the cellular level, but, she notes, that disease comes to us through stories constructed largely by a scientific culture that can and should be challenged (161). Race and ethnicity, as I have been arguing throughout this book, come to us similarly through a culture of ethnic studies grounded in diversity discourse upon which some pressure can also be put. In this chapter I present Cuadros and Ortiz Taylor as engaging in related forms of discursive challenging, crafting new narratives of race and disease that treat AIDS not as racial allegory but as an occasion to reimagine the social through the materiality of the human body.

Cuadros and Ortiz Taylor produce a sense of peoplehood and community as part of what Stacy Alaimo describes as "the material interconnections between the human and the more-than-human world [from which] it may be possible to conjure an ethics." Alaimo terms these interconnections "transcorporeality," which she argues "underlines the extent to which the substance of the human is ultimately inseparable from 'the environment'" (*Bodily Natures* 2). Transcorporeality is a useful way to understand how Cuadros and Ortiz Taylor deploy language and narrative to produce a sense of the human as returned to the fold of the natural world. From the inside-out and outside-in perspectives on corporeally imagined political community that I discuss in chapters 1 and 2 of this book respectively, I move now in chapter 3 to an exploration of the communal sense of place. These novels ask where people belong and what it means to do so. Return and integration are central to both *Coachella* and *City of God*, each of which deploys images of characters' choratic amalgamation with built and natural environments to argue for repetition and communion as modes of authentic becoming.

Before becoming, however, before authenticity, before ethics came fear. Naked fear. And death. Randy Shilts opens his now classic account of AIDS's early years with Rock Hudson's passing in 1985 as "the moment the AIDS epidemic became palpable and the threat loomed everywhere" (xxi). By 1985, though, the disease was a pandemic, too widespread to stop, and Shilts devotes his book to documenting the "drama of national failure" to protect public health in the United States. "People died," he writes, "while the public health authorities and the political leaders who guided them refused to take the tough measures necessary to curb the epidemic's spread. . . . And people died while gay community leaders played politics with the disease" (xxii). People were "dying in the streets," as Stuart Hall notes, going on, therefore to ask quite rightly, "what in God's name is the point of cultural studies?" (285).

Treichler uses Hall's question to launch her own investigation, tracing the links between reality and metaphors at the inception and during the early years of AIDS discourse (Treichler 3). There is now, as I write in the early twenty-first century, a sense that we are living in the "aftermath" of AIDS, as Julie Minich notes in "Aztlán Unprotected." What then, to paraphrase Hall, is the point of studying imaginative literature about the disease? This aftermath narrative, Minich argues, is just as misleading and dangerous as some of the problematic rhetoric around early AIDS research that Treichler describes. Despite the widely held belief that the crisis is over in the United States, Minich contends that "HIV/AIDS remains an urgent health concern" for US men of color who have sex with men (167). While Minich positions Cuadros in relation to the aftermath narrative, arguing that his work illuminates the exclusion of queers of color from contemporary AIDS discourse, I will use him, along with Sheila Ortiz Taylor, to consider the past, the height of the AIDS crisis, and literary transcorporeality.

AIDS came at the apex of the post–World War II sexual revolution and it marked, as Hall notes, "the site at which the advance of sexual politics [was] rolled back." In its wake, Hall feared that not just people but also desire and pleasure would die without the right metaphors to help them survive (285). This revolution of desire and pleasure whose imminent demise Hall laments was made possible in no small part by a very large plant that grew mainly in the jungles of southern Mexico. For generations, indigenous Mexicans had known of barbasco's healing properties (figure 3.1). The wild root, a yam varietal, grew abundantly in the south, where farmers regarded it primarily as a weed, though occasionally they would use it for fishing, throwing slices into the water to create a foam sending fish to the surface for easy collection. Farmers were careful not to throw too much into the water, however, since cows that ingested enough barbasco residue downstream tended to miscarry. Indigenous healers knew that barbasco tea could be used as an abortifacient for humans, but they also fermented it as a tonic for aching joints (Laveaga 72). Such knowledge did not circulate very widely, however, and as Gabriela Soto Laveaga explains, until 1941 "campesinos generally regarded barbasco as having little utility" (73). In the fall of that year, Russell Marker, an American chemist, ventured into the Oaxacan jungle to collect barbasco samples, from which he would eventually procure diosgenin, which can be turned into synthetic progesterone, from which all other synthetic hormones can be derived.

In her study of barbasco's impact on the social, political, and economic lives of twentieth-century indigenous Mexicans, Laveaga identifies the oral contraceptives developed at Syntex, the company Marker

Figure 3.1. Barbasco de placa (*Dioscorea mexicana*). Photo by Rillke.

established in Mexico, as the industry's primary economic driver. In 1960 the US Food and Drug Administration approved Enovid, the first birth control pill. By 1962 over two and a half million women were taking oral contraceptives, and the FDA approved Ortho-Novum, Syntex's version (Laveaga 71). The increasingly widespread use of oral contraceptives corresponds to rapidly changing sexual mores after World War II, but so do other uses of synthetic hormones that Laveaga does not discuss.

In *How Sex Changed*, Joanne Meyerowitz explores the evolution of transvestitism, transsexuals, and transgender culture in the twentieth and twenty-first centuries. She says that the emergence of the phenomenon can be explained by discoveries in endocrinology in the early part of the twentieth century, when researchers learned to attribute sexual expression to hormones and, more importantly, that because men and women shared sex hormones, it was theoretically possible for a human to change their sex (27). From the twenties until 1933, when his Institute for Sexual Science in Berlin was destroyed by the Nazis, Magnus Hirschfeld experimented with sex reassignment, news of which trickled into the United States, along with that of other doctors abroad (18). "Sex change" became a household word and concept in 1952 when the *New York Daily News* ran the headline "Ex-GI Becomes Blonde Beauty," telling the now familiar story of Christine Jorgensen, who changed her sex through a series of operations and hormone treatments in Denmark, overseen by Dr. Christian Hamburger. Jorgensen was not the first man to change sex, but she was certainly the most famous. After Jorgensen's story circulated in the United States, Dr. Hamburger received many inquires from US patients, whom he referred to Dr. Harry Benjamin.

Benjamin had studied with Hirschfeld before relocating to the United States, where he treated patients suffering from gender dysphoria. He brought transgender issues to national attention with his 1966 book *The Transsexual Phenomenon*, becoming a leader in the field and the doctor to whom many trans patients turned to ease their suffering. Along with oral contraceptives, then, we must see barbasco as catalyzing a parallel sexual revolution by significantly decreasing the price and widening the availability of sex hormones in the 1960s. While it is true that access to treatment for gender dysphoria was limited to those who could afford it and find a willing doctor (Meyerowitz 142), it is also true that by the mid-1960s—thanks to barbasco, Russell Marker, and Syntex—the widening supply and decreasing cost of synthetic hormones meant that more and more patients took matters into the own hands, administering their own medications and, in some cases, performing their own surgeries (Meyerowitz 144–45).

Thus, not only does barbasco allow people to engage in more heterosexual sex without risking pregnancy, it also allows humans to access the sexual diversity and fluidity of the natural world. In *Exposed*, Stacy Alaimo describes scientific accounts of queer animals that show how "heteronormativity has damaged and diminished knowledge in biology, anthropology, and other fields" by rendering queer sexuality unnatural

(44). Life, as Alaimo shows, is fundamentally queer, and to imagine it as such decouples generativity from reproduction and makes possible a vision of the future apart from heteronormative repetition.

The transcorporeal connections between barbasco and the human body illuminate that future vision and open humanity up to the natural world's subversive diversity of sex and gender, where boundaries are fluid and change is constant. I put forward this transcorporeality as a model for thinking about *City of God* and *Coachella*, which, I argue, work like barbasco by establishing transformative, choratic networks of text, human bodies, and the natural world. Read together, the books raise questions about what it means to be a person, searching for a kind of ontological authenticity that both authors attach to racial and ethnic identification. In both books, however, race and ethnicity are depicted not as knowable objects but as repeating patterns of connection and change. In Cuadros those repetitions lead to a vision of AIDS as a means of transforming the body into other things, while Ortiz Taylor's protagonist, Yo, a phlebotomist at a local hospital, refuses to think of blood as anything other than itself. "Blood was blood," she muses (66). In *Coachella*, things do not transform into other things as they do in *City of God*. Things are what they are. Plants, for example, die, return to earth, and are born again as plants, a cycle central to the novel's plot as well as its narrative structure.

Both texts depend on this cyclical understanding of time, arguing for a repeated return to literal and figurative roots as a means of moving beyond the confines of the self. This return to roots enables a transformative reproduction in both texts, where reproduction is depicted not as bodies interacting with other bodies to produce more bodies, but as bodies interacting with their surroundings to produce networks of *chicanidad*. Even as they are explicitly about transformation and reproduction, both *Coachella* and *City of God* remain attached to a notion of authenticity, performing a nostalgic longing for some semblance of the real.

They each depict writing as making, not representing, this unattainable real for which they long. Writing, in each, moves characters closer to the real, be it through Yo's research notebooks or the tight connections Cuadros draws between text and the body. This textual play is closely related to the temporal play in which both books engage. Their emphasis on cycles is, on one level, a rejection of linearity and the concept of the future as something we arrive at having traveled in a straight line. Both books follow circuitous narrative paths that bind time and the real through narrative, where text is a mode of both reproduction and transformation, not simply representing, but actively participating in experience.

These two Chicanx AIDS novels, that is, treat language and narrative as chora. They resist documentary status by asserting themselves as part of the process of becoming, as part of the Chicanx experience itself. This process is in productive tension with each book's investment in the real, symbolized in both by indigenous people and things. Barbasco is an indigenous thing used for centuries only by indigenous people, but its travels out of the jungle and its pharmaceutical permutations demonstrate a point the novels also make: that everything is always both becoming itself and changing into something else. *Coachella* and *City of God* show us two related ways books can engage historic events and experiences, like AIDS, while resisting ethnography. Despite their emphasis on the racialized body, Cuadros and Ortiz Taylor do not reproduce ethnic things for readerly consumption. Both use the body and notions of the organic to show that literature does more than reflect and reproduce; it produces iteratively through a recursive return to roots.

How Deep Is "Deep Indian Blue"?

At first pass, though, Gil Cuadros would seem to be moving as far away from his roots as he possibly could with *City of God*, which City Lights Press published in 1994, when he was only thirty-two years old. Two years later, Cuadros died of AIDS-related complications. A gay Chicano native of Montebello, just east of Los Angeles, Cuadros accomplished quite a bit in his short life, winning the Brody Literature Fellowship in 1991 as well as two grants from the city of Los Angeles's Cultural Affairs Department. He was also one of the first to receive the PEN Center USA/West grant to HIV-positive writers. *City of God*, a collection of related stories and poems woven together in a loose narrative of the protagonist's struggle with HIV and the dramas of his large, extended family, stands as a compelling testament to an artistic life cut tragically short.

The scant critical attention *City of God* has received rests largely on these biographical particulars, with scholars assessing his work primarily, as Alberto Sandoval Sánchez does, as an autobiographical representation of the Latinx experience of AIDS.[1] Paul Allatson and Raúl Villa complicate this approach somewhat. The former uses Cuadros to outline what he refers to as "AIDS-graphesis," which examines the role of race and class in the process by which writing transforms resistant queer bodies into objects of knowledge; the latter situates Cuadros in what he calls the "expressway generation" of artists who came of age at the same time as the Los Angeles freeways, which destroyed but also remade Chicanx spaces in Los Angeles (17). Cuadros, in Villa's analysis, owns his barrio space and is resistant to Anglo culture, but his queer identity reveals the dystopic nature of these homophobic and patriarchal racialized spaces. Likewise, Rafael Pérez-Torres, beginning from Villa's premise of Cuadros's double exclusion, reads *City of God* as a quest for spiritual transcendence that ultimately fails to catalyze collective action.

Pérez-Torres criticizes *City of God*'s theoretical solipsism, but by linking the book so closely with Cuadros the person, Pérez-Torres and others perform a similar critical individuation that Minich takes issue with. Allatson, Villa, and Pérez-Torres take for granted that Chicanx culture makes no room for *City of God*'s queer protagonist, but Minich calls this a passive reading of the protagonist's agency. In Cuadros's story "Unprotected," for example, which ends with the narrator falling asleep on a public bus "filled with Mexicanos" (Cuadros 69), Minich finds "a nascent sense of belonging" that allows the narrator to make space for himself in the hostile social landscape of public transportation ("Aztlán Unprotected" 180). Though the narrator is not entirely comfortable on the bus, he is able to fall asleep, which he had not been able to do before in his white date's apartment. Minich takes this moment as the story's primary political achievement of bringing its protagonist's sexuality into public space and forcefully making room on the bus for queer *chicanidad*.

I am less interested than Minich is in Cuadros's articulations of subjectivity and assertions of rights, but like Minich I find Cuadros's use of collectivity and communal spaces compelling. I am not sure, as Minich is, that Cuadros is committed "to telling a complete story of HIV/AIDS" ("Aztlán Unprotected" 186), but I am very interested in the relation between text and body in Cuadros's work, in how, as Pérez-Torres observes, *City of God*'s various scenes of physical disintegration leave only "the collection of stories and poems Cuadros' readers hold in their hands" (173). In this chapter I explore how Cuadros articulates the self in relation to other selves, and how text mediates the interaction of self and surroundings, how it returns the self to the "city of God."

Critics have taken Cuadros's title to be a critique of dystopic Los Angeles. George Lipsitz, for example, reads it as "ironically mocking Saint Augustine's teleological vision, contrasting the writer's own AIDS-wracked body with the metropolitan body politic suffering from its own deleterious divisions and diseases" (513). Cuadros's allusion to Augustine is clear, as is the connection he draws between his body and the city, but a parallel city surfaces here and there throughout Cuadros's work that mitigates Lipsitz's apocalyptic sense of Cuadros's writing. In the fifth century CE, Augustine is defending, in *City of God*, against charges that Christianity has brought about the fall of the Roman Empire. He structures his defense by distinguishing between the cities of God and man. "A people," he writes, referring to any sort of political group or commonwealth, "is an assemblage of reasonable beings bound together by a common agreement as to the objects of their love" (19.24). The city of man, or the "earthly" city, is characterized "by the love of self, even to the contempt of God," while the city of God is characterized by the love of God, "even to the contempt of the self" (Augustine 19.28). Los Angeles is Cuadros's earthly city, a modern-day Rome "declined into sanguinary seditions and then to social and civil wars" (Augustine 19.24). What, then, is the city of God come to redeem it?

However critics understand that redemptive city, they generally agree that Cuadros does not reach it. Allatson, for instance, reads the city of God as the quest for "Chicano queer redemption" (24), a quest that Pérez-Torres reads as having failed. "The stories," writes Pérez-Torres, "represent an ever-shrinking world of human connection where, ultimately, the characters withdraw further into their own physical suffering and spiritual enlightenment," with the end result being the impossibility, in his analysis, of "transcendence as a means of human connectivity" (172). I, conversely, read AIDS not as foreclosure, but as provoking an epistemological crisis of belonging. As AIDS wreaks havoc on the human body, consciousness emerges as a function of things besides the isolated, racialized bodies that populate the collection. Physical suffering, in other words, breaks the body down so that people can join in true communion with other objects.

This communion is not Christian in the Augustinian sense, though Christian iconography abounds in Cuadros's work. His stories maintain an uneasy faith, being simultaneously rich in religious imagery while criticizing religious hypocrisy. Baptism emerges as a trope both in the story "Baptism," where the protagonist cuts of all her hair (89), and in "Chivalry," where a child nearly drowns and then later slits his own wrists, coming to his parents Christ-like, bleeding with his arms outstretched (38). In "Holy," moreover, a mentally disturbed neighbor tapes prayer cards to the protagonist's door while he's away (72). In "Indulgences," however, the collection's opening story, the protagonist's receipt of a rosary and corresponding explanatory booklet calls into question the relationship between text and act. In Catholic tradition an indulgence is the lessening of punishment for a sin, achievable by, among other things, praying the rosary. This rosary and book about indulgence, however, appear in a story called "Indulgences" that is about the absence of forgiveness. In the story, the protagonist's family blames the patriarch's death on a female cousin, whom they physically attack after the funeral. To open *City of God* with the palpable irony of the unforgiving family giving the young protagonist empty symbols of forgiveness calls attention to the distance between rhetoric, action, and object that the stories and poems exploit, a distance Cuadros appears to close in the very next story, "Reynaldo."

There are two Reynaldos in the story, one in the present and one in the past (for our purposes here I'll refer to them as "present-day Reynaldo" and "past Reynaldo"). Present-day Reynaldo, named after his grandfather's close friend, is HIV-positive and visits his doctor, who writes him prescriptions for antidepressants and mood elevators—"twelve white sheets of paper, each with a different savior and my doctor's signature"—that Reynaldo shoves into an old diary (22). The number twelve recalls Jesus's apostles, whose creed—a declaration of faith in God and Jesus—is one of the prayers recited as part of the rosary. None of the characters in "Reynaldo" recite it, but they all maintain complicated relationships with Rosario, Reynaldo's grandmother and the woman who comes between his grandfather and past Reynaldo. "Reynaldo" thus rejects empty religious gestures but retains the magic of repeated actions of faith and ritual.

Another example of this retention and rejection can be found in the story's description of the grandfather's "flower garden" (31). Grandma

Rosario constantly tends her rose garden, and past Reynaldo's mother "set candles into rosettes" (25) on his birthday cake. "Rosary" and "rose" both have etymological roots in *rosa*, Latin for pink, and *rosarium* is Latin for "rose garden." "Reynaldo" carefully depicts roses as the flowers of Catholic tradition and the women who tend it, but the story is about male homosociality, and Reynaldo's grandfather wants flowers, not roses. The generic "flowers" that he plants to temper his desire for travel signal alternate modes of spiritual fulfillment.

Similarly, in "Sight," the protagonist acquires healing powers that allow him to shape and direct the light he perceives in other people's bodies. When an "elderly woman holds the elevator" for him, he can sense her erratic heart and the tumors in her body. She says "God," but the first-person narrator's touch banishes the word, which becomes "the warm buzz of bees and wooden flutes" while her body begins to emanate a healing amber light (97). God is not entirely banished, just rewritten, as later, in the poem "The Breath of God That Brings Life," two lovers hold a copy of the Qur'an as they listen to another man praying in the distant rain (116). The poem equates the rhythm of the prayers with the rhythm of breath and the sounds of the season's "first real rain" (115), suggesting text, in this case religious text, though pointedly not Catholic, as a means by which the human body can experience integration with the natural environment.

Religion, however, just carries the metaphor in *City of God*; it is the vehicle for the tenor of the book's ultimate vision, which relies not on faith but on escaping the confines of the self, on fully connecting with and returning to chora, the stuff of the world. Across the collection individual narrators are de-emphasized in favor of the connections the individuals build with others and that the book builds between and within the shorter pieces it comprises. The poem "Even Months after the Death, John Dreams," for example, turns on a destabilization of "John." Its ambiguous use of pronouns makes it difficult to decipher whether John is dreaming or being dreamt about: "dreams" might be a verb, or a noun modified by "John." This lexical ambiguity finds a visual corollary in "My Aztlán," where the protagonist buries beneath his house the disjointed body parts of dolls he has dismembered (55).

The narrator's doctor in "Sight," similarly, frustrated by the protagonist's refusal to take any more medications, explains the progress of his current condition by disassembling "a model of a large eye" (96). The deconstruction of the eye, a homophone of "I," suggests Western medicine's dehumanization of gay men in the late 1980s and early 1990s, but the protagonist refuses to be cowed.[2] He rejects the eye parts in favor of a new vision. "I can see," he says, "that everything, everyone in her office has a glow around their bodies." The protagonist does not need the doctor's eye/I; he has found his own eye/I that affords him a different way of being in the world (96).

The deconstruction of subjectivity and the permeable borders between subject and object are functions of form as well as imagery in *City of God*. Key images, scenes, and characters repeat and mirror each other between stories and poems. There are, as noted above, parallel baptismal references and two instances of dismemberment. Similarly, the accused cousin in "Indulgences" wears a "flimsy dress, a brownish print" (5), while the scarecrow the family passes on their way out of town at story's end is wearing a "flimsy brown dress" and has a "stake skewered up through the body" (14). The scarecrow visually represents the family's treatment of the cousin, but other instances of repetition are less easy to parse. For example, the narrator in "My Aztlán" recalls how his mother physically abused him (55) while the speaker in "At Risk" witnesses a mother abusing her son in a doctor's waiting room (121); characters eat the same exact dinner of beans, steak, and tortillas in two separate stories (11, 18); a scarf flutters "in the softest breeze" (34) in one story, and birds are described as "twisting and turning like a swath of fabric falling in air" in another (95); past Reynaldo appears as a ghost in "Reynaldo" (28), a child describes images of her mother cut, with scissors, from family photos as "ghosts caught on film" (78) in "Baptism," and the narrator confronts his own ghostly image in "Letting Go" (94).

Self-conscious intertextuality in "Holy" renders these repetitions significant rather than coincidental. Referencing the Smiths' song "Bigmouth Strikes Again," the narrator says, "Now I know how Joan of Arc felt," an intentional reference that asks readers to take *City of God*'s own intratextuality seriously as an assertion that the world and all it contains work by reference, repetition, and connection (75).[3] Repetition obviates uniqueness and singularity, rendering subjectivity and individuality less important. While Morrissey's Latinx fan base in Southern California has been well documented, the meaning of isolated instances of inter- or intratextuality in *City of God* is less important than the simple fact that they occur.[4] In other words, the repetitions are important not for what they mean but for their imbrication of the stories and poems, a formal integration that reflects how the various protagonists and speakers in *City of God* integrate themselves into a series of natural and built environments. These integrations are the key to the dissolution of self the collection works toward: connection is the first step away from the self, followed by recognition that there is no meaningful distinction between self and other.

City of God represents this idea through repeated images of merging, as when, for example, in "Chivalry," the narrator and his cousin lie down in the furrows of the family fields, crush strawberries all over themselves, and then rub their naked bodies together. "Now we're brothers," his cousin tells him (50). Likewise, "Reynaldo's" narrator, present-day Reynaldo, recalls a childhood spent daydreaming under a tree, "the roots spread open like two hands cradling him; beneath him clover spread like a blanket" (16). These two examples of people blending into the land and each other resonate with an earlier example from "Chivalry" where the wind from passing traffic spins weather vanes atop a fence as a child jumps up and down, anticipating the arrival of a truck (39). In this scene nature, technology, and humanity move in concert: the tool (weather vane) responds to the wind and registers the aftereffects of other tools (cars), while the human child registers the same influences as the weather vane; the vane spins as the child jumps.

People and place are connected more explicitly in "My Aztlán: White Place," where the narrator buries his doll's body parts (55) and body blends with asphalt as roads are described as "the veins and arteries of downtown" (54). "My Aztlán," as Minich notes, has garnered the most critical attention of all the pieces in *City of God*. "All the published scholarship on Cuadros" engages with it, she writes ("Aztlán Unprotected" 172). In the story, a "stinking drunk" (53) narrator drives home, contemplating the freeways, his childhood, his diagnosis, and the racial politics of his relationship with his dead white lover. Pérez-Torres reads the story as staking "an original claim to the city" (165), predicating that reading on the narrator's describing his childhood home as "my Aztlán" buried beneath the freeways (55), and his listing of specific events in Chicanx history whose memory the narrator must suppress in order to be with his white lover, who "played no part in these atrocities" (56). While his lover was alive, the narrator "became white too" (56), and so it is not difficult to read this story as being about the willful erasure of a Chicanx consciousness resurrected by illness and imminent death.

"My Aztlán," however, can be read as an exploration of productive *mestizaje* just as easily as it can be understood as a lament for white's erasure of brown. The narrator's declaration that he "became white" suggests a transformation from brown to white, a transformation mirrored in the geography of the city, whose brown neighborhoods were erased and whitened by the freeways.[5] The word "Aztlán," however, is etymologically white, meaning "land of the white herons" in Nahuatl, the Aztec language (Pina 43). Aztlán is always already white; it does not become so. The story describes colonial oppression, and the narrator metaphorizes the city as his "Hot latin, brown-skinned, warm, exotic, dark, dark, dark" body buried beneath the "weight, dirt and asphalt, moist skin, muscle and blood" of his white lovers (58). But Aztlán is also white, and "a milky white fluid floats" in what the narrator describes as his "body's space," suggesting a deeper, physical imbrication of white and brown.

The narrator in "My Aztlán" struggles to articulate his own theories of mestizaje while the story depicts the ambiguous "space" of his body as sensually responding to its environs. A "milky white fluid," semen, floats in this space and fractures the "marriage of [the narrator's parents'] cells," suggesting a queer ecology that opens the body to a world of connections beyond history and heredity. As "My Aztlán" comes to a close, the narrator's body transforms into something new as "ivy grows" over the rotting doll parts he buried long ago (55). This transformation is possible only in the City of God, where distinctions between human and other, natural environments and built, collapse. The narrator's family dramas, the racial politics of his past love affairs—these he longs to leave in the City of Man. At the end of the story, the narrator becomes the "veins and arteries" of the freeways (54); he can feel himself "becoming tar" as the "white clay" of his childhood home pokes through the surface asphalt; his inner whiteness blending with the metaphorical whiteness of the built environment. The caving in here, as the clay "sifts through the ceiling," is liberating rather than destructive; his body's space becomes an abstraction of liberation whose "bones shine in the dark," illuminating the City of Man (58).

The disintegration of the narrator's body allows him to fully return to the world; he becomes the light and energy of his surroundings. Falling apart paradoxically makes him whole, in other words. This process is mirrored in the collection's concluding poem, "Conquering Immortality," where the speaker explores the ruins of the Egyptian Theater in Hollywood. The Egyptian, built in 1922 to celebrate Hollywood glamour, closed in 1992 and was left to ruin until American Cinematheque bought, restored, and reopened it in 1998, two years after Cuadros's death. The Egyptian he would have known was a hollowed-out shell of its former self, a crumbling façade whose demise the speaker in the poem describes as "like the progression of a disease" (143). The derelict theater "leans outward" (148), as the speaker's objective correlative, but as he contemplates this visual representation of his physical state, he notices "that today is beautiful, / that the sand colored walls of the Egyptian, / yellow like dark mustard, / set out against this blue sky" (149). From the depths of his despair the speaker finds beauty and strength, and he enters the boarded-up theater.

"Conquering Immortality"—with images of illness, disintegration, communion, text, and history—corrals themes that circulate throughout *City of God*, but its title raises quite a few questions. It is not immediately clear whether conquering immortality is desirable or not. Would a terminally ill person not prefer to conquer *mortality* rather than *immortality*, to live rather than die? To conquer immortality, though, might mean achieving the transformative disintegration of "My Aztlán," conquering the desire for immortality altogether. Or the title might suggest conquering the fear of death, avoiding a desperate clinging to an empty life such as that visually suggested by the crumbling theater and the *Twilight Zone* episode the speaker recalls about an ancient actress whose youth is preserved by a talismanic beetle she wears around her neck (142). To conquer immortality might be to move past and through the City of Man into the City of God's immanent wholeness.

This the speaker achieves when noticing the beauty in decay. He is carried outside himself with the realization "that today is beautiful," and "the walls of this building / are sturdy like myself" (149). When he can see through his own tragedy to the "blue sky," he achieves not self-awareness, exactly, but world-awareness, a sense of his fleeting time in the order of things. "And even if the parapets are bulldozed in haste," the speaker thinks, "this sacred space can never die out" (149), just as something will remain of him even when he dies. This moment closely parallels the end of "Holy," one of *City of God*'s prose pieces. There, the very sick narrator notes that his "complexion changed from metallic gold to a deep Indian blue" (75), colors echoed in the yellow walls and blue sky of "Conquering Immortality." In both, yellow or gold is the color of confinement, of walls or able-bodiedness, while blue is the color of freedom, an idealized, pre-Contact indigeneity that frames a space apart from a debased material world. The sense of confinement versus freedom is projected also in the role the built environment plays in each piece. In "Holy," the speaker hallucinates sitting on a flowery throne, a "small flame" in his right hand, while in his left he feels "the beginning framework of a new home, the skeleton of a new being" (75). As in "My Aztlán," here the narrator's sense of self correlates to built structures, but at the end of the collection, in "Conquering Immortality," the speaker is ready to leave behind the confines of body and buildings for the expanse of the blue sky.

"Holy" hints at the leave-taking in "Conquering Immortality." Etymologically, the word "holy" refers to a state of inviolate wholeness, from whence it evolved to mean something sacred and set apart, but *City of God* largely rejects that isolation in favor of immanence. The word "holy" never occurs in "Conquering Immortality." The speaker is redeemed without rhetoric. From "Holy" to "Conquering Immortality" the religious icons and the language of the self are rejected in favor of the language of the whole; the "Indian blue" of human struggle becomes blue sky, and the speaker is finally free.

Across *City of God* this freedom is a function of text, a function most visible in "Conquering Immortality." Cuadros figures reading, writing, and interpretation as processes, both active and passive, that move the self beyond the confines of the body toward choratic communion and wholeness. For example, the decaying theater in "Conquering Immortality" reminds the speaker of the progression of his illness and how he initially tried to make sense of his symptoms, indecipherable "clues" that "fly around / like . . . decayed hieroglyphs (144). Text brings body and building together; the speaker uses words to indicate the parallel processes of reading that frame his exploration of the theater and his coming to terms with HIV. This merging of body and text recalls two other moments in *City of God*: in "Reynaldo," past Reynaldo emerges from the letters and becomes an entity with which present-day Reynaldo must engage; in "The Breath of God That Brings Life," holding a copy of the Qur'an allows the speaker to connect with the prayers he hears in the distance as he "explode[s], muscles surrender[ing] to peace" after a massage (116). In all three instances—the massage, the letter reading, and correlating the body to the theater—text moves an individual beyond himself, beyond the present time and space to a different temporal, physical plane.

Something similar happens in the Osiris section of "Conquering Immortality," though the scene of reading there is passive rather than active. In the above instances the speaker acts: he reads letters, talks to ghosts, holds a Qur'an, and tries to decipher the hieroglyphs of his own body. Osiris, conversely, is read and written. He does nothing, is acted upon. His brother, Seth, kills him, but his wife, Isis, "found him and brought him back to life" (146). Seth then kills Osiris again and scatters his dismembered remains across Egypt, leaving Isis to find and reassemble the body parts. Osiris's story of being destroyed and then rebuilt mirrors the speaker's journey from diagnosis to immanence. The dismemberment here echoes the dismembered dolls in "My Aztlán" and the disarticulated eye in "Sight," but the crucial difference in *City of God*'s concluding piece is the speaker's passivity. In "Sight," the disarticulated eye leaves the narrator with the ability and desire to heal others; in "My Aztlán," the narrator takes action against the dolls. In "Conquering Immortality," however, the speaker is finally able to let go and do nothing at all.

This letting go is figured as a play of active and passive voice. After a series of lines in the active voice describing what Seth and Isis do, Osiris finally takes action: "Osiris became the god of the dead." This action, however, is followed by descriptions of death-related décor in the passive voice and a confusion of subject and object: "In many inscriptions written on sarcophagi, / an invocation can be read, / "Greetings O thou art chief of the great . . . / I am Osiris." "Thou" might be the god Osiris, but the next line equates "I" with Osiris. In the ambiguity of these lines "I" and "thou" become one, a reading supported by the section's final line: "All the dead become Osiris." That conflation of subject and object is reinforced by the descriptions of reading and writing in the passive voice. The phrases are redundant (written inscriptions and read invocations); reading and writing are so important the speaker must use two words to describe them when one would suffice. They are, however, in the passive voice, which subordinates subject to object. In a radical departure from the rest of *City of God*, the subject who reads and writes is less significant than that which is written and read.

The read and the written hold great illocutionary power in the Osiris section, conflating subject and object. "You" and "I" become one through Osiris's dismantling, and this story then becomes an allegory of both the speaker's relationship to his failing body and the reader's experience of *City of God*. Seven years into his diagnosis, the speaker sees his "life as a series of facades / each layer in erosion," reminding the reader of the decaying theater but also suggesting the peeling away of protective layers of self. From here the poem moves through descriptions of "my mouth," "my calves" (148), foregrounding "me" until arriving once more at the passive voice: "Forgotten is career and income" (149). Not "I have forgotten about," but "forgotten," an active passivity whereby, just as Osiris's dismemberment conflates subjects and objects, the speaker enters infinite time and space as he feels the layers of his body fall away. He conquers immortality, he returns to the infinite roots of himself, when he lets his layers go. The speaker remains "protected by myth," circulating in communal, textual space.

How Soon Is Now?

Cuadros's textual continuation is less about the endurance of the I and more about the conflation of subject and object, the merging with Osiris, or passing from the City of Man into the City of God, figured ultimately as leaving behind both time and the body. Sheila Ortiz Taylor, on the other hand, imagines time and the body as things to be inhabited, not abandoned. As one character puts it, in the past, "everything had seemed to mean itself and something more," whereas now, "everything will agree to be itself and nothing more" (46). The body simply is. The cities of God and man are not opposed in *Coachella*; they are the same. Like *City of God*, *Coachella* is about AIDS, but Ortiz Taylor, unlike Cuadros, figures the body itself as a mode of transcorporeal connection to the earth. Watching Marina rock her baby from a distance, for example, the protagonist, Yo, imagines that rocking as a rhythm evolving into a shadow moving across the desert, "burning herself into the landscape and into the moment in which the bucket still swings from Yo's hand" (32). The physicality of the moment becomes a pulse of space and time, integrating Marina into the landscape and connecting her with Yo, caught in the shadow of Marina's maternity.

Ortiz Taylor understands this choratic integration of selves and the environment as a cornerstone of the Cahuillan traditions indigenous to the Coachella region. For both Ortiz Taylor and Cuadros indigeneity is a central concept, though each deploys it differently. For Cuadros indigeneity is an important touchstone on a series of journeys in which characters attempt to leave human concerns behind in favor of something more real, beautiful, and true. The speaker's perception shifts in "Conquering Immortality," for example, from "Indian blue" to the "blue sky," from the human to the expansive world beyond. For Ortiz Taylor, by contrast, indigeneity is the expanse. The real, the beautiful, and the true surround Ortiz Taylor's characters in the blood networks, threatened by AIDS, connecting the Cahuilla to the earth. *Coachella* resists thinking of blood in metaphorical terms. In her lab Yo considers it "quantifiable, essential, compelling life fluid" (66). The same blood runs through all humans; there is not indigenous blood and Anglo blood. Once Yo realizes "a pattern," wherein patients receiving blood from her lab are falling prey to a mysterious illness the hospital is reluctant to identify as AIDS, she begins to understand the dangers of metaphoric thinking (54). The blood does not point away from itself toward abstractions of race; it means itself and nothing more, a pattern of disease.

Gary Luna, Yo's uncle, embodies a similar tension between metaphor and materiality. Luna is a native Cahuillan who, despite being dead, regularly visits characters in the novel, imbricating "reality" and real "Indians" with questions of time. Luna connects the characters to each other and their heritage in ways meant to combat the carnivalesque indigeneity on offer at the spa (45) and county fair (65), where indigeneity is figured as something to buy rather than as a way of being in the world. With Luna and images of blood, *Coachella* asks what blood *really* is and what it *really* means to be Indian. Blood and indigeneity work along parallel tracks in the novel, woven together by narrative deployments of time and temporality. Time is a mode of both content and form in *Coachella*. It is, in other words, a way for Ortiz Taylor to represent things, but time is also what the novel is essentially about; arguments about the real in *Coachella* are temporal at their core.

Ortiz Taylor uses different experiences of time to represent opposing worldviews. There is, for instance, Ellen, a dutiful daughter, for whom time "keeps diminishing" as she administers lethal doses of morphine to her terminally ill mother. For Ellen, the caretaker, "time is compacting, becoming a distillation" to an encompassing and inescapable now (160). David, on the other hand, Marina's abusive husband, experiences time as an engulfing never. He "is not a patient man" (108) and feels himself to be "doing time" (164) as he waits for his wife's return. For David, time expands; he is always waiting, always trying to reach a temporal horizon.

Ortiz Taylor opposes Ellen's now to David's never, but both represent a kind of measureless infinity that is reflected by the non-time in which Yo and Marina's interactions take place. When planning for her and Marina's future and deciding what to do about David, Yo tells her father not to act just yet. "The time is coming," she says (115). Yo and Marina's time is neither now nor never; it is anticipated. It is "that ambiguous zone between afternoon and evening" during which Yo and Marina swim at novel's end. There is no pattern to their swimming, the narrator remarks (181), but the "patterns of shadows" they cast "could be just one creature swimming" (182). In this ambiguous time the two women merge and become one "creature" in ways that recall Yo's earlier vision of Marina's rocking as a "shadow of a woman zigzagging across the landscape" (32). In both moments the temporal ambiguity signals a planetary consciousness and dissolution of self and other.

In Yo and Marina's measureless time, Ellen's now, and David's never, then, we see three distinct views of otherness: a rejection of otherness altogether, a care for the other, and a destruction of the other. Time represents various humanistic dispositions, but it is also the primary way action in the novel is framed. *Coachella* is broken into chapters with specific dates as titles, beginning on February 15, 1983, and ending on June 1, 1983. Though Marina and Yo's measureless time clearly signals the ethical orientation the novel champions, indicated also through Ortiz Taylor's present-tense narration, these chapter titles do measure out time and move chronologically from mid-winter to mid-spring. The chapters trace a clear arc, but significantly they begin and end mid-season, in periods of ambiguous transition like the dusk at novel's end. The action ends, furthermore, at the height of spring, June 1, a time of beginnings, flowerings, and new life, the culmination of a natural cycle.

Coachella is concerned thematically as well as formally with cycles, which humans are consistently depicted as disrupting. Yo's father, Crescencio, and her cousin Jaime, for example, disagree over proper gardening techniques. Crescencio (whose name conjures the Spanish verb *crecer*—to grow) operates his own small landscaping business, tending to private clients while appreciating the natural desert landscape where "plants took care of themselves" (5). Jaime wants Crescencio to leave all that behind to work with him on the golf course that he, "in his big green tank truck," sprays regularly "with a mixture of fertilizer and Diazinon" that is corroding the skin on his hands (128). Jaime is depicted as misguided. The characters that readers are meant to admire and identify with, by contrast, maintain an awareness of their connection to the earth and the inevitability of their return to it, like Josie, Jaime's mother, who prepares natural remedies for her son. His hands are one ill effect among several described in the novel of attempts to alter the earth's natural cycles by force of human will.

These interventions all end badly. Readers learn about the Mexican state of Guerrero, for instance, flooded in order "to bring water to the ugly towns springing up all along the Tamaulipas border" (126). There is also one of the city of Coachella's major industries, cosmetic surgery, transfusions from which are spreading HIV to wealthy clients like Ellie, Ellen's mother. Attempts like this to disrupt the flow of nature lead ultimately to destruction, a point that escapes many of the novel's characters. Jaime, to illustrate, resists Crescencio's careful landscaping. David, Marina's abusive husband, similarly feels himself trapped by Marina and Yo's non-time. Instead, he moves ever forward, steadily closer to Marina as the novel progresses, destroying instead of nurturing.

Less destructive, though no less impatient, is Ellie's husband, George, who cannot understand her passing as a moment in an eternal cycle of becoming. "The light has gone from the world" for George, who has only a linear conception of time (162). Likewise, Ellie's friend Biscuit thinks that being a woman is all about linear time: "time to get breasts, time to get your period, time to go steady, get engaged, get married, time to have babies, get on the pill, go through the change, stop her stomach from pooching. And now maybe it was time to start in on her face. Rejuvenate it" (13). For George and Biscuit, time moves inexorably forward, leaving ruin in its wake. Ellie herself succumbs to this temporal vision when she tries to turn back time with cosmetic surgery. Only on her deathbed does she begin to understand herself as part of an interconnected, cyclical network of being, "waiting like a dry root for the water to reach her through intricate conduits of irrigation" (40), comforted only by the "sound of earth being turned over around her roots" (42). Ellie finally sees herself as both subject and object, as both having and being a root, as dying but on the verge of rebirth.

Through this attention to interconnected cycles *Coachella* appears to be advocating for something like what Alaimo describes as an ethics that is "not merely social but material." Alaimo's ethical terrain comprises the "unmappable landscapes of interacting biological, climatic, economic, and political forces" achievable only by "thinking across bodies." *Coachella*'s conflation of water, blood, plants, and human bodies does "catalyze the recognition that the environment, which is too often imagined as inert, empty space or as a resource for human use is, in fact, a world of fleshy beings with their own needs, claims, and actions," as Alaimo puts it, though she is not discussing Ortiz Taylor's work (*Bodily Natures* 2). Humans, however, remain at the philosophical core of Ortiz Taylor's novel, which fetishizes certain kinds of people, like women and native Cahuillans, even as it tries to decenter the human.

At the end of the novel, for example, Crescencio mawkishly observes that "woman marks [man's] time, shapes his days by her cycling" (183). Crescencio is also the vehicle for *Coachella*'s linkage of race and temporality. The novel opens with his meditation on George's timed sprinklers, which work "by the clock, like everything gringo. It's time, it's time they always say," he thinks (3). This opening sequence explicitly correlates notions of time to race: Anglo time is linear and destructive—treating plants as if they were on an "assembly line" would kill them, thinks Crescencio (4)—while mestizo and indigenous time is cyclical and regenerative.

As the novel progresses, these temporal meditations become coded as an authenticity contest between Indians when Sal Greenfeather, owner of the Palm Springs Spa Hotel, is set against the undead Gary Luna, who, in Yo's estimation, "just kept to the path. That was all. Did not make pronouncements" about his tribal affiliations as Sal does (65). The mineral springs, mud baths, and treatments on offer at Sal's spa exploit "women's cosmetic anxieties with the best of them," and the novel presents this manipulation as an indication of Sal's inauthenticity. His view of time is linear, like George's and Biscuit's, not cyclical, like Crescencio's. *Coachella* stakes Luna's authenticity, by contrast, on his ability to inhabit indigenous time, to move between the afterlife and the present.[6] He cannot always be seen but his presence can be felt, as at the end of the novel when Crescencio experiences Luna's presence as "a warmth filling the cab" of his truck (184), or earlier when Josie senses him as she watches a news report about HIV in the US blood supply (156). Luna functions in the novel as a force that comes and goes while retaining the power to influence action in the present: he signals to Josie that HIV and AIDS are important, and he helps Crescencio kill David.

Luna's present absence takes on increasing significance as the novel unfolds. A sprinkler goes off, for example—"so faithful you could set your watch by it"—as George contemplates "the knowhow that created this oasis out of barren desert, a life out of nothing" (27). The novel depicts the golf course as an artificial imposition with Jaime's chemically afflicted hands, but also by taking issue with George's idea that "know-how" creates something out of "nothing" in the desert. He sees the oasis as man-made, whereas Yo understands an oasis as the result of "something pushing its way past obstacles, seeking easy movement, freedom." She comes to this theory by comparing fault line maps to topographical maps and realizing that green space in the desert occurs "because the fault had buckled up and let water seep or rush up to the surface from underground rivers" (25). Where George sees the desert as "nothing," Yo understands that there is no such thing as nothing. Nothing is always something in the process of becoming.

Coachella depicts the idea of present absence in a variety of contexts besides the fullness of the landscape. There is, of course indigeneity as represented by the unassuming, ever-returning Gary Luna. Marina, though, voices the idea directly as she appreciates the whiteness on the patio of the Casa Diva Guesthouse. The gleaming outdoor furniture reminds her at first of bones and death, but then she remembers that white "is the presence of all colors. Whatever is absent is also present" (19). The concept surfaces again in a later conversation between Marina and

Josie while the two are hiking in the San Jacinto Mountains. The women quietly appreciate the desert beauty, and Josie says, "I could say a whole lot about all of this, but I ain't going to" (98). Josie's reticence suggests the inability of language to convey the fullness of the visual scene. Language also, the novel explicitly argues, is incapable of representing the reality of AIDS, as Yo comes to appreciate when she realizes that she and her friends "never said AIDS" when explaining a friend's illness to Marina. The word, itself an acronym that gestures not to one thing but rather to a collection of conditions, is inadequate to the range of experiences, feelings, and subject positions HIV pulls into its network. Language is thus the defining present absence in *Coachella*.

The notion of language as a present absence grounds *Coachella*'s arguments about race and ethnicity, the authenticity of which is one of *Coachella*'s primary thematic concerns. The novel also understands, however, that authenticity can be neither represented nor written; like the land, Josie's feelings, and HIV, it spills beyond linguistic confines. People cannot tell by looking, for example, that Ellie is Mexican. "Oh, you couldn't see it so much by her skin; una guera. It was the way she turned her head and looked at you. It was in the manner of her listening. La sangre" (5). Her race is not conventionally legible, but it leaves a trace. Biscuit is similarly confounded in her attempts to read race when she visits Sal's spa and notes that an employee "doesn't look Indian but you never could tell" (43). She is sure another employee is "definitely Indian" because she seems "like she knows something but is not about to say what" (45). Biscuit's observations echo the novel's own argument that race cannot be locked into visual or narrative systems; it is like the water underneath the desert floor, pushing up and through the surface, leaving only traces of itself and patterns to be discerned. Biscuit, however, has a deep faith in race as a portal to the real. Armed with spiritual beliefs based on Indian kitsch marketed to Anglos such as herself, Biscuit is sure that the Cahuillan gods "can help her decide" what to do with her body (45).

Coachella, on the other hand, discounts Biscuit's position. There is no Indian truth; there are no Indian things. There is only a constant becoming, and that becoming is a function of connecting as characters come together, moments in time overlap, and images form patterns through repetition. These moments of connection are also moments of return to the root, to the folds of the text and the world; moments of regeneration that fuel another cycle of forward movement. These connections and returns are similar to the repetitions in *City of God*, though repetition in *Coachella* is even more explicit, especially with "all those test tubes of blood, a pattern" emerging in Yo's lab (54). "Connect those dots," Yo tells herself as she tries to read the pattern. The blood draws everyone together, an idea mirrored in a later image of Yo mashing beans, "the rhythm of her hand and wrist coaxing the individual beans into a blended, textured substance" (91). There is no objective, racial reality that stands outside the network of blood; there is only the reality of patterns and mixing, of nodes in the texture of the beans.

Scenes as well as images repeat in *Coachella*, as they do in *City of God*. There is, for instance, George looking at the golf course and Yo contemplating the desert, as described above. Yo wrings out a rag while washing her car (31), for another example, while a few pages hence Marina squeezes a sponge under her faucet (38). Much later, after an argument, both women are described, pages apart, in the same position staring at each other's trailers (104, 106). Yo and Marina are represented in the novel's form as well as its content as connected, like the women patients, and like the many instances of the same woman Ellie imagines George will marry after she dies. "His need will create the woman," Ellie thinks, as she imagines George "pregnant with wives, each of them somehow her sister" (146). Such paralleling and repetition renders narrative a function of this becoming. Narrative does not represent; it shapes experience. Language, as Treichler argues, is real. Like chora, language and narrative mark the place from which the real emerges at the same time they are the things by which the real is known. Neither *reflects* authenticity, in other words; they are modes of *becoming* authentic.

Coachella's structure, which relies on patterns, repetitions, and connections, embodies and performs the kinds of authenticating networks it describes. The Cahuillas so inserted themselves into the natural fabric of things that "nothing got lost," Crescencio observes; they used "everything God gave them" (61). *Coachella* works similarly, drawing objects into its network of textual becoming. The novel will not represent indigeneity for the reader, but it will, like the storyteller Yo encounters at the fair, chant "way beyond ground leases and mudpacks . . . to touch the mineral spring of kinship they might have carried safely to this spot" of reading (68). The chant, the novel, text itself brings people together as one with the world around them in a move that can be variously described as romantic pastoral or implicit ecological critique.

Language, in the midst of such ambiguity, is depicted as a present absence, like when Josie tells Marina how much she could say but will not (98). Later on during that hike, Marina finds a used roll of film, "pictures taken, lost" (99). She eventually takes the film to be developed but never picks up the pictures. Thus, while Marina's discovery of film and the narrator's description of her being "lost in the art of the desert" on the one hand posit her as the visual answer to Josie's reticence, visual fullness does not attend to the emptiness of language (99). Words and pictures operate in concert, like "the song of the crickets underlying everything" at the end of the novel, like Yo's notebook and Marina's artist's eye for color and form. No one system, visual or linguistic, supersedes the other in *Coachella*. They are both incomplete and imperfect means of drawing humans closer to the infinite.

How Clear Is the Authentic Trace?

People move closer to the infinite in *Coachella*, but they never really arrive. Yo says, in the early stages of her romance with Marina, that "she'd like to know everything, the way you can when you read a novel," and yet this novel gives readers no answers (137). Marina's photos remain unseen, and characters continue to die of AIDS, though the word itself is repressed. "Nunca AIDS," Marina complains to Yo (103). Nobody tells Marina that Gil has it, and Yo resists revealing her suspicions to Ellie, assuring Josie that "the time is coming around" for them to let her know (115). The time never comes, however, and Ellie dies without knowing. The temporal condition of not knowing—never for Marina and not yet for Ellie—thus is a constitutive feature of the novel's plot and form. "Yo said the time would come," thinks Crescencio at the end of the novel (175). It "would" come, but whether or not it ever does arrive is unclear. The verb remains conditional, as do the fates of all the characters in the novel.

In this deferral, this present absence, *Coachella* pushes back against the power of AIDS discourse to condition the experience of the disease, much as Cuadros does when his characters in "Sight" and "Reynaldo" reject their doctors' prescriptions. Treichler says that "an illness always constructs its metaphoric double, which speaks truth as faithfully as any biomedical diagnosis" (172). We might see Cuadros and Ortiz Taylor, then, challenging biomedical discourse as Treichler says is necessary in order to make apparent how clinicians understand and subordinate culture to the putative objective reality of science (160). We might also understand *Coachella* and *City of God* not as attempts to define AIDS or articulate a particular experience of it, but rather as tracing its networks. In *Exposed*, Alaimo suggests that new forms of politics will arise from "the material-semiotic entanglements of the world." Thinkers, activists, and writers must look therefore not to "how each object exists in isolation" but rather to how "objects are entangled—economically, politically, and substantially across bodies, ecosystems, and built environments" (187). This, I argue, is how Cuadros and Ortiz Taylor should be read. AIDS allows Cuadros's narrators to push beyond the limits and fictions of their bodies, whereas *Coachella* asserts the body's inescapable materiality. In both books, however, AIDS catalyzes connections to and integration with the natural and built environments in which the human body is enmeshed, carrying us back finally to barbasco.

Barbasco is an occasion to think through what makes something authentic and real. The yam is a very large root deeply imbricated with indigenous Mexican farming practices. Its authenticity can also be read, however, as a function of its ability to generate multiple networks of trade and commerce linking indigenous Mexicans to Mexico's GDP, and inserting Mexico into global pharmaceutical markets. Authenticity in *Coachella* and *City of God* operates with a similar tension of materiality and abstraction. Both books are concerned with indigeneity, but not as something one can know, buy, or experience. Indigeneity in each book is a tool for what Alaimo describes as "thinking as the stuff of the world." Racial and ethnic heritage are important to Cuadros's and Ortiz Taylor's protagonists, but they all "analyze, theorize, critique, create, revolt, and transform as someone whose corporeality cannot be distinct from biopolitical systems and biochemical processes" (*Exposed* 185). History and social justice are important to these characters, but they reject the politics and aesthetics of the self.

In each book the protagonist's sense of self relies on a rejection of individuality in favor of transcorporeal communality. Cuadros and

Ortiz Taylor are usually read in the context of progressive queer expression, but this privileges individuality in ways that vitiate the political force of queer attachment. In her discussion of queer ecologies, Alaimo discusses the "multitude of animal cultures that disrupt human—even feminist, even queer—models" (*Exposed* 57). To fully appreciate Cuadros and Ortiz Taylor, then, we must think of their queerness as more than human. They do not present queer ethnic selves in commoditized literary form so much as they use queerness to depict human selves as part of an interconnected, transcorporeal web of being. *Coachella* and *City of God* reconceive the human body as a crucial, galvanic component of this web, and, like the authors in the next chapter, the books refuse to let the human body evaporate into historical mist. They will not lose the materiality of the human body even as it expands into something more than human. In their discursive constructions of AIDS, Cuadros and Ortiz Taylor divorce the body from the Chicanx experience of AIDS, or more precisely, they make that experience be about something besides the human self. To understand how the body can remain even as it expands to something beyond itself, I turn in the opening pages of my next, and final, chapter to the bio-digital installation art of Rafael Lozano-Hemmer.

4

WASTE

The Trash Fiction of Alejandro Morales, Beatrice Pita, and Rosaura Sánchez

In 2010 the city of Santa Monica commissioned the Mexican Canadian artist Rafael Lozano-Hemmer to build a large-scale installation for Glow, its all-night art event featuring original works from international, national, and local artists designed to engage audiences by bringing art into unexpected places. Lozano-Hemmer, who represented Mexico in the 2007 Venice Biennale, is known internationally for his new media works that deploy digital technologies to build what he describes as "platforms of participation where the public may establish relationships with each other, with the built environment, or with certain curated contexts" ("Digital Art" 32). Lozano-Hemmer's idea of participation platforms structures my reading in this chapter of two Chicanx science fiction (SF) novels: Alejandro Morales's *The Rag Doll Plagues* (1992) and *Lunar Braceros*, by Rosaura Sánchez and Beatrice Pita (2009). The books mediate the apparent gulf between Lozano-Hemmer's abstracted, artistic bodies and the material bodies of those who perish crossing the US-Mexico border. Taken together, these objects—books, bodies, digital installations—explore the potential of the body to intervene in what Achille Mbembe calls necropolitics, the "subjugation of life to the power of death" (186). For Glow, Lozano-Hemmer explored this potential with *Sandbox*, which used infrared surveillance equipment to project live images of people on the beach to small sandboxes where participants were invited to reach out and touch the tiny people, while their hands were simultaneously magnified and projected in real time back onto the beach (figures 4.1 and 4.2).

Sandbox is number 17 in Lozano-Hemmer's *Relational Architecture* series, all of the pieces in which use the viewer's body, usually in the form of biometric data, to reconfigure the human experience of

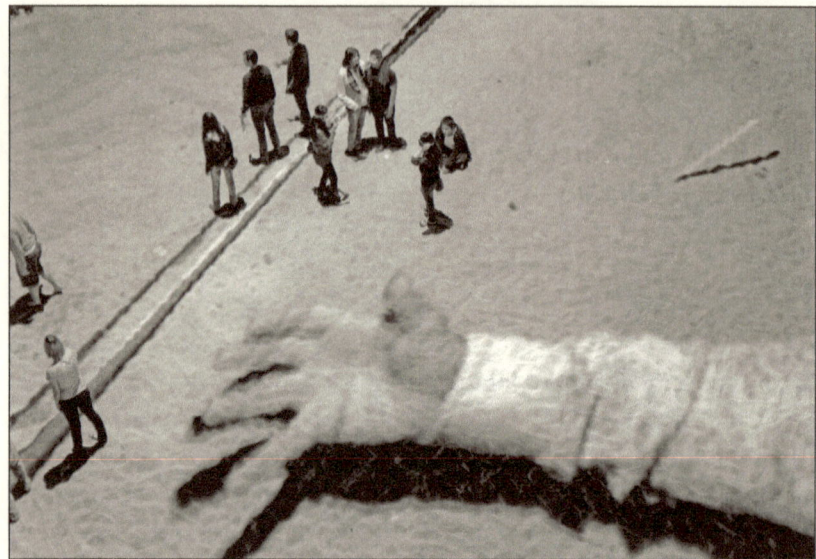

Figure 4.1. Human hand magnified and projected onto the beach. Rafael Lozano-Hemmer, *Sandbox, Relational Architecture 17*, 2010. Santa Monica, California. Photo by Antimodular Research.

space and time. *Pulse Park* (*Relational Architecture* 14, 2008), for example, was composed of a series of lights placed around the central oval field of Madison Square Park in New York City (figure 4.3). The flickering pattern of the lights was modulated to the heart rates of individual observers as read by a sensor installed in a sculpture at the north end of the lawn (figure 4.4). The pattern moved sequentially down the row of lights as new visitors made contact with the sensor, so viewers could see their own illuminated biometrics moving through space in temporal relation to other visitors.

Pieces like *Pulse Park* perform Rosi Braidotti's notion of the self as "differential and constituted through embedded and embodied sets of interrelations" (138) and the subject as "marked by the interdependence with its environment through a structure of mutual flows and data transfer" (139). These installations also allow Lozano-Hemmer to fulfill one function of his art: "to amplify and empower the public." Conversely, Lozano-Hemmer also seeks "to create predatorial environments that police, track, brand, or classify the public" in order to trouble an unthinking embrace of technology and undermine "the fallacy that advanced surveillance equipment can make our cities safer from terrorists" ("Digital Art" 32). *Sandbox* straddles the divide between these two aims. It uses infrared surveillance technology similar to that found at the US-Mexico border, and its stated aim is to illuminate the asymmetries of power. This is all accomplished in a very playful way, however, using surveillance technology to create what Lozano-Hemmer calls "environments of connection" rather than of suspicion (Lozano-Hemmer, "Glow"). By purposefully misusing the technology to distort the size of the participants' bodies, Lozano-Hemmer collapses three spatial

Figure 4.2. Participants play with sand and each other. Rafael Lozano-Hemmer, *Sandbox, Relational Architecture 17*, 2010. Santa Monica, California. Photo by Antimodular Research.

Figure 4.3. Blinking lights represent observers' biometric data. Rafael Lozano-Hemmer, *Pulse Park, Relational Architecture 14*, 2008. Madison Square Park, New York City. Photo by James Ewing.

scales—the small box, the big beach, and the normal human scale—in the service of creating a shared public, anti-corporate, cooperative space.

In *Sandbox*, space becomes an event, a trick of the light defined by the movement of real and virtual bodies coordinating in real time on the beach, the sandy border between land and sea. Consider now a different kind of spatial event, with bodies on a different sandy border: the Sonoran Desert between the United States and Mexico. The bodies found here are not tricks of light; they are harrowingly real, and we know them by their traces: 1,146 men's underpants, 64 rosaries, 11 packages of Q-tips, 64 candies, 9 spoons, 49 dentures, 4 compasses, 21 cloves of garlic, 1 calculator watch, 249 bras, 1 Barney stuffed toy, 139 sets of keys, 18 makeup compacts, 34 pairs of eyeglasses, 7 decks of cards, 19 containers of hair gel, 1 carton of milk, 4 pornographic magazines. Those are just a few of the items featured on "The Things They Carried," John Stobbe's hand-drawn poster, designed for the Colibrí Center for Human Rights (figure 4.5). These objects were found along with the unidentified bodies of migrants who died crossing the US-Mexico border. According to Robin Reineke, Colibrí's executive director, these objects are key to identifying remains often rendered unidentifiable by the harsh desert climate (Human Rights Watch, *Torn Apart*).

The Colibrí Center's main mission is to identify and match these remains with families searching for loved ones last seen crossing the border. They also advocate for immigrant rights and border demilitarization. Since the mid-1990s, when the US government began increasing surveillance and personnel along its border with Mexico, there has been a sharp increase in migrant deaths as people are pushed toward

Figure 4.4. Sensors read observers' biometric data. Rafael Lozano-Hemmer, *Pulse Park, Relational Architecture 14*, 2008. Madison Square Park, New York City. Photo by James Ewing.

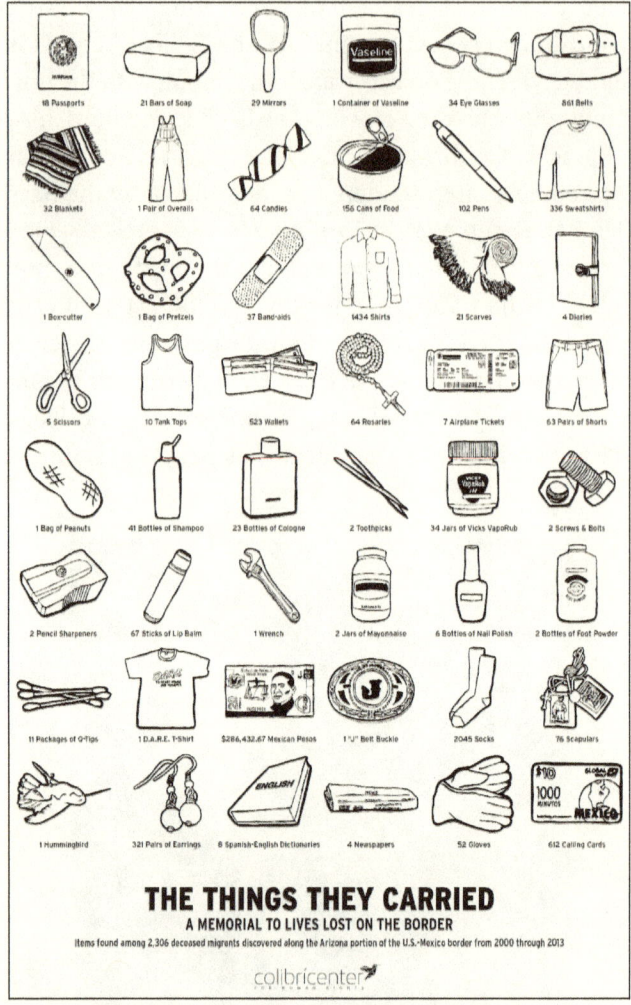

Figure 4.5. "The Things They Carried: A Memorial to Lives Lost on the Border" (detail). Hand-drawn poster created by John Stobbe for the Colibrí Center for Human Rights, 2014.

less patrolled, more dangerous points of entry. Eight migrant remains, for example, were brought into the Pima County Medical Examiner's Office, which works closely with Colibrí, in 1995, compared with 71 in 2000, 200 in 2005, and 225 in 2010, grim flashpoints in a general upwards trend (Colibrí Center).

By "flashpoints" I mean to indicate the exact opposite of *Pulse Park*'s artistic biometrics. The bodies Colibrí collects catalyze a different kind of machinic interaction. If we think of *Sandbox* as a play machine built of bodies and surveillance, "The Things They Carried" signals a terror machine.[1] The brown bodies of the dead migrants interact with surveillance technologies and border spaces in ways that bear very little resemblance to the playful environments of connection generated by the primarily white bodies we see in the videos and photographs documenting *Sandbox*. And while the bodies in Lozano-Hemmer's projects become absorbed into the story of the play machine, the migrant bodies in the desert refuse, in their insistent materiality, absorption into the terror machine.

Case in point: the gruesome 2014 discovery of mass migrant graves in Falfurrias, Texas. The *Corpus Christi Caller-Times* broke the story of a team of researchers working on a volunteer basis to exhume and identify migrant remains in a government-owned cemetery in Brooks County, Texas. In the summer of 2013 the researchers and their students exhumed 110 remains; in 2014 they exhumed 52 plots that contained more than 52 bodies. Alongside and in between coffins, the researchers found skulls in biohazard bags, body bags containing the comingled remains of multiple bodies, and kitchen garbage bags full of bones. These plots date back to 2005, while the improperly disposed-of bodies, researchers believe, date from 2009. Both can be traced back to Funeraria del Angel Howard-Williams, which contracts with the county to dispose of the bodies at $450 apiece. When questioned by the *Caller-Times*, Funeraria del Angel claimed that it had no records pertaining to the plots in question; a spokesperson for its parent company, Howard-Williams, later said that while it did have some records, "this does not amount to confirmation that Howard-Williams was involved in depositing the remains in the manner the researchers described" (Collette). Apart from themselves, it would seem, the bodies left no trace.

To date, the people in these mass graves are literally undocumented, as far as researchers have been able to tell. They are rendered unidentifiable by the one word that has been officially attached to them: "illegal." Eddie Canales, an immigrant rights activist in Brooks County, argues that because the dead migrants were seen as "illegals," they were afforded no respect, putting his finger on how the politics of border militarization forces a shift in perception from real human to immaterial abstraction (Collette). These bodies enter the discursive world not as individuals who have loved and lost, but as "illegals" that can be manipulated by various sides of a contentious, seemingly irresolvable debate.

As Braidotti describes "refugees and asylum seekers," the bodies in these mass graves are also "another emblem of contemporary necropower because they are the perfect instantiation of the disposable humanity that Agamben also calls homo-sacer" (127). These migrant corpses comprise one category of "the disposable bodies of the global economy" upon whose deaths the comfortable lives of others depend (Braidotti 111). Their vulnerability marks a common bond between humans and other species threatened by the current global political economy, thus offering occasion to take up Braidotti's invitation to rethink death and dying, to articulate "an affirmative posthuman theory of death" (111). The migrant bodies embody the homo-sacer's fundamental ambiguity. As Agamben reminds, the homo-sacer was, in Roman law, an outcast, a banned person who might be killed with impunity. *Sacer* grounds the English "sacred," but for the Romans it meant simply set apart, both cursed and hallowed (Agamben 79). The migrants are casualties of posthuman inhumanity, and yet they remain with us; their unidentified bodies and the things they carried are holy.

They are holy because they have the potential to make us think beyond our selves, to imagine a politics beyond the human subject that accounts for the vulnerability of all living things. Building on Mbembe's work, Braidotti notes that our contemporary, global political economy deconstructs individual subjectivities into generic categories of people that power the machines of capital and the state. If we are to effectively resist this, she argues, death must cease to be the horizon of experience (Braidotti 110). The migrant corpses are necropolitical waste marking the inhumanity of the posthuman, but the bodies return; they will not be so easily disposed. Taking up Braidotti's challenge to "rethink death . . . as another phase in a generative process" (121), in this chapter I use the corpses to ground "an ethics that respects vulnerability while actively constructing social horizons of hope" (Braidotti 122). Their bones, their objects will not be absorbed and abstracted. They insist upon themselves, and in their refusal to become historical ephemera they serve as useful analogs to the status of the human body in *The Rag Doll Plagues* and *Lunar Braceros*.

In both of these novels the human body refuses to become historical trash. It resists being contained, diminished, or narrated away in celebratory descriptions of cyborgs and synthetic organs. In *Lunar Braceros*, the protagonist, Lydia, remembers what Lysa Rivera calls the "future history" of labor exploitation in the borderlands (418). In Lydia's recent past, which is the reader's distant future, poor people are contained on state-controlled reservations and all manner of "waste" is being sent to the moon for deep burial. "Waste management, population management, it was all part of the same thing in the end for the state," says Lydia (15). *The Rag Doll Plagues* describes a similar future history of human detritus. The human body irrupts into the present of each narrative, however, seizing its place in the future at the same time as tremendous efforts are being made to contain it.

This irruption renders *The Rag Doll Plagues* and *Lunar Braceros* exemplary science fiction (SF) novels, a genre broadly understood as using scientific discoveries or advanced technologies—real or imagined, earthly or otherworldly—as integral to plots generally depicting social or environmental change. Don D'Ammassa identifies SF as one of three types of speculative fiction, the other two being fantasy and supernatural or horror stories. D'Ammassa gives a capsule overview of SF's development in the introduction to his *Encyclopedia of Science Fiction*, moving from the fantastical tales of Jules Verne to the more serious and scientific writing of H. G. Wells, through the pulp magazine period, the advent of paperbacks, and the explosion of "new wave" SF writing starting in the 1960s, which is when, in the United States, we see writers like Ursula Le Guin and Samuel Delany making their marks.[2] D'Ammassa is more interested in chronologizing Le Guin and Delany than in exploring the politics of race and gender in SF, but those intersections have received a fair amount of attention from others.

SF's embrace of technological possibilities—space travel, time travel, body modifications, and environmental manipulations, to list just a few—has proved fertile ground for writers of color and queer writers seeking to call into question the status quo, argues Catherine Ramírez in her foundational article "Afrofuturism/Chicanafuturism: Fictive Kin." Ramírez discusses black and feminist writers who took control of what was once a predominantly white and male genre, transforming it into a "politically charged medium for the interrogation of ideology, identity, historiography, and epistemology" (186). Chicanafuturism, she contends, borrows extensively from Afrofuturism, which Ramírez explains as the umbrella term for works of art exploring the relationship between blacks, technology, and the legacies of humanism. Chicanafuturist works interrogate the promises of science and technology for people of color who, Ramírez notes, "are usually disassociated from [those] signifiers of civilization, rationality, and progress" (188). People of color tend to be fixed in a racialized past, she argues, while the future is imagined either as white or entirely without race.

Chicanafuturist works disrupt these colonial narratives, seizing SF tropes in order to plot people of color firmly in the future. Ramírez borrows from Gloria Anzaldúa in order to distinguish Chicanafuturism from Afrofuturism, placing heavy emphasis on Anzaldúa's "alien" consciousness (Anzaldúa, "La Prieta" 43). Ramírez reads Anzaldúa's alien state as an attack on Cartesian subjectivity rooted in the particulars of the Mexican American experience of Anglo nationalism and heteropatriarchy (189). Cathryn Merla-Watson and Ben Olguín build on Ramírez's groundbreaking work in their introduction to a collection of articles dedicated to what they call "Latin@futurism." Emphasizing border militarization and the increasing globalization of capital, Merla-Watson and Olguín assert that "Latin@ cultural production obscures colonialist boundaries between self and other, between the technologically advanced and the primitive, between the human and the nonhuman and between the past and the future." Chicanx and Latinx artists since at least the 1970s, they argue, have mined SF in order to "defamiliarize the ways in which the past continues to haunt the present and future" (135). We cannot imagine the future, they say, unless we fully reckon with the ghosts of colonial modernity.

Ernest Hogan, who brought Chicanx SF to wide attention with novels like *Cortez on Jupiter* (1990) and *High Aztech* (1992), concurs. The power of Chicanx SF, Hogan argues, is in its ability to push back against corporate aesthetic control, to use science and technology not as surface decoration but to profoundly interrogate the past, present, and future. "We need never-ending revolution," he writes, "to keep science from becoming nothing but a corporate franchise" ("Chicanonautica Manifesto" 133). Such traces of corporate, marketable SF are visible throughout *Lunar Braceros* and *The Rag Doll Plagues*, which tread familiar SF territory. Each catalogs a dystopic future history of first border militarization, then border disintegration and conglomeration as space shape-shifts under the feet of poor, largely indigenous people of color. Characters travel through time in *The Rag Doll Plagues*, and in *Lunar Braceros* they take round trips to and travel all across Earth's moon in elaborately described space vehicles. In both novels, moreover, readers encounter devastating epidemics and cyborg interactions. *Lunar Braceros*, in particular, takes its science very seriously, featuring heads of state who hold PhDs in astronomy (23) and references to actual NASA projects like the Terrestrial Planet Finder (7). They avoid the co-option and commodification Hogan fears, however, by pushing back against these generic trappings in the ways Hogan deems necessary.

The surface distractions of science and technology run parallel to explicit musings in both novels about writing and textuality, signaling that the topical critiques in both have their analogs in narrative form. In this chapter I explore the tension between form and SF content in *Lunar Braceros* and *The Rag Doll Plagues*, arguing ultimately that the novels' most effective modes of critique lie not in their descriptions of the techno-future, but in the ways they narrate the relationship between technology and the body. The structures of the books in particular, competing and interwoven narrative threads in *Lunar Braceros* and recurring metalepsis in *The Rag Doll Plagues*, suggest, I show, the tensions and inconsistencies of their social critiques.

These critiques coalesce around both books' understanding themselves engaging late capitalism's objectification of people of color, as well as the destruction of both democracy and the environment. They do this in part with narrators who imagine themselves as, to a certain extent, heterodiegetic, as standing apart from and describing the workings of the neoliberal machine. Their critiques are more interesting, however, when read as embodied rather than mimetic, when functioning the way José Luis Barrios describes Lozano-Hemmer's installations as "aesthetic activations of the paradoxical registers that are internal to or inherent in machines." Lozano-Hemmer's work "does not represent anything," Barrios continues, "but rather accomplishes, by aesthetic means, the material history of the technics" (226). In this chapter I propose Barrios's reading of Lozano-Hemmer as an interpretive lens for *Lunar Braceros* and *The Rag Doll Plagues*. The novels' deployments of the body are "aesthetic activations" that disrupt neoliberal narratives just as the dead migrant bodies and the things they carried do.

Put another way, we might say that *Lunar Braceros* and *The Rag Doll Plagues* understand themselves as representing the ways technology and capital impinge on the human body, but their significant interventions happen almost accidentally in depictions of the body's becoming machine. These novels are more interesting if, instead of reading them as describing body and machine as antagonists, we read them choratically as writing machines that reconfigure social relations and political space, working parallel to the machines of play and terror described above. *Lunar Braceros* and *The Rag Doll Plagues* want to assert the brown body as a world of meaning unto itself, but necropolitics relies on just this sort of atomization, and the novels seem not entirely aware of their deconstructed subjects' radical potential.

Jodi Melamed amplifies that kind of potential in *Represent and Destroy*, where she discusses the emergence of what she calls "race liberal orders" after World War II (x). In this moment, "formal anti-racism" becomes the accepted way of talking about race and masks the material inequalities conditioning the lives of people of color in the United States (11). It is very difficult to value diversity, in her analysis, without reifying capital's normalizing epistemes (9). A focus on individual subjects, whose diversity can be celebrated, shifts attention away from systemic inequality, says Melamed. Her argument exemplifies Bruno Latour's observation in "Why Has Critique Run out of Steam?" that "the new spirit of capitalism has put to good use the artistic critique that was meant to destroy it" (231). Latour provocatively wonders whether "explanations resorting automatically to power, society, discourse had outlived their usefulness" (229) and suggests that criticism shift attention from explaining facts to instead exploring "the rich and complicated qualities of the celebrated *Thing*" (233).

Latour's philosophical motivation, upon which Mitchum Huehls draws in *After Critique*, is to dispute the modernist legacy of a divide between subjects and objects that Latour traces back to Heidegger.[3] Things are never just facts that exist beyond the confines of an unfettered subject, says Latour. We should explore, not explain, things with "a multifarious inquiry launched with the tools of anthropology, philosophy, metaphysics, history, sociology to detect how many participants are gathered in a thing to make it exist and to maintain its existence" (246). From this, Huehls builds a theory of reading that eschews a clear distinction between subjects and objects. Such a distinction only empowers what he calls the "neoliberal circle," which lays claim to both subjective and objective representations, flattering our sense of individuality while appealing to our longing to be part of a group (10). If we "insist on a critical politics that challenges one way of looking at the world with a different way of looking at the world," then we will only ever run into political dead ends, Huehls claims, because neoliberalism has "captured both sides of the subject-object relation that grounds representation itself" (15). *Lunar Braceros* and *The Rag Doll Plagues* rely explicitly on the kind of critical politics dependent on a subject-object split that Huehls, Latour, and Melamed deem ineffective, but, drawing on these three thinkers, I hope to accomplish something more in this chapter than what Latour refers to as the explanatory "critical trick" (241). We get less from reading the body in these two novels as a fetishistic critical fantasy and more from thinking it through as a Latourian *thing* that draws multiple participants, human and nonhuman, into its web of concern.

Objective Bodies

As she is for Catherine Ramírez, Gloria Anzaldúa is a useful touchstone here. "The whole time growing up," writes Anzaldúa, "I felt I was not of this earth. An alien from another planet—I'd been dropped on my mother's lap" ("La Prieta" 40). This sense of alienation stems from her body's primal betrayal: early-onset puberty, including menstruating when only three months old (39). This physical disorientation breeds a sense of her own otherworldliness, which Anzaldúa roots in her appreciation for books. In the same paragraph where she describes herself as "dropped on [her] mother's lap," Anzaldúa relates how "[her] father dropped on [her] lap a 25¢ pocket western," in which she encounters the forms of racism that would go on to condition her adult life (40). Equating her own body with a book, Anzaldúa connects her physical disorientation to a tropological racism that she is able to see and renarrate because of her alien consciousness; writing about race is, for Anzaldúa, a choratic, corporeal metaphysics of "western" political and geographic space.

Something similar is happening in both *The Rag Doll Plagues* and *Lunar Braceros*, though they understand themselves to be using the body quite differently from Anzaldúa. The action in both novels unfolds under the multifaceted shadow of biopolitical control, ranging from the global north's managing brown bodies for profit to manipulating public health as a primary tool for maintaining political power. In *Lunar Braceros*, "bio-labs seeking to create artificial organs, new medications, enhanced bodies, and to artificially develop new species had free rein" (14), and in the final section of *The Rag Doll Plagues*, wealthy citizens keep Mexicans "like expensive pets" because their blood fends off the incurable epidemic resulting from the toxic waves of trash attacking the coast (193). In the opening section of *The Rag Doll Plagues*, moreover, we learn that the protagonist was sent to colonial Mexico to "assess the medical needs of His Majesty's colonies" because the king knows that the revolutionary spirit is "contagious" and that his control of the empire depends on the physical well-being of his subjects (16). The physical health of the indigenous population likewise underpins corporate empire in *Lunar Braceros*, where indigenous people are "laborers and service workers" (37) highly valued for their pure blood and ability to produce antibodies (22).

The plots of each novel revolve around similar ideas about the simultaneous corporatization of both political space and the human body. *Lunar Braceros* tells Lydia's story in four, interwoven threads: (1) Lydia's bildungsroman from her childhood on the reservation through the political activism that lands her first in prison then to the moon to work off her sentence; (2) the future history of states, conglomerated into mega-political units, as corporate shills monetizing the bodies of the disenfranchised through various biotechnical means; (3) the science and history lessons that Lydia is ostensibly giving to her son and his friends in Chingananza, the commune where Lydia and her husband, Frank, live after their escape from the moon; and (4) descriptions of their post-moon life on the commune. These threads all lead to the novel's catalyzing plot event, where Lydia and Frank return north to continue organizing to overthrow the reservation system. *The Rag Doll Plagues*, less explicitly political, is divided into three sections corresponding to distinct geographic spaces and historical periods: first, colonial Mexico ("Mexico City"); then late 1970s–early 1980s Los Angeles ("Delhi"), and finally the "region from the center of Mexico to the Pacific Coast" ("LAMEX"), known in the late 2000s as "the LAMEX Coastal Region of the Triple Alliance" (134). Dr. Gregorio Revueltas is sent from Spain to Mexico City in the first section to attend to matters of public health; his descendants, also doctors named Gregory, are the protagonists of the second and third sections, each of which describe devastating plagues decimating the human population. In both novels, the survival of the global north depends upon its ability to physically exploit poor people of color in the global south.

Both novels respond to this corporeal commodification by asserting the mysterious sanctity of the human. The indigenous blood in *Lunar Braceros*, for example, is pure because the Guaraní villagers live in utopic isolation in the rainforest beyond the reach of modern contaminants, "uncompromised from exposure to antibiotics and pollution" (22). Conversely, the brown bodies in "LAMEX," *The Rag Doll Plague*'s final section, have been inexplicably "transformed genetically to produce a blood that was able to sustain life in the most polluted conditions on earth" (165). Whether picturing indigeneity as apart from or imbricated with industrial capital, both novels fetishize the native while criticizing power's desire and ability to capitalize on indigenous bodies. Even as the books hold up the body as a defense against capital, that is, their veneration of it completes Huehls's neoliberal circle by participating in the same kind of objectifying discourse.

This kind of privileging presents problems throughout each book. For example, in *The Rag Doll Plagues* the reader is meant to understand "Mexico City" Gregory's revulsion at the "immoral racial mixtures" (11) openly engaging in "hedonistic carnal acts" (28) as evidence of his prudish racism. Later sections of the novel are no more progressive or anti-racist, however, though they clearly understand themselves as such. Sandra, "Delhi" Gregory's hemophiliac girlfriend, is a wealthy Jewish actress with no Latinx heritage but possessed of a passion for Mexico, where she traveled in her youth and "chose an Indian" with whom to have a romantic adventure (97). Similarly colonial is the strange attraction the homeboys of Orange County feel to her performance in *Blood Wedding*, by the Spanish poet and playwright Federico García Lorca (91). Likewise, "several Indian men and women" tend lovingly to this white woman's body when, having contracted HIV after a blood transfusion and dying of AIDS, Sandra visits a *curandero* in Tepotzotlán. They clothe her in a "transcultural, transhistorical" dress that Gregory describes as "Indian and modern" (125). The dress allegorizes Sandra's own physical and ideological border crossings, but "Delhi" Gregory's juxtapositional description suggests that "Indian" is not "modern"; the dress crosses over into Sandra's present from the mists of indigenous time, and the actual Indians who people this chapter, like her earlier homeboy fans and her Indian lover, are locked in a fetishized past whence they can never be Sandra's coevals.

The transcendence Gregory imagines for Sandra is predicated on maintaining indigeneity as an idealized object in the past, an "other" distinct from Sandra's present "self." Lydia's lessons on histories of mestizaje in *Lunar Braceros* are similarly contradictory. She tells Pedro that ultimately class supersedes race as a category of political organizing (62), but she relies heavily on a racialized idea of herself as mestiza, which might very well be a generative mixing but relies still on colonial ideologies of race. "Ultimately, capital can undo any ties or links on the basis of race, ethnicity, language or color," she tells Pedro, urging him to remember that "it's the system" (31). Lydia wants to have race both ways: as both a subject and object of capital, as insignificant, subordinate to capital, but of supreme importance. She tells Pedro, "If as Indians or cholos we have been oppressed, it will be as Indians or cholos that we will rise up" (63). Even as she recognizes the constructed nature of these categories, her desire to privilege the purity of indigenous blood makes it impossible for her to escape racial categories of identification.

Evident in both *The Rag Doll Plagues* and *Lunar Braceros*, then, is that as much as both books seek to undermine hierarchies of the human, they depend on these categories to stake out resistant subject positions. To further illustrate, even though characters in both books understand themselves as polyamorous sex and gender radicals, they rely on heteronormative understandings of human sexual behavior and family structure. Lydia takes pains to explain to Pedro, for example, that he is "as much [her] son as Frank's, Leticia's, Maggie's, Tom's, and Betty's" (119). His biological father, Gabriel, deposited sperm to fertilize Lydia's eggs. They froze the resulting embryos, one of which was carried by Maggie, Leticia's partner, who eventually birthed Pedro, for whom Tom and Betty care when Lydia and Frank, Pedro's adopted father, go north.

It truly did take a village to create Pedro, but that creation relies on the same biotechnology Lydia opposes, and she raises Pedro in a heterosexual family unit.

The Rag Doll Plagues works at similar gendered cross-purposes. "Delhi" Gregory and Sandra engage in some vaguely sadomasochistic knife play (94), while "LAMEX" Gregory enjoys "multiple modes of copulation" with his girlfriend, Gabi, a hard-partying cyborg (147). Their behavior is meant to contrast "Mexico City" Gregory's refusing offers of "sexual alleviation" with "delightful virgins" (22). His prudishness, however, does not undermine the novel's ostensible sexual adventurousness nearly as much as "LAMEX" Gregory's heteronormative desire to "love a woman and have children, like normal people did in the late twentieth century" (199), or the "gender requirements" of the life-saving blood transfusions he discovers (187), which work only when the transfused blood has come from a donor of the recipient's opposite sex (168).

Both books foreground the human body as full of radical, transformative potential, but that potential is foreclosed in each. "Mexico City" Gregory, for instance, learns, from a drunken traveller at an inn, of a cross-dressing nun who is daring in battle while rebelling against colonial authority (14). The pope grants her a dispensation to live as a man, a state-sanctioned gender transgression that the book does not develop. Similarly, "LAMEX" Gregory has strong physical feelings that "events had planned in themselves their own occurrence" that he should not resist (134). He senses himself as part of an energized network here, just as when he "sensed" himself at the beginning of a great adventure after his "chance meeting" with a Mexican soldier (148). These moments could be opportunities for rethinking the boundaries of the body, but *The Rag Doll Plagues* does not follow them through. As in *Lunar Braceros*, the body always stands apart even when each novel wants most to use the body to break down hierarchical dualities of subject and object.

Nevertheless, each novel depicts a range of self-organizing, complex ecosystems—environmental, political, and social—that have direct impacts on physical bodies. The human body appears, in these instances, as part of a transversal (to borrow Braidotti's word) or transcorporeal (to borrow Stacy Alaimo's) flow, as an object among objects, functioning in non-hierarchical relation to other things, despite the novels' explicit articulations of the human body as distinct and special.[4] The clearest example of this in both books is the body's response to pollution. People worry "about the ecology of the earth" (149) in *The Rag Doll Plagues*. They understand themselves as part of a living system and feel "some kind of disharmony" (150) resulting from vast amounts of mobile, animate trash (166) that causes fatal illnesses (138) as well as neurological damage (155). In *Lunar Braceros*, by contrast, "the relocation of waste was definitely giving Earth some breathing room" (59). In both books the waste has an adverse effect on the human body, but while *Lunar Braceros* maintains the purity of uncontaminated, indigenous blood as an antidote to the illnesses of capitalism (22), *The Rag Doll Plagues* imagines a "human quantum biological leap" (180) in the "renegade blood of Mexicans" whose environmental adaptations render them the singular cure to LAMEX's plague (181).

Pollution notwithstanding, in neither book does the human body fully integrate with its surroundings, a corporeal exceptionalism analogous to the social and political webs each novel documents. The modes of resistance in each book are anthropocentric, focused on human impact at the expense of human transversality. Whether in the colonias (Morales 173) or the communes (Sánchez and Pita 115), each novel emphasizes networks while asserting the individual. *Lunar Braceros* illustrates this paradox nicely in its allusion to Samir Amin's work on delinking, which, Lydia recounts, "turned out, in fact, to be quite difficult in real historical time."[5] Amin contends that underdeveloped countries need their own markets apart from global systems of exploitation, but, as Lydia observes, "There was no way to compete with the multinational corporations" (111). Can an economy survive independent of global capital flows? Can an individual exist independent of the group? *Lunar Braceros* puts forward a tentative yes, but the novel leaves its own contradictions open-ended and unresolved.

A similar tension between human autonomy and interdependence appears around cybernetics and biotechnology in each novel, with the protagonists discounting both in favor of an unwavering faith in the superiority of the unadulterated human body. In *Lunar Braceros*, for example, Lydia grapples with the benefits and threats of fertility treatments, digitizing brain waves to help dementia patients, and two-way communication devices implanted directly in the brain. Despite their potential benefits, these technologies lead to a darker side of biopolitical control in *Lunar Braceros* and, in Lydia's analysis, are best avoided. Likewise, "LAMEX" Gregory does not want a computerized arm, though he understands that he will likely lose his job over this refusal (143). The Triple Alliance Directorate may think that computer implants will close the gap "between us and perfection," Gregory thinks, but the technology, he theorizes, will only ever trap humanity "in the asymptote of knowledge" (182). Humans will, in other words, always be close to perfection, but will never quite get there, and advanced technologies only highlight, never close, that infinite distance.

On the one hand, this kind of technological resistance resonates with N. Katherine Hayles's judicious warnings against a celebratory "metanarrative about the transformation of the human into a disembodied posthuman" (22). In *How We Became Posthuman*, Hayles supplants that seemingly inevitable narrative of progressive disembodiment by telling the history of cybernetics as a series of historically specific struggles between human and machine. Like Hayles, *Lunar Braceros* and *The Rag Doll Plagues* may be exploring the tension rather than embracing the technology. They may also, as Braidotti does, be retaining the embodied human as the sign of subjectivity necessary for a "sustained political analysis of the posthuman condition" (42). On the other hand, the narrators of these novels feel almost like Luddites in their fetishistic attachments to their sanctified bodies. Their resistance to technological dystopia undermines their own theories of interconnection.

Both books posit the inviolate human body as the last bastion of resistance against machines of the capitalist state, but one might also, as Braidotti does, embrace the permeable borders of the human body as the beginning of a new political imaginary. Braidotti wants to develop an "affirmative ethics" that propels "new social conditions and relations into being, out of injury and pain." Her "posthuman necro-political and legal theory" eschews legal subjectivity in favor of "singularities without identity who relate intimately to one another and the environment in which they are located." This gives us, she argues, a posthuman, postidentitarian politics grounded in shared vulnerability across species, which engenders a "politics of survival" that challenges us "to think with and not against death" (128). Life, Braidotti asserts, "cannot be bound or confined to the single, human individual" (135), and so a life-affirming politics must conceive itself as a "transversal inter-connection or an 'assemblage' of human and non-human actors" as embodied sites of resistance (45).

In their treatments of time and temporality, *Lunar Braceros* and *The Rag Doll Plagues* approach this kind of networked assemblage. They both describe connections between people, places, and things across time, and time travel is, of all the novels' shared features, the most prototypically SF. Still, even this relies on a privileging of the human body as index of subjectivity. The "Gregory" figure, for example, links all three sections in *The Rag Doll Plagues* both by the repetition of his name and with metaleptic appearances by "Delhi" Gregory and his grandfather Papá Damián in both "Mexico City" and "LAMEX." At the end of each section, moreover, each Gregory cries an "ancient tear" (66, 129, 200), building up the corporeal connective tissues between sections just as human illness does. AIDS in "Delhi" and the plagues of "LAMEX" produce symptoms like those of "La Mona" in "Mexico City"; in fact, the healers at Tepotzotlán call Sandra's condition "La Mona" (122). In *Lunar Braceros*, similarly, the characters understand time only in so far as it has an impact on their bodies. One of their primary missions on the moon, for example, is "to investigate the long term impact of space on the human body" (24); thus they understand the lunar day in terms of its excessive heat (44). While they can theorize the existence of other temporal dimensions, which might open up new ways of understanding the moon's impact on the body, they can see these dimensions only in dreams (102). In each book, then, the body offers glimpses of connection across time and space, but more often than not the limits of human sensory and cognitive perception foreclose those possibilities.

The Space of Time

Put another way, in each novel time and temporality signal liberatory possibilities just beyond the limits of comprehension. Despite Lydia's admission that "of course we are not, never have been, and never will be" the center of the universe (80), each book rationalizes temporal possibility away by containing it within the boundaries of things already known. Time does not exceed the limits of scientific knowledge in *Lunar Braceros*, which uses black holes (84, 94), brane theory (102), and dark matter (110) to argue that time and space are inherently social phenomena. The

Rag Doll Plagues retains that sociality of time but eschews hard science in favor of narratology with different characters representing certain philosophies of narrative time. "Delhi" Gregory's parents teach him "to walk through the past to live in the present and to work for a better future" (69), but Sandra's illness, which "Delhi" Gregory describes as a journey through a place where "time was not as we knew it" (106), destabilizes that sequential comfort. Bypassing this temporal phenomenology, "LAMEX" Gregory, observing treasure-hunting scuba divers, thinks about their search as the quest for "a chrono object of a drowned chronotope in our time" (178).[6]

Morales's direct allusion to Bakhtin here emphasizes space and time as functions of each other, an idea mirrored in *Lunar Braceros*, though in the latter the time of space and the space of time are primarily functions of sense experience. The distance between lunar colonies, for instance, is described in terms of the braceros' travel time, but their "mag-shuttlettes" confuse their sense of space-time because they cover vast distances so quickly (44). Equally destabilizing for the braceros is the difference between the lunar and Earth days. Lydia tells Pedro, "We divided the hours as if we were on Earth, even though on the moon it was still the same day" (78). *The Rag Doll Plagues* eschews the temporality of sense in favor of historical sensibility, depicting space-time in terms of the evolution of place. Mexicans, muses "LAMEX" Gregory, "were trapped in a historical and geographical bowl" (181), in which are stacked layers of time that *The Rag Doll Plagues* can be read as systematically peeling back. The novel embodies Sandra's desire to "explore the recently found archeological sights" around the Templo Mayor (95) in "Delhi."[7] There, all layers past, present, and future exist simultaneously in the same space, spilling over each other into a bundle of confused times paralleling the braceros' temporal confusion on the moon.

Each book conveys the sense that thinking creatively about time will enable new perceptions of space and that this reconfigured space-time will remake society. Space is primarily "a product of social relations," Lydia tells Pedro. She hopes that when he grows up he will "be involved in the production of new spatial relations" that will reorganize the class and race hierarchies that still constrain their lives (25). A similar sociality of space is evident in *The Rag Doll Plagues*, which emphasizes the spatial politics with historicizing descriptions of Southern California barrios, "the real Aztlán," that shape social relations in the region (71), conditions only exacerbated in the future history of the Lower Life Existence (LLE), Middle Life Existence (MLE), and Higher Life Existence (HLE) enclaves of LAMEX (137). Of course, there is also LAMEX itself, a vast political conglomeration whose shifting borders echo the New Imperial Order's reconfiguration of southwestern US space in *Lunar Braceros* (8–9).

These shifting spaces are depicted in each novel as working in the service of capital. Lydia, to illustrate, tells Pedro that she and her fellow activists "were especially interested in making a statement against property and enclosure" because space is so closely linked with race and class (34). Physical space and conceptual space, despite being metaphorical vehicles for the tenor of state power, are, nevertheless, highly unstable in both books. That instability remains unexplored, however, because neither book is able to present it as anything other than a function of its characters' sense experience. For example, "LAMEX" Gregory observes that "everything oscillated" in Mexico City. Buildings, air, flies, and dead trees move (163), and piles of waste "rose like giant tortoises which undulated" (166) as he searches for subjects on which to test his experimental cure. The ground beneath the characters' feet is always moving in *The Rag Doll Plagues*, and the universe that contains *Lunar Braceros*' Chicanx waste workers "is unending," Lydia tells Pedro, "always expanding," potentially contracting and imploding (33). Space has its own catalyzing energy that, in each novel, remains subordinate to time.

Both novels are invested in puncturing what Walter Benjamin refers to as the "homogeneous, empty time" of capital, in which each minute and hour is equivalent to the next and follows upon another in unending progression (*Illuminations*, Thesis 13, 261). *The Rag Doll Plagues* and *Lunar Braceros* seek "time filled by the presence of the now" and attempt "to make the continuum of history explode" by depicting the quest for multiple times to exist in the same place (Benjamin, *Illuminations*, Thesis 14, 261). Both are equally, if differently, unsuccessful. *Lunar Braceros* conflates time by observing that the multiple days they experience are really just one lunar day (78). Lunar time is now, even though the braceros divide their time into earthly rhythms. Alternative temporal models are inaccessible, however, once the braceros finally understand their importance. The "Director and Lab Researchers" that Maggie sees in her dream are "beyond [their] time-space, in another brane or dimension" (102). "Mexico City" Gregory symbolizes this same limit. He tries to shake hands with "Delhi" Gregory and his grandfather Papá Damián, but "enormous monoliths of time, places and people circulated among us, always preventing us from consummating our handshake" (23). They can see and communicate with each other; they can move into each other's time, but they cannot touch. While alternative time-spaces represent modes of resistance to the spatializing work of capital, both novels have difficulty carrying them off and rely instead on returns of the historical repressed to do the work of temporal irruption.

History takes center stage in *Lunar Braceros*, where Lydia's prison work assignment entails "revising historical accounts not favorable to the Cali-Texas government" (38). With historical knowledge figured as a weapon against the state, *Lunar Braceros* weaves historical fact throughout its future historical fiction. Lydia's husband, Frank, for instance, is descended from Chinese immigrants to Mexico who fled Los Angeles after the 1871 Chinese massacre (48), and Lydia's ancestors include actual historical figures like Pacomio (118) and Mariano Vallejo (55), who serve as touchstones for her later activism. *The Rag Doll Plagues*, by contrast, refers to historical figures like Juan Vicente de Güemes and Catalina de Erauso mostly for realistic effect rather than to advance the narrative.[8] The description of *Ramona* tours in the "LAMEX" section, which deliver Indian, Mexican, and Spanish cultural history as performance, only reinforces this notion of history as a decorative object.[9] The tours, like Lydia and Frank's ancestry, create space in the narrative for the oppositional histories of racialized, gendered violence. But, while indigenous history might be an enduring story that has not quite faded away, it is contained and packaged as entertainment, having no real impact on the power structure of "LAMEX."

History is repeated in *The Rag Doll Plagues*, in other words, but to little effect. *Lunar Braceros* runs into similar difficulties. "How to attain social change?" Lydia asks Pedro, rhetorically. "We've gone over this subject time and time again," she says, repeating the same answers but encountering the same problems as time goes by. If, on the moon, the braceros encounter "Chinese workers" and "African miners," just as they would have done in Pacomio and Vallejo's nineteenth-century California, then how effective can these historical invocations be (78)? The novel's strategy of repetition recalls Benjamin's assertion that history is not a series of facts and causes; the historian does not relate a "sequence of events" but instead observes a "constellation" between eras that, taken together, comprise the "time of the now" (Benjamin, *Illuminations*, Addendum A, 263). In the case of *Lunar Braceros*, if all days are the same day, if all time is now, if history is endlessly repeating, then perhaps the progression of capital's homogeneous and empty time can be interrupted. That does not happen in *Lunar Braceros*, however, where the same problems and answers circle endlessly around each other; nor is any social change evident in *The Rag Doll Plagues*, where the cycle of disease and destruction continues at novel's end despite "LAMEX" Gregory's dropping off the grid.

Time and temporality nevertheless remain at the core of the social problems each novel identifies, but these problems cannot be addressed with historical data. History's irruptions, figured as a temporal hybridity, meet the same fate Néstor García Canclini describes for cultural hybridity in a Latin American context. García Canclini's ideas on hybridity differ significantly from those of Homi Bhabha, which have achieved wider recognition in the United States. Bhabha sees hybridity as a site of resistance to colonial authority, and this is certainly how both *Lunar Braceros* and *The Rag Doll Plagues* appear to be deploying their historical data. For García Canclini, by contrast, hybridity is the means by which Hispanic elites maintain hegemony over black and indigenous populations in postcolonial Latin America.[10] *Lunar Braceros* and *The Rag Doll Plagues* embody the process García Canclini describes, by which power absorbs hybridity and difference. The spatial and temporal differences that both books present as oppositional wind up reifying the forms of power they seek to undermine. The body and the narrative structures that emerge around it, rather than historical data, stand as the more productive sites of resistance in each.

The body has its own time, as *The Rag Doll Plagues* makes clear. "Fear extends time," thinks "Mexico City" Gregory when talking to the drunken man at the tavern (14), and he describes the nuns at the hospital as "forever smiling," which only emphasizes his fear (33). Later, the ghostly figures of Papá Damián and "Delhi" Gregory indicate to him wordlessly that he "had no time to waste" as he prepares for a cesarean section; the time of the body, put another way, is beyond words (59). The temporal body is silent, as are the mute, smiling nuns in "Mexico

City" and the taciturn driver at Sandra's healing retreat in "Delhi," who "gestured with her fingers" instead of speaking (116). Likewise, "LAMEX" Gregory and his assistants find that "talk was superfluous" as they manage the toxic health crisis, "communicating through sight and touch" instead (173). Paradoxically, in its refusal of language, the time of the body becomes, in both books, as in Dagoberto Gilb's work discussed in chapter 1, the time of writing.

Narratives of Futures Past

The time of writing eludes human perception in *The Rag Doll Plagues* and *Lunar Braceros*. "Delhi" Gregory must escape the flow of time in order to write about Sandra (104). At his mother's house, suspended in time, he listens to his mother's memories, struggling to document his present as his mother recounts her past. Other scenes of writing similarly create a sense of suspended time upon which the structures of past, present, and future depend. A blind man sits near "Mexico City" Gregory and his fiancée, Renata, holding a "tireless unsatiable quill" with which he seems to document everything the lovers say (65). The image of the diligent scribe-out-of-time reappears when "Delhi" Gregory and Sandra travel to Mexico City and see Papá Damián writing about them in an outdoor café (115). *Lunar Braceros*, with the reiteration of Lydia and Frank's initial encounter with their lunar predecessors' corpses, likewise figures writing as an eternal, necessary act that simultaneously creates and upends time. We see Lydia and Frank seeing the bodies on three separate occasions (9, 18, 56). These repetitions, like "LAMEX" Gregory's "asymptote of knowledge," push the reader increasingly closer to the truth of those dead bodies without ever quite touching it, signaling the narrative act as necessary and constant, if always incomplete.

Writing may be a function of Benjamin's eternal now, but it is also very much rooted in the materiality of the present in both novels. In part this is an intertextual effect, with both novels establishing links to other texts that root them in time. *The Rag Doll Plagues* stages multiple scenes in libraries, and "Grandfather Gregory's library," which contains many of his own self-authored works of fiction, is very important to "LAMEX" Gregory (141). So is Colombian author Andrés Caicedo, whose cult classic *Que viva la música!* (1977) serves as this section's barometer (169).[11]

Lydia and Gabriel, in *Lunar Braceros*, similarly understand their post-prison options through the work of Brazilian poet Manuel Bandeira (39), and Lydia explains the intersections of race and class to Pedro with the words of José Mariátegui (63).[12] More important than direct textual reference, though, is the way that writing and text are figured in each book as integral to the body.

The body itself is a readable text in *The Rag Doll Plagues*, when, for example, the viceroy and his daughters are exiled from "Mexico City" and "their cruel lot grotesquely grew on their faces and bodies" (63), or when "Delhi" Gregory describes Sandra as having "become the text that I loved" (86). "LAMEX" Gregory loves his grandfather's books so much he "placed the cool, almost living skin-like paper to [his] lips and desired the people" who live within their pages (142). In *The Rag Doll Plagues* bodies *are* texts, texts *are* bodies, and narrative is figured as a creative force that brings bodies into new being, as when Dr. Antonio tells "Mexico City" Gregory that his students "map the human anatomy" as they dissect cadavers, or when the Tepoztecatl *curandera* crafts a "*nahuatl* narrative" of Sandra's body in "Delhi" (122).

The privileging of text is not mere neo-Luddism in either novel, however. "LAMEX" Gregory explains the ghostly presence of his ancestors, Gregory and Papá Damián, as effects of technology. "Delhi" Gregory's "self-description, once computerized, was so intense that in hours he became a computer ghost and now appeared to assist and guide me through this world, which I believed to be real" (141). The force of his digital writing, in other words, manifests in bodily form traveling across time and space. Presence in *Lunar Braceros* is also a paradoxical function of digital text. Characters signal their well-being to each other from afar by means of encoded digital messages, but when Frank receives a message from his bother Pete, whose dead body he has already seen, he understands that text can be manipulated to conjure presence in the face of absence (72). When Pedro suggests that maybe Lydia and Frank's vision of Pete was really "Uncle's ghost," Lydia tells him, "No m'hijo, unfortunately there are no ghosts; we are only matter, material stuff that decays, dust to dust, as they say" (71). Text has real power, that is, but neither text nor technology can surpass the limits of the body.

Text is "sacred," nevertheless, as "Delhi" Gregory acknowledges when he "blessed the pages which held the story of [his] time" with Sandra

(95). Surpassing representation, text both creates and is created by the body. It is a portal through which the body passes into other worlds, and it is, as it has been in all the works I have discussed in *Racial Immanence*, a choratic tool for reconfiguring the real. "Curve after curve, I heard his voice," Gregory writes of his initial encounter with Papá Damián's otherworldly presence. In the vision, Papá Damián "nam[ed] the streets and towns that we passed on the way down the mountain" (96). This spatial narration is analogous to the many scenes of writing the body in *The Rag Doll Plagues*, where, for instance, procedures are "duly recorded" (57) in medical diaries to be discovered in libraries of the future: "treasure[s] of leather-bound books from the eighteenth and nineteenth centuries" (116) housing entire sections of "books describing Indian medicine" sharing shelf space with "personal journals written by Spanish doctors who lived centuries before" (117). Compared with the "results of the UCLA blood test" that Sandra's doctor reads aloud to her "with his prescribed 'bad tidings' medical bearing" (104), these books tell a remarkably different story about Sandra's body.

Writing is world-making in *The Rag Doll Plagues*; it amplifies and gives meaning to the materiality of flesh. "Mexico City" Gregory, to illustrate, does not answer personal letters from home (47, 64), but he does keep a medical diary (58), signaling the novel's interest in turning writing away from social artifice toward the real, human matter of the body. Preparing to amputate the leg of a toxic attack victim, "LAMEX" Gregory sees Papá Damián and Grandfather Gregory "watching." He wants their help, "but instead they frantically wrote down everything they observed." As he longs for a "computerized arm and hand," "LAMEX" Gregory realizes that his patient has died (152). Humans, he hypocritically thinks, listening to the demolition crews outside, "had a bad habit of erasing the calamities caused by our mistakes" (152). He has himself just been on the verge of erasure through amputation, however, and so this passage argues through multiple imagistic trajectories that technology will not erase the body. Cybernetic arms will not save the toxic attack victims; human arms will. "LAMEX" Gregory must have faith in his body, the bodies of others, and the powers of observation and writing to build a better world.

Reading is also a vital part of this world-building process in both *The Rag Doll Plagues* and *Lunar Braceros*. *The Rag Doll Plagues* explicitly foregrounds interpretation and analysis through "LAMEX" Gregory's meditations on genre, which he calls "oppositional binar[ies]" (141), and his full-bodied reading process. Reading, for "LAMEX" Gregory, is an active process of consumption "with [his] eyes" followed by a physical "passing [the words] to [his] brain" (141). Text becomes a part of his body. *Lunar Braceros* makes a comparable, if less material, argument. Lydia brings with her to the moon a "text-pad" on which she stores thousands of science, literature, and history texts, along with some literary games that involve solving mysteries and writing stories (45). This she leaves with Pedro when she heads north, along with a collection of "nanotexts with lunar posts, lessons, bits and pieces of conversations, and notations with friends" (5). Lydia enjoys writing games, but she is no author. She acknowledges as much when she admits that, though she hopes they "will be of some help," the writings she left Pedro are "fragmented." Lydia understands that, above all, "preparing him for what is to come" means training Pedro to be a good reader.

"How do you make sense of your life?" Lydia asks. "Perhaps in the telling, in the writing, in the recollection of people, through memory, dialogues, and scenes, it'll all make some sense to him" (58). The novel closes with a note from Pedro to his Uncle Ricardo, in which he says that "these memoirs" the reader has just finished were the last he has heard from Lydia in eight years. When he says, in the novel's concluding lines, that he is heading north to find her, that he's "not a kid anymore [and] can help out," the reader understands that reading and interpreting his mother's "bits and pieces" have revolutionized Pedro, much in the same way one expects *Lunar Braceros* is meant to revolutionize its readers by emphasizing the transformative and activist potential of reading.

Written with the Body

In positing readers as activists, *Lunar Braceros* suggests that effective modes of resistance to neoliberal encroachments can be found in text, not tech. Such an argument undermines the novelty of the new: the NIO's technologies of oppression are just surface distractions from a much older social dynamic. "The mission sounds a lot like the reservation, Mom," observes Pedro (54) right before Lydia wonders to herself about the way things can seem "so like a distant past and yet not so different from what is going on today" (58). In *Lunar Braceros*, technology evolves though the underlying problems remain the same, as do the strategies of resistance the novel depicts. Even Lydia recognizes that the consciousness raising and agit-prop upon which she and her colleagues rely "did not lead to much, much less an insurrection." She says, "It's time for a new strategy," but then immediately suggests "a new version of the old urban guerilla tactics that were declared defunct two centuries ago" (116). *Lunar Braceros* recognizes the need for, but is unable to imagine, the new, just as Maggie is unable to access the alternate dimensions of which she dreams (102). *The Rag Doll Plagues* is at a similar loss. For all its fantastical cyborgs and time traveling, the novel remains profoundly conservative. It fetishizes indigeneity from a position of white privilege, is heteronormative, is deeply suspicious of digital technologies, and appears uninterested in interrupting the exploitative cycles of history it describes. While on the surface, then, both novels seem full of radical potential, they engage modes of resistance that power both produces and absorbs.

The Rag Doll Plagues and *Lunar Braceros* do undermine narratives of power, however, through their use of bodily metaphors. These allegorize distinct narrative devices in each book that put pressure on the links between text and temporality. Death, for example, in *The Rag Doll Plagues* symbolizes change and return, the imbrication of all matter. "Do not be ashamed of your decaying body," the *curanderas* tell Sandra in "Delhi." "God and the energies of the earth are calling you to join them in their metamorphosis of all of us" (119). Identifying the stable fibrinogen, which forms scabs by weaving protein strands into mesh barriers, in the infected blood helps "LAMEX" Gregory discover a cure for the plague, thus repeating that earlier emphasis on connection in "Delhi" (167). Connections, networks, and imbrications have formal as well as topical significance for the novel. The sections repeat and overlap, are linked just as all people and things, material and immaterial, must be. Life is "never ours," "Delhi" Gregory's mother tells him, echoing Braidotti's zoë-centric assertion that "the life within me is not mine" (Braidotti 135). "We were not who we were, in the past, in the present, in the future. Our life, ourselves, belonged to others and those others belonged to us," Gregory muses. Our selves are convenient fictions—"My lonely collective face was everyone's face," he thinks—and the real events of our lives are always unfolding elsewhere from where we are, "always further away, outside me, from me, but never in my control" (Morales 110). At novel's end this has evolved into "LAMEX" Gregory's realization that all selves are the same selves, acting in the same places, at the same times (200).

These same ideas galvanize *Lunar Braceros*, where the human body drives the engine of history. Ancestry symbolizes humans' physical link with the past, and the novel depicts endless iterations of colonial history and corporeal exploitation across a range of textual forms and topics. The physical trauma of history does not disappear or pass away. It repeats like the multiply narrated scenes in the novel; it fractures and sutures itself together in new forms like the interwoven narrative threads that surface in Lydia's memories, lessons, nanotexts, and reflections. History endures like the bodies of the murdered braceros on the moon, like the migrant bodies in their Texan mass graves. In *The Rag Doll Plagues* and *Lunar Braceros*, the human body refuses to become part of the detritus of history, refuses to be deleted like the historical data in Lydia's prison work program, or forgotten like Gregory's books.

The body's resistance to its own erasure in both novels is a function of textuality against technology. Digital, biological, and scientific technologies ground notions of progress and immediacy that each novel eschews in favor of the immersive and circular temporality of reading and interpretation, depicted as somatic and sensory. The body's resistance in these books is also the resistance of race to the notion that technology, variously manifest, will allow humans to transcend the body. The particularities of the body ground the imperial humanism, with its hierarchies of difference, that Braidotti so eloquently decries (16). Moving beyond those hierarchies charts a course to a more just, sustainable, and equitable future, but it does not require leaving the body behind. *The Rag Doll Plagues* and *Lunar Braceros* both make this same argument by construing time as unable to progress past the human body; the body is always now, never past. "LAMEX" Gregory is "transfigured into all those that have gone before [him]" because we are all made of the same stuff (200). There is only ever one body sharing the same space, and we are all always writing and rewriting the same text.

The Rag Doll Plagues and *Lunar Braceros* achieve this kind of relational posthumanism structurally, but not topically. At the level of content, the body remains "sacer," while formally plots converge and overlap; characters repeat and reflect each other; the texts themselves are fractured, repetitive, and circular. The novels even describe self-energizing systems that evoke Braidotti's vital materialist understanding of matter as "intelligent and self-organizing" (35). Still, matter, technology, and the human remain distinct; technology is something that humans use to manipulate matter in these novels, whereas Braidotti understands the three as symbiotic. For Braidotti, humans are synergistic, relational confederations of intelligent, self-organizing stuff, while for *The Rag Doll Plagues* and *Lunar Braceros* the human body is a sign of subjectivity that stands apart from the material world.

That marks a significant political difference between the novels and the relational posthumanism they gesture toward but never quite attain. In both books, human bodies signal individual subjects. Freedom of the body is figured as individual freedom, and selves stand in opposition to states and corporate control. This begets novels where one worldview is critiqued and supplanted with another (Chingananza opposes the reservation in *Lunar Braceros*; El Mar de Villas eludes enclosure in one of the "existence areas" in *The Rag Doll Plagues*), and highly symbolic, somewhat heavy-handed discursive modes. Take, for example, the vampiric north literally living off the blood of the south in *The Rag Doll Plagues*, and Pedro in *Lunar Braceros* making sure the reader understands the reservation as an allegory for the mission (54). These referential narrative techniques run the novels around the "neoliberal circle" that Mitchum Huehls describes (10) and away from the just, ethical futures on the horizons of their stories.

Rather than tagging bodies to individual subjects, we might think in terms of the material confederations Braidotti describes. She offers alternate conceptions of political agency that rely on embodiment but see the body as contiguous with rather than opposed to culture and technology. This, she argues, "produces a different scheme of emancipation and a non-dialectical politics of human liberation" (35). Politics does not have to be a critical, oppositional project of articulating counter-subjectivities; it can instead be an ongoing self- and world-making process that must continuously engage and negotiate dominant forms of power and value. This Braidotti calls an "affirmative politics" that "respects vulnerability while actively constructing social horizons of hope" (122). It allows different possibilities for the body to emerge in *Lunar Braceros* and *The Rag Doll Plagues* than the novels imagine for themselves, possibilities brought to life in Rafael Lozano-Hemmer's art.

Lozano-Hemmer's work imagines the human body in relation to the world, as Braidotti's affirmative politics demand. His installations weave human bodies into complex webs of space, time, machine, and community. *Pulse Park* and *Sandbox* defamiliarize the body by rendering it as distorted light in space and time; they disconnect the body from the self, creating collective art built around and upon the body's materiality. There are no divisions in Lozano-Hemmer's work: no us and them; no human and machine; no self and other. All his art begins from flesh and blood; everything flows from the body; everything meets in the body; the body conditions all. Pieces like *Sandbox* and *Pulse Park* demonstrate how we are all implicated in the body's power, and how our own bodies are vulnerable and subject. We must care for each other, Lozano-Hemmer's work asserts, as if, and because, we all share the same body in the same space, and that shared body is implicated in the infinite nexus of flesh and machine that buried those migrant bodies in Falfurrias. Lozano-Hemmer's art manifests Braidotti's politics of continuity and negotiation, an evolving politics that unearths the dead migrants, that collects and catalogs their things, that asserts their textuality, their materiality, and emphasizes their status as fleeting moments of time when a particular constellation of the life we all share endured. *Lunar Braceros* and *The Rag Doll Plagues*, in their insistence on the body, work similarly despite their oppositional politics and the divide they imagine between human and machine. Through them we can begin to imagine the embodied politics of an ethical future for all beings.

Coda

Accordions of Abjection: Genealogies of Chicanx Punk

So what now? Well, first and foremost, we need to feel.
—Junot Díaz

"What now?" asks Junot Díaz, writing in the *New Yorker* in November 2016, just after Donald Trump was voted president of the United States. Trump's election forces recognition that in the twenty-first century a significant enough number of US citizens were willing to support what Díaz describes as a "toxic misogynist, a racial demagogue who wants to make America great by destroying the civil-rights gains of the past fifty years" ("Under Trump"). How to carry on, Díaz wonders, in the face of so much hate? How, moreover, to grapple with the vulnerability of *latinidad*; how to move through the world under a president who calls Mexicans rapists, criminals, drug dealers, and enemies of the United States (Reilly). What kind of ethical future can we hope for, really, when so many bodies are threatened? What now, indeed. And what good does reading do anyone?

Now, says Díaz, we need to "connect courageously with the rejection" and "mourn all these injuries fully, so that they do not drag us into despair" ("Under Trump"). We must feel things and let those feelings extend outwards to form solidarities and create the motivating energies to build better tomorrows. "Because let's be real," Díaz cautions in conclusion, "we always knew this shit wasn't going to be easy. Colonial power, patriarchal power, capitalist power must always and everywhere be battled, because they never, ever quit" ("Under Trump"). People cannot fight without hope, though, and Díaz offers "radical hope" as that which we must *do*—not *have*—now. We must feel our pain, sense our loss, and actively hope for a future we cannot yet imagine.

Where does reading fit, then? Why think about literature? Throughout *Racial Immanence* I have argued for reading as an intra-action of body and text. In the preceding chapters I demonstrate reading as producing an experience wherein *latinidad* can be sensed and perceived, wherein race is immanent and productive. I have challenged my own readers to think of reading not as representing but as conducting sensory experiences between entities, as generating feelings and making space for radical hope. Reading in this way asks us to linger with rather than interpret the text. Granting the immanence of race reconfigures the space and time of reading and writing; it posits both as world-making performances that reimagine the social.

In conceiving reading as a performance of politics, I have been most inspired by the political theorist Cristina Beltrán, who cautions against seeing embodied political actions like protests or demonstrations as preludes to participation in the electoral process. She argues that "the embodied action of Latinos does not simply reflect but actively *constructs* communities and solidarities within the public realm" (17). Beltrán sees the physical performance of politics—marching in the streets, for example—as producing a shared sense of belonging and ownership that makes new political imaginaries possible. Her understanding of embodied politics has informed my own ideas about reading throughout *Racial Immanence*, but here I want to extend Beltrán's theory to something more playful.

What now? Chicanx punk.

Punkero aesthetics most clearly articulate the sensibilities of the artists I explore in this book. Punk has been widely studied in the British context as a working-class art form with an overt social consciousness, but it has always had an ambiguous relationship with race. With few exceptions, the history and significance of Chicanx and Latinx punk are rarely recognized in studies of the genre, and "race," if it is discussed at all, refers mostly to African American musicians, or to white punks' racial anxieties. In *Loca Motion*, however, Michelle Habell-Pallán reveals a history of brown punk that addresses social inequality and racism, forming cross-cultural alliances among a diverse body of artists in 1970s and 1980s Los Angeles.[1] Inspired by but independent from British and Anglo-American punk scenes, Chicanx punk is simultaneously a political object and an affective mode that pushes us toward radical hope. It is the purest expression of racial immanence, and I trace its emergence to early articulations of the US-Mexico border.

Interlude 3: The Diary

In 1827, after Henry Ward, the British ambassador to Mexico, had raised concerns over the steady progress of US citizens into Mexican territory, the Comisión de Límites (Boundary Commission) left Mexico City with a charge from President Guadalupe Victoria to assess the true nature of Anglo settlement in Mexico's northern frontier. The Comisión was also to ascertain the effects of aggressive US removal policies on Mexican indigenous groups and determine with which tribes, if any, Mexico should formally ally. Leading this endeavor was General Manuel de Mier y Terán, accompanied by several assistants, including José María Sánchez, who served as the expedition's draftsman and kept a detailed diary of the Comisión's work.[2]

Terán and his men found, as Ward had claimed, that Anglo-American and European settlement was happening rapidly, and they predicted that the people there would soon become ungovernable. Upon reaching Austin on April 27, Sánchez notes that its "population is nearly two hundred persons, of which only ten are Mexicans, for the balance are all Americans from the North with an occasional European" (271/46).[3] These settlers are largely, in his estimation, "lazy people of vicious character" (271/46), slave owners who cannot be bothered to cultivate their own land.[4] Sánchez warns that Stephen Austin, founder of the settlement, has "lulled the authorities into a sense of security" and that "the spark that will start the conflagration that will deprive us of Texas, will start from this colony" (271/47).[5]

Throughout his diary Sánchez uses different strategies to assert Mexican sovereignty over Texas. These revolve mostly around language and who has the right to name Texan space, rights predicated, in his analysis, on proper sentiment. Through his meditations on the natural environment, Sánchez constructs himself as a *feeling* subject who can properly desire, and thus *deserve* the land, as when he describes the effects of the nighttime sounds in Texas as filling "the soul with a strange melancholy known and felt only by sensitive hearts" (255/25).[6] The reader must assume that Sánchez possesses such a heart since he is able to experience (and write about) such sweet melancholy.

Feeling is physical as well as emotional in Sánchez's diary, and he deploys the human body in striking ways. At one point the expedition is crossing a river where he remembers an important battle had taken place during Mexico's war for independence from Spain, and he mentions that one can still find the bones of Mexican soldiers in the dirt there (256/26). From this Sánchez observes that though the United States will likely force Mexico out of what he sees as incontrovertibly Mexican space, the soil under Anglo-American feet will always be made out of decomposing Mexican bodies.

Sánchez enthusiastically embraces this macabre image just as he embraces Terán after the latter is attacked by mosquitoes. A "numberless legion" of the insects bite Terán and his men "everywhere" one night in Austin. As dawn breaks the soldiers see "the terrible onslaught that these cursed insects had made upon [them], leaving [them] full of swollen spots, especially on the face of the general, which was so raw that it seemed as if it had been flayed" (273/48).[7] Sánchez lovingly nurses his general back to health, however, as all the soldiers, swollen and *horroroso*, go about their business.

As the tension builds, and incidents of Mexican-Anglo antagonism increase in the diary, Sánchez celebrates abjection more frequently. He even disparages himself by telling the story of coming upon an exceedingly "unattractive" place to camp and suggesting to his fellow soldiers that they name it after him (270).[8] Sánchez knows that his rational arguments for Mexican sovereignty will be ineffective, and his nuanced linking of feeling, language, and rights will fall on deaf ears. His ultimate response to the futility of Terán's mission is to leverage the abject Mexican body as a rejoinder to both US aggression and the ineptitude of the Mexican government.

Sánchez's strategy of performative, aggressive abjection is the essence of punk. It resonates with the Latinx hard-core scenes that emerged across the United States in the 1990s, when bands like Los Crudos, Bread and Circuits, and Kontra Attaque formed in response to political events such as the 1994 uprising in Chiapas as well as domestic anti-immigrant and anti-Latinx legislation. Los Crudos are trailblazers of the scene, and their front man, Martin Sorrendeguy, is, as I write, still an incredibly productive artist and activist, collaborating most recently with Alice

Bag, an epigraph from whom opens this book. One of Los Crudos' signature songs, "That's Right We're That Spic Band," expresses many of the same themes evident in Sánchez's diary: "That's right motherfucker. / We're that spic band! / You say you call yourself a punk? / Bullshit! / You're just a closet fucking Nazi. / You are bullshit! / You just don't understand us? / Bullshit! / You just fucking fear us!" The song asserts a "spic" identity, as Sánchez asserts *mexicanidad*; it refuses to be misunderstood, as Sánchez does in all his discussions of language and naming; and Sorrendeguy delivers his lyrics in a deafening roar at speeds that defy comprehension, a performative analog to Sánchez's applauding the atrocious.

Like Los Crudos (whose name translates as "The Unrefined," or more colloquially as "The Hungover"), Piñata Protest, twenty-first-century Chicanx punk rockers from Texas, embrace the unpolished coarseness of punk that I claim as a thread tying them to Sánchez. Their jocular ferocity presents quite a contrast, however, to Los Crudos' raw, 1990s solemnity. "No mames güey, soy vato bien perron," sings Álvaro del Norte on "Vato Perron" from the band's 2013 album *El Valiente*.[9] He continues, "a los chingones, les canto esta canción / I'm in a gang, I also do voodoo / I am mojado, y qué? What's it to you?"[10] From the playful "I" of the opening lines the song moves to a communal "we" at the close; "Vatos perrones we won't go away / We're here to stay, live for today." Differences in tone aside, both "That's Right We're That Spic Band" and "Vato Perron" evidence a similar tension between I and we. In each the "I" is working in the service of "we"; both reject the singular and leverage the communal. Nevertheless, these songs perform different kinds of work in the world. Los Crudos is mobilizing punk aesthetics to further racial justice agendas, but I mean something different when I say that Chicanx punk is the purest expression of racial immanence. For that claim to be true, punk must be something other than a subject position; it must be something other than Sorrendeguy's earnestness, something more like Piñata Protest's irreverence and its lead singer Álvaro del Norte's accordion.

Del Norte's instrument of choice is the accordion, which is the musical thing focusing Sánchez's ire in his diary (figure C.1).[11] As a young musician, del Norte initially rejected the accordion-infused sounds of the norteño (northern Mexican) music his traditional Mexican family

Figure C.1. Álvaro del Norte, lead singer and accordion player for Chicanx punk band Piñata Protest. Photo by Carlos J. Matos.

favored, but he eventually found his way back to the instrument (Vigil). "Somewhere along the history of rock & roll, the accordion got lost," says del Norte, asserting that to play an "unorthodox instrument" in a musical style with such a rigid orthodoxy as punk "is quite a musically rebellious statement in itself" (in Moser). Bringing the accordion to bear on punk is also a way to harness the insurgent energies of the genre to Mexican ends. "I don't think punk rock spoke anything about my culture or geographic background," del Norte told one interviewer. "If anything, punk rock was a way to rebel against my own heritage" (Vigil). The accordion, however, changes everything.

The accordion carries colonial history in its bellows. It is prevalent in Mexican music, particularly norteño, because of German migration to Texas. The accordion was first patented in Berlin in 1822 and is believed to have come to the Americas with traveling German merchants and migrants who settled Texas in large numbers. By 1850 Germans constituted more than 5 percent of the total population of Texas, forming what has come to be known as the German belt, centered around Austin (Jordan). The "occasional European" Sánchez sees in Austin is almost certainly a

German. The accordion, therefore, signals cultural mestizaje, but also colonization and encroachment, which is exactly what Sánchez railed against in his diary.

Accordions and polka rhythms reverberate throughout traditional Mexican music, but the instrument inhabits a liminal zone between permanence and impermanence. It symbolizes change, but it also risks becoming an immutable icon of *mexicanidad*. In Piñata Protest the accordion is both/and, Mexican and something else. It resists colonization narratives at the same time that it resists commoditized stereotypes of Mexican music and punk rock. In "Vato Perron" del Norte sings, "I am mojado, y qué? What's it to you?" (I'm a wetback, and what do you care?) He is also, he tells his audience, "el mero mero," the best of the best. The song simultaneously performs and explodes stereotypes; it takes abject and facile images of what it means to be Mexican American and says, "Yes, I'm all these things: I'm a drunk, and a gangster, but I'm *bien perron*." The objects by which you think you know Mexicans, del Norte asserts to his listeners, are not real, but he does not tell listeners what *is* real. Del Norte refuses the teleology of interpretation; in "Vato Perron" he lingers in "today"; he "won't go away."

Del Norte revisits this lingering in "Life on the Border," where he sings of being "nameless not aimless." That song is an homage to the in-between. "Life on a line, on a tightrope / the border's my life, all that I know," runs the song's refrain, but del Norte is not singing about Gloria Anzaldúa's *nepantla*, the "tierra desconocida," or "liminal zone" of discomfort and fear signaling transition and transformation ("(Un)natural Bridges" 243). Del Norte *conoce su tierra*, he knows his land. It is made of Mexican bones and filled with the bodies of dead migrants such as those discovered in Falfurrias, Texas.[12] He is not afraid or transitioning; he has "no side to declare, no need or desire, / I'm not stuck . . . I'm weaving and dancing, ascended, sublime" ("Life on the Border"). These differences can easily be attributed to gender. Of course del Norte is unafraid: he is a young, able-bodied, cis-gendered man in a world made for men. But he is Mexican.

What does it mean to *be* Mexican? Why does art by and about Chicanxs matter? I have been weaving around and dancing with these questions throughout *Racial Immanence*. It is impossible to ascend above them to some sublime plateau of interpretive confidence, del Norte's charismatic swagger notwithstanding. I take his lyrics as a gesture of radical hope. The video for "Vato Perron" is a cacophony of such gestures. It features a performance of the song in a packed bar where fans crowd-surf along with a large, rainbow-colored, donkey-shaped piñata. The band's performance is cut with interludes of fans posing and interacting with this stuffed donkey. In the final sequence, del Norte destroys his accordion, and the closing shot features its remains alongside the now-shattered piñata.

The parallel destruction of the piñata and the accordion is a gesture of radical hope. It makes space for the accordion to be reimagined; it makes time for an endless today that will not go away; and it makes it possible to remain nameless not aimless. Del Norte's refusal to be afraid, his resistance to interpretation, his embrace of Mexican things but rejection of Mexican stereotypes, these are all *puro* punk. They are punk like the accordion, punk like ugly José Sanchez, and punk like the sick and swollen General Terán. They are punk like *Homeboy Beautiful,* and punk like Los Crudos, punk like the bodies in Falfurrias . . . all of which insist on a materiality energized by a racial immanence that comes together in fleeting, performative moments of *chicanidad.*

ACKNOWLEDGMENTS

In 2018 Jordan Peele became the first African American to win an Oscar for best original screenplay. His acceptance speech gave me goose bumps because, in part, it seemed like a historic occasion, but also because his description of making his directorial debut, *Get Out*, resonated so much with my experiences writing this book. "I stopped writing this movie about twenty times because I thought it was impossible," Peele told the audience. "I thought it wasn't going to work. I thought no one would ever make this movie." Likewise, my writing was peripatetic, and I often wondered what kind of academic press would ever want to publish it. Peele and I both persevered. As he recounts, "I kept coming back to it because I knew if someone let me make this movie that people would hear it and people would see it." I'm pretty sure that *Racial Immanence* will not, as *Get Out* did, earn over $250 million worldwide, but I am just as grateful to all the people who helped me write this book as Peele was for his mentors and collaborators. "I want to dedicate this to all the people who raised my voice and let me make this movie," he said, concluding, "I love you all. Thank you so much" ("90th Oscars"). To the many people who helped bring *Racial Immanence* from my brain to readers' hands: I love you and owe you infinite thanks.

Thanks, first and foremost, to Eric Zinner, the best editor a person could ever hope to have. He may have laughed when I first described *Racial Immanence* to him, but he believed in me and offered encouragement and support as I took this ball and ran with it over the years I spent writing. *Un abrazo fuerte pa' ti*, Eric. Next, to Nina Eidsheim, a goddess among colleagues. I love you, Nina, for being brilliant, for your hustle, for funding my manuscript workshop, for amplifying my voice . . . for everything. You are an exemplary woman supporting other women, and my greatest goal is to be able to pay it forward one day.

Stacy Alaimo, Michael Hames-García, and Uri McMillan: nothing but love for you three for helping this book live up to its potential. Thank you for your generosity and for all your amazing intellectual work, which has been so generative to my own. Thanks also to those who funded your efforts and travels to California to discuss *Racial Immanence*: my chair, Lowell Gallagher, whose support has been crucial in ways too expansive to enumerate here; the Friends of English at UCLA; David Schaberg, UCLA dean of humanities; and Chris Dunkel Schetter, UCLA's associate vice chancellor for faculty development.

Maite Zubiaurre and Reem Hanna-Harwell, where would I be without you? You've been my champions through days both dark and bright. I'm not sure I could have finished writing this book without you both on my side. *Mil gracias.* For your research help, Kim Calder and Miriam Juárez, *estoy muy agradecida.*

I am blessed with some phenomenal colleagues at UCLA and beyond. Partners in crime, sisters and brothers in battle, *los amo a todos.* Special shout-outs: Eliza Rodríguez y Gibson, thanks for listening to so many conference presentations about Piñata Protest. Carlos Gallego, Rodrigo Lazo, and Jesse Alemán, thanks for soliciting articles that allowed me to work through the early rumblings of this book. Rafael Pérez-Torres, thanks for slogging through so many of my drafts, for all the lunches, all the hugs, and for always listening. Josh Guzmán, thanks for being so kind, so sweet, so smart, and for helping me unlock the mysteries of what I was trying to tell myself. Anahid Nersessian, thanks for being you. Fred D'Aguiar, thanks for helping me see myself in a whole new way. Justin Torres, thanks for being totally rad. Mitchum Huehls, thanks for love, for support, for keeping me from going totally off the rails, and for being with me every step of the way, yea, though we have definitely walked together through the valley of some shadows.

Thank you to my brother, Andrew. I love you for sushi by flashlight, for making me laugh in the angry depths of despair, and for telling me how smart I was when I needed to hear it most.

And finally, thanks to everyone who has called this book in its various stages too "gimmicky," too theoretical, not theoretical enough, too white, too brown, not brown enough . . . not "rigorous" enough. Your derogation helped me push even harder against the burden of liveness. I love you all for letting me know I was on to something immanent and real.

NOTES

INTRODUCTION

1 See, for example, Esther Cepeda, who argues that Cubans' historically elite immigration status creates resentment in other non-Latino communities and renders them unattractive candidates to Latino voters.

2 In *Shelby County v. Holder* in 2013, the court invalidated a section of the Voting Rights Act of 1965 that had required nine states with particularly severe histories of racial discrimination to obtain federal approval for any change to their election laws.

3 In a study of Latino college degree completion rates by national origin, Ponjuan et al. found that, in 2012, South Americans saw the highest percentage of men earning college degrees: 28.4 percent. Other Hispanics were next with 27.13 percent, followed by Cubans at 21.2 percent, Puerto Ricans at 21.0 percent, Central Americans at 17.4 percent, and, finally, Mexicans at 17.2 percent (63). Ponjuan et al. limited their study to men, but their findings suggest that academic representation of Latinxs by national origin is incommensurate with representation in the population at large; Mexican Americans, that is, are underrepresented in higher education while South Americans and Cubans are overrepresented. It is possible to speculate, by extension, that while a more inclusive Latinx studies has real intellectual justification, the institutional push to frame Latinx rather than Chicanx scholarly questions adumbrates internecine conflicts around class and citizenship.

4 *The Social Imperative* is only the most recent and visible flashpoint in a long tradition of reading for representation in Chicanx literary history. Raymund Paredes said it first and most succinctly in his landmark article "The Evolution of Chicano Literature" (1978). "What exactly is Chicano literature?" he asks in his concluding paragraph. "Chicano literature," he answers, "is that body of work produced by United States citizens and residents of Mexican descent for whom a sense of ethnicity is a critical part of their literary sensibility and for whom the *portrayal* of their ethnic experience is a major concern of their art" (104, emphasis added here and in the following quotes). Following the path blazed by Paredes, later twentieth- and twenty-first-century scholars of Chicanx literature have attended to a wide range of things besides "ethnic experience," but remain heavily invested in "portrayal." To illustrate, in *Chicano Poetry: A Critical Introduction* (1986), Cordelia Candelaria relies mainly on prosodic and formalist analysis but asserts, "Chicano literature grew directly out of raza oral traditions and their evocative *reflections* of the culture" (20). Ramón Saldívar's deconstructive study *Chicano*

Narrative: The Dialectics of Difference (1990) concerns itself primarily with "the social world *represented* in the writings of Chicano men and women" (4). A few years later, his brother José published *Border Matters: Remapping American Cultural Studies* (1997), a book examining "issues of expression and *representation* in folklore, music, and video performance art" (ix). Rafael Pérez-Torres explores a range of things that "mestizaje *represents*" in *Mestizaje: Critical Uses of Race in Chicano Culture* (2006). Finally, a cluster of books published around the time of this writing have representational and communicative concerns at their core: Elda María Román is interested in "texts that *portray* racialized subjects' desire for financial solvency" (3); Jennifer Harford Vargas explores "an overarching concern on the part of Latina/o writers to *represent* resonances and dissonances between hierarchies of power and modes of repression in the Americas" (6); and Ylce Irizarry "assumes that narrative is, above all, a *communication* between the author(s) and implied but not necessarily identified audience(s)" (9). Since Paredes published his article in 1978, Chicanx and Latinx literary studies have evolved tremendously. It is, as I hope my examples show, an exciting, diverse, and growing field. We have yet to seriously question one of our underlying assumptions, however: that words *portray, represent, reflect*, and *communicate*. In *Racial Immanence* I grant that this is so, but I also explore the racialized politics of representing and communicating while asking whether that is all that words can do.

5   See, for example, Díaz's page on Genius, a site that crowdsources annotations and invites artists to annotate their own work.
6   The "Pastry War" erupted as France tried to secure trade arrangements with Mexico equal to those enjoyed by Britain and the United States. Fighting erupted when a French national demanded remuneration for damage his bakery suffered at the hands of the Mexican army.
7   This honor is actually hotly contested. "Many are the claimants for the honor of capturing Santa Anna's cork leg," writes East in "Santa Anna's Cork Leg" (166).
8   In this Viego is explicitly indebted to Rey Chow's notion of "coercive mimeticism." In *The Protestant Ethnic and the Spirit of Capitalism*, Chow argues that subjects become ethnic through a system of social pressures to imitate a stereotyped ethnicity promoted by the dominant culture and produced through autobiographical or confessional literature.
9   José Muñoz articulates the necessity of such disruptions in *Disidentifications* and theorizes the temporal dimension of queer Latinx politics in *Cruising Utopia*.
10 Political community, says Connolly, relies on a sociality best understood as a kind of emergent causality occurring between bodies in space and time. Social experience, he explains, is mediated by the human ability to mimic the behavior and movement of others, producing physical and emotional knowledge that works in tandem with cognitive, linguistic knowledge. Sociality and social change, in other words, rely on the ability to perceive others, not just cognitively, but spatially and temporally as well (183).

11 Connolly, too, argues that the suspension of time is a key strategy for upending political expectations and creating the possibility of change. Building on Brian Massumi's work, Connolly argues that new media can exploit the half-second delay between perception and experience by defamiliarizing space and time, thus enabling new political formations (194).

12 California Proposition 6 was an initiative on the November 7, 1978, statewide ballot. Known as the Briggs Initiative, had it passed, it would have banned gays and lesbians from working in California's public schools. Proposition 13, which severely limited property taxes in the state, passed on the June 1978 ballot and remains controversial.

13 It may be more accurate to say that the biological evidence for distinct races is fuzzy. Since the sequencing of the human genome in the early 2000s, scientists have come to the consensus that there is only one human race. Genetic variation tends to be regional and correlates, in some cases, to socially constructed racial categories, but this is inconsistent and imprecise. See Yudell et al.

14 Even if, as Timaeus argues, the universe is formed in imitation of an ideal model (29a), it still must exist somewhere and be made from something. If, in other words, fire is a fleeting imitation of ideal fieriness (49d), what we experience as fire still happens in the same universe that contains the ideal fiery form, so what is it made out of and where does it happen? What else is there, asks Timaeus, besides "Model Form" (48e) and "model's Copy" (49a)? There is, writes Plato, "the receptacle," which is the "nurse of all Becoming" (49a). The Greek word Plato uses for this is "chora" (space), not "hyle" (matter), as Judith Butler notes in *Bodies That Matter* (42), but he is unclear about what happens in the receptacle and how it functions.

15 NAFTA liberalized trade, eliminated most tariffs, and sought to protect intellectual property between the United States, Canada, and Mexico. It enjoyed bipartisan support and has benefitted the economies of all three partners, but has remained controversial, with US-based critics arguing that it shifts US production, jobs, and manufacturing to Mexico.

CHAPTER 1. RACE

1 Hassig says that the central face is either that of Tonatiuh, the sun god, or Tlateuctli, an earth deity (69). He prefers the latter reading. Villela, Miller, and Robb spell the latter "Tlatecuhtli," and allow for the possibility that the central figure is a hybrid or unknown entity (1).

2 Francisco "Pancho" Villa was born a peon on an hacienda in San Juan del Río, in the north of Mexico in 1878. He became a populist revolutionary hero after aiding Francisco Madero's overthrow of Pofirio Díaz in 1910 and remained a force to be reckoned with in Mexican politics, advocating for progressive land reform and indigenous rights, until his assassination in 1923.

3 Leys refers to anti-intentionalism as the "dominant paradigm" in emotion studies and defines it as the belief that "affective processes occur independently

of intention or meaning" (437). Intentionalism, or cognitivism, contests the anti-intentionalists' belief that action and behavior are predicated on affective programs that are "independent of consciousness" (Leys 443). They see the opposition of affect and cognition as a false dichotomy and argue that the two are far more intertwined than science has yet to discover.

4 The evolution of sense in Gilb's writing occurs across genre. That is, while I consider here both short stories and novels, the narrative explorations I am most interested in with my analyses occur on such a micro-level as to function in longer works as they do in shorter texts.

5 In his discussion of what he calls "homeboy cosmopolitanism," Diawara theorizes hip-hop as a "transnational cultural form" (237) that can help young African American men move beyond the "trap of racial immanence," which he defines as the idea that black men are hegemonically confined to a limited set of social roles.

6 In *After Finitude* (2008), Meillassoux takes philosophy to task for being unable, or unwilling, to separate thinking from being, for operating on the assumption that things that cannot be thought effectively do not exist. Though Graham Harman and other philosophers have argued the finer points of correlationism (the idea that our thoughts must correspond to objects in the world, that every thought correlates to a thing and vice versa) with Meillassoux, together they share a distaste for anthropocentric philosophical models. I return to this kind of speculative theorizing in my conclusion.

7 Tobin Siebers, for one, advocates a theory of "complex embodiment" (27), and Sharon Snyder and David Mitchell have focused on "the outer and inner reaches of culture and experience as a combination of profoundly social and biological forces," an "interactional space" they contend the field has yet to theorize (7).

8 For example, Robert McRuer and Abby Wilkerson argue, in their introduction to *GLQ*'s special issue on disability and sexuality, that queer and disabled identities draw political force by insisting on making the invisible visible: the body for the disabled; sexuality and desire for the queer. McRuer and Wilkerson read their linkage in queer and disability activism as powerful critiques of the global, neoliberal public sphere.

9 Carol Breckenridge and Candace Vogler, for example, contend that "feminism, sexuality and gender studies, and critical race theory meet at a point of incomprehension when faced with the corporeality of the disabled body" (350). Siebers, for his part, agrees, and argues further that race is immutable while disability is a shifting signifier and can potentially condition all human identities (26).

10 Ellen Samuels's *Fantasies of Identification,* for example, is notable for its direct disarticulation of categorical identity. Jennifer James and Cynthia Wu, by contrast, trace the intersection of race and the body in "multiple identities" maintained by social hierarchies (8). Additionally, Douglas Baynton sees disability as a "constitutive element of social relationships" that reinforces social hierarchies of race and class. Similarly, Harriet Washington details the uses of African American bodies

in scientific experiments benefiting mainly Anglo-Americans in *Medical Apartheid*. Julie Minich's analysis in *Accessible Citizenships*, where she looks to representations of disability as models for alternative political communities, nuances this relationship somewhat, but she is still very much invested in staking identitarian claims (5).

11 My argument here is a version of that espoused by Lennard Davis, who advocates a "post-identitarian" approach according to which the body mediates history and culture. Gilb pushes back against identity politics in ways that echo Davis, but Davis's strong reaction against cultural diversity is far afield from the territory Gilb stakes out in his writing. Davis does not reject identity politics so much as he laments disability studies' absence from the rhetoric of diversity, ultimately pitting the two against each other. See, for example, Davis's article "Why Is Disability Missing from the Discourse on Diversity?"

12 The foundational text explicating this difference is *Racial Formation in the United States* (2015 [1986]) by Michael Omi and Howard Winant, which I discuss further in the introduction to this book. In their development of critical race theory, Richard Delgado and Jean Stefancic have built on Omi and Winant's work showing how legal institutions frame and codify shared notions of race and identity. See, for example, their edited collection, *Critical Race Theory: An Introduction* (2017 [2001]).

13 In the first volume of *Time and Narrative*, Ricoeur argued that "between the activity of narrating a story and the temporal character of human experience there exists a correlation that is not merely accidental but that presents a transcultural form of necessity" (52). That is, in all languages and cultures, a primary purpose of storytelling is to render time legible.

14 It is Libet's research and Massumi's interpretation of it that raise Leys's ire. Broadly speaking, Libet's work explored the relationship between unconscious neural activity and conscious decisions to act. In a series of experiments Libet found there to be a half-second delay between bodily action and the first sign of brain activity. See Leys (452–55) for a critique of Libet's methodology and findings.

15 Merleau-Ponty explains, "Between the alleged colors and visibles, we would find anew the tissue that lines them, sustains them, nourishes them, and which for its part is not a thing, but a possibility, a latency, and a *flesh* of things" (*The Visible and the Invisible* 132). Gilles Deleuze and Félix Guattari found this formulation a bit too metaphysical and contemplative. Flesh was "too tender" to support the force of becoming (*What Is Philosophy?* 179), according to them; in his study of Francis Bacon, Deleuze rejected "flesh" in favor of a theory of "meat," which he defines explicitly as "not dead flesh" (*Francis Bacon* 17). Though my focus here is on lived experience and the materiality of race, Gilb's catachrestic descriptions of violence and physical contact render "flesh" more suitable than "meat" to a discussion of his fictional worlds.

16 The collection was Gilb's first published work to appear after he suffered a stroke of his own in 2009.

17 Here Mr. Sanchez's writing functions as a kind of "minor literature" in relation to the major literature of Western medicine. I use "minor" not to indicate Mr. Sanchez's status as a minority subject but rather in the Deleuzo-Guattarian sense of minor literature as an act of becoming as described in their *Kafka: Toward a Theory of Minor Literature*.

18 Object-oriented ontology takes issue principally with Kant's idea, which I mention above, that objects conform to the human mind and so are, essentially, products of human consciousness. Object-oriented ontologists, by contrast, believe that objects exist outside human perception, have an impact on each other, and should not be subordinate to human consciousness. In his introduction to *The Quadruple Object* (2011), for example, Harman writes that our working definition of "object" should include "those entities that are neither physical nor even real." He continues, "along with diamonds, ropes, and neutrons, objects may include armies, monsters, square circles and leagues of real and fictitious nations." All objects, Harman argues, "must be accounted for by ontology, not merely denounced or reduced to despicable nullities" (1).

19 Gilb's insistence on narrative as enacting rather than representing the relationship between body and brain renders Alcoff's analysis of racial feeling as inadequate to his task. Similarly, the work of postpositive realists such as Satya Mohanty and Paula Moya, who are inspired by Alcoff and with whom my analysis has some affinity, is equally insufficient to explain Gilb's narrative experimentation. Mohanty's *Literary Theory and the Claims of History* (1997), Moya's *Learning from Experience* (2002), and especially Moya and Michael Hames-García's edited collection *Reclaiming Identity* (2000) all take identity to be a subject's constructed narrative about their accumulated experiences, narrative being an integral part of identity and having a solid foundation in the real. *Identity Politics Reconsidered*, edited by Alcoff, Moya, Mohanty, and Hames-García (2006), further consolidates these assumptions under the aegis of the "future of minority studies." Gilb, on the other hand, foregrounds the very question of narrative itself, not just refashioning it, but asking how language intersects with experience, especially corporeal experience, to form our notions of self, our identities. My reading of his work thus resonates less with postpositive realism and more with Peggy Phelan's project in *Unmarked*, which takes up explicit renderings of corporeal absence in art and performance as a rejoinder to "cultural activists [who] have also assumed that 'selves' can be adequately represented within the visual or linguistic field" (10).

CHAPTER 2. FACE

1 My exploration of the body is similar to Rosemarie Garland-Thomson's approach to disability in *Extraordinary Bodies*, where she reads physical disability in literature as "a repository for social anxieties about such troubling concerns as vulnerability, control, and identity" (6). Disability, she says, is determined by "the ways that bodies interact with the socially engineered environment and conform to social expectations," which allows her to argue that the significance of dis-

ability is to be found in social relationships rather than physical flaws (7). Helio's deformity works a bit differently than those Garland-Thomson explores, however, since he is a primary focalizer and Garland-Thomson's thesis is predicated on her observation that "main characters almost never have physical disabilities" (7). She is concerned with the politics of disability as spectacle, while *Face* takes up the sensual experience of deformity.

2   The process is described in the Theatre's "Organizational History," which talks about performances like *After Eurydice*, for example, as "a ritual piece celebrating sexual consciousness," which was "the culmination of an anthropological, sociological and political workshop process," and *Threesomes*, an "entirely developmental piece," which "placed the performer directly before the audience in all his/her personal authenticity, without the usual disguise of non-autobiographical textual material." Gary Geerdes, writing in the *Los Angeles Free Press* about an *After Eurydice* rehearsal, describes how the actors collectively choreograph Eurydice's final scream, and Pineda, responding to a request to sit in on a rehearsal, explains that because "the nature of our work is very volatile," the majority of their rehearsals are closed (Letter to Tzivia Stein).

3   "I do not see how I could successfully place your manuscript with a publisher," wrote one agent (Hoffman), while another more helpfully opined, "I do think you will have a hard time finding an American publisher for the novel. It reads as if it were a European book, and the introspective aspect of the narrative, together with the terribly upsetting story behind it, will not easily lend itself to a marketable book" (Siegel).

4   Pineda's papers at Stanford contain correspondence about Pereira with the Brazilian embassy and plastic surgeons in the United States, as well as a copy of *Basics of Dermatalogic Surgery*, heavily annotated in Pineda's handwriting. The collection also includes a small composition book, where the first few pages of *Face* are handwritten, interspersed with diary entries about a trip to Mexico and philosophical meditations on time and experience.

5   Performance photos from *TIME/PIECE* feature four performers, including Pineda. They appear to be building a ladder-like structure, which is supported also by strings and scarves. In some photos the actors are tying pots, pans, and each other together with this same string; in others they are eating, kissing each other, and climbing over one another.

6   Pineda attributes her epigraph to M. Merleau-Ponty in *Phénoménologie de la perception*, with no page reference. While it summarizes Merleau-Ponty succinctly, it is not a direct quote. Merleau-Ponty writes,

   As for the novel, although its plot can be summarized and the "thought" of the writer lends itself to abstract expression, this conceptual significance is extracted from a wider one, as the description of a person is extracted from the actual appearance of his face. The novelist's task is not to expound ideas or even analyse characters, but to depict an inter-human event, ripening and bursting it upon us with no ideological commentary, to such an extent that any change in the order of the narrative or in choice of viewpoint would alter the literary meaning of the event. A novel, poem, picture or musical work are individuals, that is, beings in which the expression is indistinguishable from the thing expressed, their meaning, accessible only through direct contact, being radiated with no change of their temporal and spatial situation. It is in this sense that our body is comparable to a work of art. It is a nexus of living meanings, not the function of a certain number of mutually variable terms. . . . The arm seen and the arm touched, like the different segments of the arm, together perform one and the same action. (*Phenomenology of Perception* 151)

7 Jacob Riis was a Danish American journalist, photographer, and social reformer who devoted his career to drawing attention to poverty in New York City. His *How the Other Half Lives: Studies among the Tenements of New York* brought wider attention to the plight of the poor and was the first book to make extensive use of halftone photographic reproduction. Walker Evans began to make a name for himself in the 1930s as a photographer with the Farm Security Administration documenting the effects of the Great Depression. He is also well known for the portraits he took from 1938 to 1941 of subway riders in New York City with a camera hidden under his coat. These are collected in *Many Are Called*, with an introduction by James Agee, intended as a counterpart to the duo's *Let Us Now Praise Famous Men*. Edward Weston was one of the most important twentieth-century US art photographers; his innovations in technique and content had widespread influence.

8 Documentary photography seeks to realistically record events of social or historical significance (for an account of the history of and the debates surrounding the form, see Wells).

9 Though she does not cite him directly, Pineda appears to be in dialogue with Emmanuel Levinas, who grounds his "first philosophy" of Being, social justice, and the language that binds us all in the face-to-face encounter. "Meaning is in the face of the Other, and all the recourse to words takes place already within the primordial face to face of language," he writes (278), asserting earlier, "We call justice this face to face approach, in conversation" (71). A significant difference between Pineda and Levinas, however, can be found in their respective emphases on immanence and transcendence. Levinas sees the face as a portal to transcendence: "The dimension of the divine opens forth from the human face. A relation with the Transcendent free from all captivation by the Transcendent is a social relation" (78). Pineda, on the other hand, grounds her communal ideal in sensual experience and a rejection of transcendence.

10 Terazzo is a composite floor and wall covering, available in tile form, in which small chips of marble, granite, and other stones are bound together and polished to create a uniform surface.

11 Pineda studied from this same book (Composition Book).

12 As I discuss in my introduction, the Latinx population in the United States is growing exponentially, and the largest growth area is in US births, not immigration. As a result, "Hispanic" (to borrow from the US Census Bureau) and Spanish-language media have, in recent years, outperformed non-Hispanic, Anglo-dominant media outlets, including newspapers, but particularly when it comes to network TV. Univision, the largest US Hispanic network, is competitive with the big four (Fox, CBS, ABC, NBC) when it comes to audience size and has seen consistent revenue increases since 2000 (Guskin and Mitchell).
13 Claudia Rankine borrows this idea in *Citizen*, which includes an image from a later period similarly altered by her husband, the filmmaker John Lucas (91).
14 Thomas Skidmore's *Brazil: Five Centuries of Change,* which explores—among other things—the role of indigenous peoples and African slaves in cultural formation in colonial Brazil, is an unparalleled resource for more on Brazilian racial politics.
15 Though she resists identifying him as black in the novel, in the screenplay of *Face* Pineda describes him as "mixed race" (1) and of "mixed blood" (2) (*Face:* Filmscript, draft 2). An earlier draft of the same screenplay also specifies the setting as "The vast Bay of Rio de Janeiro" (*Face:* Filmscript, draft 1). Though several versions of a screenplay exist, the movie of *Face* has to date not been made.
16 John Cutler demonstrates the consequences of this disregard in "Towards a Reading of Nineteenth Century Latina/o Short Fiction," where he argues that such texts demonstrate Latinxs experiencing the conditions of modernity with iconoclastic narratives that resist traditional literary histories, explode generic convention, and push against national boundaries.
17 In "Feeling Mexican," I use "Latino dismodern" to describe how the nineteenth-century Mexican American novelist María Amparo Ruiz de Burton deploys a spectrum of physical ability in order to reconceive politics as a dependent field of collective, interdependent action.

CHAPTER 3. PLACE
1 See his "Breaking the Silence, Dismantling the Taboos."
2 Shilts describes this situation compellingly, and the statistics Minich cites from the Centers for Disease Control demonstrate how this is still the case for queer of color communities in the United States.
3 "Bigmouth Strikes Again" is a dramatic monologue in which a lover laments his cruelty to his partner. The refrain reads, "And now I know how Joan of Arc felt / Now I know how Joan of Arc felt / As the flames rose to her Roman nose / And her Walkman started to melt."
4 See, for example, my "¿Soy Emo, Y Qué? Sad Kids, Punkera Dykes and the Latin@ Public Sphere," a relatively late entry in the lively discussion whose genealogy I trace.
5 See Villa for a full discussion of this process and its impact on Chicanx cultural production.

6 This marking of cyclical time as indigenous finds its uneasy correlate in my first chapter's discussion of the legacies of colonial readings of indigenous time and the Aztec Sun Stone.

CHAPTER 4. WASTE

1 I intend "machine" here as a gesture toward the machinic becomings that Gilles Deleuze and Félix Guattari describe in *Anti-Oedipus* and *A Thousand Plateaus*, where connections between actors, human and nonhuman, generate an active, anti-teleological ethics.
2 Ursula Le Guin is the author of the Earthsea fantasy series and many other books, upon which have been bestowed nearly every major honor of the SF field, including the Nebula, Hugo, and Locus awards. She has also won a National Book Award and a Newberry and is regarded as a pioneering female voice in a previously male-dominated field. Samuel Delany, a queer African American writer lauded for his fantasy and erotic fiction as well as his creative memoirs, has, like Le Guin, won many awards and is regarded similarly as a trailblazer.
3 This is Latour's central argumentative thread in *We Have Never Been Modern*.
4 Alaimo defines transcorporeality, as I explain in chapter 3, as the notion that human materiality is inextricable from its environmental surroundings (*Bodily Natures* 2); Braidotti's transversality is similar, though it can include nonliving objects (45).
5 In books like *Delinking: Towards a Polycentric World*, Amin, a dependency theorist who, along with Immanuel Wallenstein, helped to develop world systems theory, argues for "delinking" as a direct counter to globalization.
6 Bakhtin uses "chronotope" to indicate the formal structures (genre, emplotment, and symbols) by which novels depict the imbrication of space with time. See "Forms of Time and the Chronotope in the Novel," essay 3 in *The Dialogic Imagination*.
7 In 1978 municipal electrical workers in Mexico City discovered a stone monolith depicting Coyolxauhqui, the Aztec moon goddess. Specialists determined that the disc must have formed part of the Templo Mayor, once the center of Aztec life, which had been destroyed and buried after the Spanish conquest. From 1978 to 1982 archaeologists excavated the site, unearthing over seven thousand ancient artifacts, now housed in the Templo Mayor museum. This work required the demolition of thirteen buildings, four of which dated back to the nineteenth century and had preserved colonial architectural elements.
8 In October 1871, approximately eighteen residents of Los Angeles's Chinatown were lynched when a conflict between two Chinese men drew police attention, leading to bystander involvement and vigilante justice. Mariano Vallejo (1807–1890), member of the californio (Mexican Californian) ruling elite, was once the most wealthy and powerful man in California and was the Mexican military commander of the state at the time of the transfer to US rule in 1848. Pacomio

(c. 1794–1840) was a Chumash carpenter and police commissioner in Monterey, where Vallejo spent his childhood, who led the Chumash Revolt of 1824. Juan Vicente de Güemes was viceroy of New Spain from 1789 to 1794. Catalina de Erauso's (1585–1650) name is never mentioned in *The Rag Doll Plagues*, but she is the real-life cross-dressing nun, whose dictated memoirs were published posthumously in 1829.

9   In *The Rag Doll Plagues*, "LAMEX" Gregory recounts how "dozens of buses with fourth-life people toured through the Oakridge estates and headed down the mountain to attend the performance of *Ramona*, a play that depicts Indian, Mexican, and Spanish cultures two hundred years ago in the region" (133). The play, based on Helen Hunt Jackson's novel of the same name, has been performed continuously since 1923 at the Ramona Bowl in Hemet, CA.

10 See Bhabha's *The Location of Culture* and García Canclini's *Hybrid Cultures* for evidence of this distinction. Alberto Moreiras offers a pointed critique of the inapplicability of hybridity theory to a Latin American context. It is in danger of becoming, he writes in 1999, "a sort of ideological cover for capitalist reterritorialization—and even a key conceptual instrument for the very process of naturalization of subaltern exclusion" (377).

11 Caicedo's novel follows teenaged María del Carmen as she renounces her upper-middle-class comfort to explore the musical underground and party culture of Cali, Colombia. Caicedo, who committed suicide the day the novel was published, has taken on cult status as an author widely regarded as a transitional literary figure between the "Boom generation" and later twentieth-century Latin American aesthetics.

12 Bandeira (1886–1968) was one of Brazil's most significant twentieth-century poets. His experimental, quotidian symbolism marked the turn from *modernismo* to *vanguardismo* with unique stylistics. Mariátegui (1894–1930) was a Peruvian writer and influential Latin American socialist. His journalism and essays in political philosophy continue to influence social movements in Peru.

CODA

1   I discuss the racial politics of punk scholarship and give a more detailed history in my article "¿Soy Emo, y Qué?," where I argue for a transnational *latinidad* predicated on feeling.

2   In "The Mexican Lieutenant," I offer a thorough analysis of Sánchez's diary, which I read against Ralph Waldo Emerson's "Nature" to put forward a theory of hemispheric romanticism.

3   "Población es de cerca de doscientas personas, entre las cuales solo se cuentan diez mexicanos, pues los demás son Americanos del Norte, y uno u otro extranjero europeo" (46). The English quotes come from Carlos Castañeda's translation of José María Sánchez's "A Trip to Texas in 1828"; the original Spanish is from Jorge Flores's 1939 edition of the diary.

4   "Pues es gente en mi entender viciosa y holgazana" (46).

5 "Adormecidas a las autoridades ... de esta colonia ha de salir la chispa que forme el incendio que nos ha de dejar sin Tejas" (47).
6 "El alma de una dulce melancolía que sólo saben sentir y apreciar los corazones sensibles" (25). Castañeda translates *dulce*, which means "sweet," here as "strange," which highlights the dark, disorienting, and desolate setting.
7 "Inmensidad de zancudos ... por todas partes ... el horroroso estragón que estos malditos animales habían hecho en nosotros que estábamos llenos de hinchazones, principalmente el General que parecía lo habían sangrado de la cara, según los lastimado que estaba" (48).
8 Though the entry is labeled "Campo de Sánchez," the paragraph describing its naming is missing in Flores's Spanish edition.
9 "Don't mess with me, I'm a bad ass."
10 "And this song is dedicated to all the rest of you bad asses ... So what if I'm a wetback."
11 I use "thing" here in a Latourian fashion to indicate a gathering rather than an object, as I explain in my introduction.
12 I discuss the discovery of these bodies in chapter 4.

WORKS CITED

ARCHIVAL MATERIAL

Hoffman, Berenice. Letter to Cecile Pineda, 18 July 1983. Cecile Pineda Papers, M1176, Department of Special Collections, Stanford University Libraries.

Johnson, Carl. "Santa Anna's Lost Leg," n.d. Santa Anna Papers, Illinois State Military Museum, Springfield.

Maricón Collective. *Homeboy Beautiful*, issue 2, n.d. Maricón Collective Ephemera Collection, Chicano Studies Research Center, UCLA.

Pineda, Cecile. Composition Book, n.d. Cecile Pineda Papers, M1176, Department of Special Collections, Stanford University Libraries.

———. *Face*: Filmscript, draft 1, 1989. Cecile Pineda Papers, M1176, Department of Special Collections, Stanford University Libraries.

———. *Face*: Filmscript, draft 2, 1989. Cecile Pineda Papers, M1176, Department of Special Collections, Stanford University Libraries.

———. Letter to Yaffa Corteen, 29 July 1979. Cecile Pineda Papers, M1176, Department of Special Collections, Stanford University Libraries.

———. Letter to Andrzej Ekwinski, April 1983. Cecile Pineda Papers, M1176, Department of Special Collections, Stanford University Libraries.

———. Letter to Tzivia Stein, 14 Dec. 1978. Cecile Pineda Papers, M1176, Department of Special Collections, Stanford University Libraries.

Siegel, Rosalie. Letter to Cecile Pineda, 8 July 1983. Cecile Pineda Papers, M1176, Department of Special Collections, Stanford University Libraries.

Theatre of Man. Organizational History, circa 1975. Cecile Pineda Papers, M1176, Department of Special Collections, Stanford University Libraries.

Viking. Press release, 29 April 1985. Cecile Pineda Papers, M1176, Department of Special Collections, Stanford University Libraries.

PUBLISHED MATERIAL

Agamben, Giorgio. *Homo Sacer: Sovereign Power and Bare Life*. Palo Alto, CA: Stanford University Press, 1998.

Agee, James. *Let Us Now Praise Famous Men; A Death in the Family, and Shorter Fiction*. New York: Library of America, 2005.

Agence France-Presse. "A Man Reconstructs His Own Face." *San Francisco Chronicle*, 21 May 1977, 12.

Alaimo, Stacy. *Bodily Natures: Science, Environment, and the Material Self*. Bloomington: Indiana University Press, 2010.

———. *Exposed: Environmental Politics and Pleasures in Posthuman Times*. Minneapolis: University of Minnesota Press, 2016.

Alcoff, Linda Martín. *Visible Identities: Race, Gender, and the Self*. New York: Oxford University Press, 2006.

Alcoff, Linda, et al. *Identity Politics Reconsidered*. New York: Palgrave Macmillan, 2006.

Allatson, Paul. "'My Bones Shine in the Dark': AIDS and the De-Scription of Chicano Queer in the Work of Gil Cuadros." *Aztlán: A Journal of Chicano Studies* 32.1 (2007): 23–52.

Amin, Samir. *Delinking: Towards a Polycentric World*. London: Zed Books, 1990.

Anzaldúa, Gloria. "La Prieta." *The Gloria Anzaldúa Reader*. Ed. AnaLouise Keating. Durham: Duke University Press, 2009. 38–50.

———. "(Un)natural Bridges, (Un)safe Spaces." *The Gloria Anzaldúa Reader*. Ed. AnaLouise Keating. Durham: Duke University Press, 2009. 243–48.

Augustine. "The City of God." Trans. Marcus Dods. New Advent. www.newadvent.org.

Bag, Alice. "Incorporeal Life." *Alice Bag*. Don Giovanni Records, 2016.

Bainbridge, Simon. "People of the World." *British Journal of Photography* 154.7616 (2007): 19–25.

Bakhtin, M. M. *The Dialogic Imagination: Four Essays*. Trans. Michael Holquist. Austin: University of Texas Press, 1981.

Barad, Karen. "Posthuman Performativity." *Material Feminisms*. Ed. Stacy Alaimo and Susan Hekman. Bloomington: Indiana University Press, 2008. 120–54.

Barrios, José Luis. "Nothing Is More Optimistic Than Stjärnsund: The Paradoxes of Enthusiasm." *Rafael Lozano-Hemmer: pseudomatismos = pseudomatisms*. Mexico City: Museo Universitario Arte Contemporáneo, UNAM, 2015. 222–37.

Barthes, Roland. *Camera Lucida: Reflections on Photography*. Trans. Richard Howard. New York: Hill and Wang, 1981.

Baynton, Douglas. "Slaves, Immigrants, and Suffragists: The Uses of Disability in Citizenship Debates." *PMLA* 120.2 (2005): 562–67.

Beltrán, Cristina. *The Trouble with Unity: Latino Politics and the Creation of Identity*. Oxford: Oxford University Press, 2010.

Benjamin, Harry. *The Transsexual Phenomenon*. New York: Julian, 1966.

Benjamin, Walter. *Illuminations*. Ed. Hannah Arendt. Trans. Harry Zohn. New York: Schocken, 1969.

———. "The Work of Art in the Age of Mechanical Reproduction." *The Photography Reader*. Ed. Liz Wells. New York: Routledge, 2003.

Bennett, Jane. *Vibrant Matter: A Political Ecology of Things*. Durham: Duke University Press, 2010.

Bergson, Henri. *The Creative Mind: An Introduction to Metaphysics*. 1934. Mineola, NY: Dover, 2012.

———. *Matter and Memory: Essay on the Relation between the Body and the Mind*. 1896. Trans. N. M. Paul and W. S. Palmer. New York: Zone Books, 1990.

———. *Time and Free Will: An Essay on the Data of Immediate Consciousness*. 1889. Trans. F. L. Pogson. London: Dover, 2001.

Bhabha, Homi K. *The Location of Culture*. New York: Routledge, 1994.
Biggers, Jeff. "Pineda Unbound: An Interview with Cecile Pineda." *Bloomsbury Review* 24.4 (2004): 3, 24.
Braidotti, Rosi. *The Posthuman*. Cambridge: Polity, 2013.
Breckenridge, Carol A., and Candace Vogler. "The Critical Limits of Embodiment: Disability's Criticism." *Public Culture* 13.3 (2001): 349–57.
Brik, Ossip. "What the Eye Does Not See." *The Photography Reader*. Ed. Liz Wells. New York: Routledge, 2003.
Bruce-Novoa, Juan. "Deconstructing the Dominant Patriarchal Text: Cecile Pineda's Narratives." *Breaking Boundaries: Latina Writing and Critical Readings*. Ed. Asunción Horno-Delgado et al. Amherst: University of Massachusetts Press, 1989. 72–81.
Butler, Judith. *Bodies That Matter: On the Discursive Limits of "Sex."* New York: Routledge, 1993.
Caicedo Estela, Andrés. *Que viva la música!* Lima: Grupo Editorial Norma, 2001.
Candelaria, Cordelia. *Chicano Poetry: A Critical Introduction*. Westport, CT: Greenwood, 1986.
Cepeda, Esther J. "Why Latinos Are Cool on Cruz and Rubio." *Hispanic Trending*, 9 Feb. 2016. www.hispanictrending.net.
Chen, Mel Y. *Animacies: Biopolitics, Racial Mattering, and Queer Affect*. Raleigh: Duke University Press, 2012.
Chow, Rey. *The Protestant Ethnic and the Spirit of Capitalism*. New York: Columbia University Press, 2002.
Christie, John S. *Latino Fiction and the Modernist Imagination: Literature of the Borderlands*. New York: Routledge, 1998.
Colibrí Center for Human Rights. Fact Sheet, 2015. www.colibricenter.org.
Collette, Mark. "Mass Graves of Migrants Found in Falfurrias, TX." *Corpus Christi Caller Times*, 26 June 2014. www.caller.com.
Connolly, William. "Materialities of Experience." *New Materialisms: Ontology, Agency, and Politics*. Ed. Diana Coole and Samantha Frost. Durham: Duke University Press, 2010. 178–200.
Los Crudos. "That's Right We're That Spic Band." *Discographia*, La Vida Es Un Mus Discos, 2016.
Cuadros, Gil. *City of God*. San Francisco: City Lights, 1994.
Cutler, John Alba. "Towards a Reading of Nineteenth Century Latina/o Short Fiction." *The Latino Nineteenth Century*. Ed. Rodrigo Lazo and Jesse Alemán. New York: New York University Press, 2016. 124–45.
D'Ammassa, Don. *Encyclopedia of Science Fiction: The Essential Guide to the Lives and Works of Science Fiction Writers*. New York: Facts on File, 2005.
Davis, Lennard J. "Why Is Disability Missing from the Discourse on Diversity?" 25 Sept. 2011. NOND: National Organization of Nurses with Disabilities. www.nond.org.
Deleuze, Gilles. *Francis Bacon: The Logic of Sensation*. 1981. Trans. Benn Linfield. London: Continuum, 2005.

Deleuze, Gilles, and Félix Guattari. *Anti-Oedipus: Capitalism and Schizophrenia*. Minneapolis: University of Minnesota Press, 1983.

———. *Kafka: Toward a Theory of Minor Literature*. 1975. Trans. Dana Polan. Minneapolis: University of Minnesota Press, 1986.

———. *A Thousand Plateaus: Capitalism and Schizophrenia*. London: Athlone Press, 1988.

———. *What Is Philosophy?* 1991. Trans. Graham Burchell and Hugh Tomlinson. London: Verso, 1994.

Delgado, Richard, and Jean Stefancic, eds. *Critical Race Theory: An Introduction*. 2001. New York: New York University Press, 2017.

Diawara, Manthia. *In Search of Africa*. Cambridge: Harvard University Press, 1998.

Díaz, Junot. *The Brief Wondrous Life of Oscar Wao*. London: Faber, 2008.

———. "Junot Díaz—*The Brief Wondrous Life of Oscar Wao* (excerpt)." Genius, https://genius.com. Accessed 10 March 2017.

———. "Under President Trump, Radical Hope Is Our Best Weapon." *New Yorker*, Nov. 2016. www.newyorker.com.

Donahue, Peter. "Self-Reflexive Storytelling and Narrative Borders in Dagoberto Gilb's *The Last Known Residence of Mickey Acuña*." *Southwestern American Literature* 24.2 (1999): 33–39.

Duncombe, Stephen. *Notes from Underground: Zines and the Politics of Alternative Culture*. Bloomington, IN: Verso, 1997.

Durán, Diego. *The History of the Indies of New Spain*. 1581. Trans. and ed. Doris Heyden. Norman: University of Oklahoma Press, 1994.

Dyer, Jack. "The Final Shinsult." *King of The Hill*. Fox, 15 March 1998.

East, Ernest. "Santa Anna's Cork Leg." *Illinois Libraries* 36 (1954): 163–70.

———. "Santa Anna's Wooden Leg." *Chicago Westerners Brand Book* 11.7 (1954): 49–51.

Evans, Walker. *Many Are Called*. New Haven: Yale University Press, 2004.

"Experimental, Improvised Drivel." *San Francisco Bay Guardian*, 10 March 1977, n.p.

Fellner, Astrid M. "The Wounded Male Body: Cecile Pineda's *Face*." *SKASE Journal of Literary Studies* 1.1 (2009): 62–74.

García Canclini, Néstor. *Hybrid Cultures: Strategies for Entering and Leaving Modernity*. Minneapolis: University of Minnesota Press, 1995.

Garland-Thomson, Rosemarie. *Extraordinary Bodies: Figuring Physical Disability in American Culture and Literature*. New York: Columbia University Press, 1997.

Geerdes, Gary. "After Eurydice." *Los Angeles Free Press*, 19 Jan. 1973, n.p.

Gilb, Dagoberto. "The Death Mask of Pancho Villa." *The Magic of Blood*. New York: Grove, 1993. 17–26.

———. *The Last Known Residence of Mickey Acuña*. New York: Grove, 1994.

———. "please, thank you." *Before the End, after the Beginning*. New York: Grove, 2011. 3–24.

Gonzales-Day, Ken. *Lynching in the West, 1850–1935*. Durham: Duke University Press, 2006.

González, Marcial. *Chicano Novels and the Politics of Form: Race, Class, and Reification*. Ann Arbor: University of Michigan Press, 2009.

Guerlac, Suzanne. *Thinking in Time: An Introduction to Henri Bergson*. Ithaca: Cornell University Press, 2006.

Guskin, Emily, and Amy Mitchell. "Hispanic Media: Faring Better Than the Mainstream Media." *The State of the News Media: An Annual Report on American Journalism*. www.stateofthemedia.org. Accessed 7 April 2015.

Guzmán, Joshua Javier, and Christina A. León. "Cuts and Impressions: The Aesthetic Work of Lingering in Latinidad." *Women and Performance: A Journal of Feminist Theory* 25.3 (2015): 261–76.

Habell-Pallán, Michelle. *Loca Motion: The Travels of Chicana and Latina Popular Culture*. New York: New York University Press, 2005.

Hall, Stuart. "Cultural Studies and Its Theoretical Legacies." *Cultural Studies*. Ed. Lawrence Grossberg et al. New York: Routledge, 1992. 277–94.

Hames-García, Michael. "How Real Is Race?" *Material Feminisms*. Ed. Stacy Alaimo and Susan Hekman. Bloomington: Indiana University Press, 2008. 308–39.

Harford Vargas, Jennifer. *Forms of Dictatorship: Power, Narrative, and Authoritarianism in the Latina/o Novel*. New York: Oxford University Press, 2018.

Harman, Graham. *Immaterialism: Objects and Social Theory*. Cambridge, UK: Polity, 2016.

———. *The Quadruple Object*. Alresford: Zero Books, 2011.

———. "The Well-Wrought Broken Hammer: Object-Oriented Literary Criticism." *New Literary History* 43.2 (2012): 183–203.

Harris, Neil. *Humbug: The Art of P. T. Barnum*. Boston: Little, Brown, 1973.

Hassig, Ross. *Time, History, and Belief in Aztec and Colonial Mexico*. Austin: University of Texas Press, 2001.

Hayles, N. Katherine. *How We Became Posthuman: Virtual Bodies in Cybernetics, Literature, and Informatics*. Chicago: University of Chicago Press, 1999.

Hogan, Ernest. "Chicanonautica Manifesto." *Aztlán: A Journal of Chicano Studies* 40.2 (2015): 131–34.

———. *Cortez on Jupiter*. New York: T. Doherty Associates, 1990.

———. *High Aztech*. New York: Tor, 1992.

Honma, Todd. "From Archives to Action: Zines, Participatory Culture, and Community Engagement in Asian America." *Radical Teacher* 105 (2016): 33–43.

Huehls, Mitchum. *After Critique: Twenty-First-Century Fiction in a Neoliberal Age*. Oxford: Oxford University Press, 2016.

———. *Qualified Hope: A Postmodern Politics of Time*. Columbus: Ohio State University Press, 2009.

Human Rights Watch. *Torn Apart, Robin Reineke, Colibrí Center for Human Rights*. 2015. https://youtu.be/yR9tARIVxvw.

Ibarra, Ana. "Stefan Ruiz: Beyond the Comfort Zone." *Elephant* 10 (2012): 56–61.

Irizarry, Ylce. *Chicana/o and Latina/o Fiction: The New Memory of Latinidad*. Champaign-Urbana: University of Illinois Press, 2016.

James, Jennifer, and Cynthia Wu. "Editors' Introduction: Race, Ethnicity, Disability, and Literature: Intersections and Interventions." *MELUS* 31.3 (2006): 3–11.

Jameson, Fredric. *Postmodernism, or, The Cultural Logic of Late Capitalism*. Durham: Duke University Press, 1991.
Johnson, David E. "Face Value (An Essay on Cecile Pineda's *Face*)." *Americas Review* 19.2 (1991): 73–93.
Jordan, Terry. "Germans." Texas State Historical Association, 15 June 2010. https://tshaonline.org.
Kevane, Bridget. "From Here to Oaxaca." *New York Times*, 20 Nov. 2011, BR23.
Latour, Bruno. *We Have Never Been Modern*. Cambridge: Harvard University Press, 1993.
———. "Why Has Critique Run out of Steam? From Matters of Fact to Matters of Concern." *Critical Inquiry* 30 (Winter 2004): 225–48.
Laveaga, Gabriela Soto. *Jungle Laboratories: Mexican Peasants, National Projects, and the Making of the Pill*. Durham: Duke University Press, 2009.
Levinas, Emmanuel. *Totality and Infinity: An Essay on Exteriority*. 1961. Trans. Alphonso Lingis. Norwell, MA: Kluwer Academic Publishers, 1991.
Leys, Ruth. "The Turn to Affect: A Critique." *Critical Inquiry* 37.3 (2011): 434–72.
Lippard, Lucy. "Concrete Sorrows, Transparent Joys." *Kathy Vargas: Photographs, 1971–2000*. Ed. Lucy Lippard and Ma-Lin Wilson Powell. Austin: Marion Koogler McNay Art Museum, distributed by University of Texas Press, 2000.
Lipsitz, George. "Learning from Los Angeles: Another One Rides the Bus." *American Quarterly* 56.3 (2004): 511–29.
Lomas, Laura. *Translating Empire: José Martí, Migrant Latino Subjects, and American Modernities*. Durham: Duke University Press, 2008.
López, Marissa. "Feeling Mexican: Ruiz de Burton's Sentimental Railroad Fiction." *The Latino Nineteenth Century*. Ed. Rodrigo Lazo and Jesse Alemán. New York: New York University Press, 2016. 168–90.
———. "The Mexican Lieutenant: Emerson, Texas, and the Sentimental Politics of Language." *Western American Literature* 45.4 (2011): 385–409.
———. "¿Soy Emo, y Qué? Sad Kids, Punkera Dykes and the Latin@ Public Sphere." *Journal of American Studies* 46.4 (2012): 895–918.
Lozano-Hemmer, Rafael. "Digital Art and the Platforms for Participation." *Aesthetica* no. 36 (Sept. 2010): 30–33.
———. "Glow, Santa Monica Beach, Santa Monica, United States, 2010." 2010. www.lozano-hemmer.com.
Mao, Douglas, and Rebecca L. Walkowitz, eds. *Bad Modernisms*. Durham: Duke University Press, 2006.
———. "The New Modernist Studies." *PMLA* 123.3 (May 2008): 737–48.
Martínez, Ibsen. "Romancing the Globe." *Telenovelas*. Westport: Greenwood, 2010. 61–67.
Massumi, Brian. *Parables for the Virtual: Movement, Affect, Sensation*. Durham: Duke University Press, 2002.
Mbembe, Achille. "Necropolitics." *Biopolitics: A Reader*. Ed. Timothy Campbell and Adam Sitze. Durham: Duke University Press, 2013. 161–92.

McRuer, Robert, and Abby L. Wilkerson. "Introduction." *GLQ: A Journal of Lesbian and Gay Studies* 9.1–2 (2003): 1–23.

Meillassoux, Quentin. *After Finitude: An Essay on the Necessity of Contingency*. London: Continuum, 2008.

Melamed, Jodi. *Represent and Destroy: Rationalizing Violence in the New Racial Capitalism*. Minneapolis: University of Minnesota Press, 2011.

Mendiola, Jim. "Vato Perron." 2014. www.pinataprotestband.com.

Merla-Watson, Cathryn, and B. V. Olguín. "Introduction: ¡Latin@futurism Ahora! Recovering, Remapping, and Recentering the Chican@ and Latin@ Speculative Arts." *Aztlán: A Journal of Chicano Studies* 40.2 (Fall 2015): 135–46.

Merleau-Ponty, Maurice. *Phenomenology of Perception*. 1945. New York: Routledge, 1978.

———. *The Visible and the Invisible: Followed by Working Notes*. 1964. Evanston, IL: Northwestern University Press, 1968.

Meyerowitz, Joanne J. *How Sex Changed: A History of Transsexuality in the United States*. Cambridge: Harvard University Press, 2002.

Michaels, Walter Benn. *The Beauty of a Social Problem: Photography, Autonomy, Economy*. Chicago: University of Chicago Press, 2015.

Minich, Julie Avril. *Accessible Citizenships: Disability, Nation, and the Cultural Politics of Greater Mexico*. Philadelphia: Temple University Press, 2014.

———. "Aztlán Unprotected: Reading Gil Cuadros in the Aftermath of HIV/AIDS." *GLQ: A Journal of Lesbian and Gay Studies* 23.2 (March 2017): 167–93.

Miranda, Carolina. "The Bold and the Beautiful." *ARTNews* 111.8 (Sept. 2012): 31.

Mohanty, Satya P. *Literary Theory and the Claims of History: Postmodernism, Objectivity, Multicultural Politics*. Ithaca: Cornell University Press, 1997.

Morales, Alejandro. *The Rag Doll Plagues*. Houston: Arte Público, 1992.

Moreiras, Alberto. "Hybridity and Double Consciousness." *Cultural Studies* 13.3 (1999): 373–407.

Moser, Margaret. "El Valiente: The South Texas Authenticity of S.A. Accordion Punks Piñata Protest." *Austin Chronicle*, 16 May 2013. www.austinchronicle.com.

Moya, Paula M. L. *Learning from Experience: Minority Identities, Multicultural Struggles*. Berkeley: University of California Press, 2002.

———. *The Social Imperative: Race, Close Reading, and Contemporary Literary Criticism*. Palo Alto, CA: Stanford University Press, 2016.

Moya, Paula M. L., and Michael Roy Hames-García. *Reclaiming Identity: Realist Theory and the Predicament of Postmodernism*. Berkeley: University of California Press, 2000.

Muñoz, José Esteban. *Cruising Utopia: The Then and There of Queer Futurity*. New York: New York University Press, 2009.

———. *Disidentifications: Queers of Color and the Performance of Politics*. Minneapolis: University of Minnesota Press, 1999.

National Public Radio. "Guest DJ Junot Diaz: 'It Takes Guts to Be Alive.'" *Alt.Latino*, 12 May 2016. www.npr.org.

"The 90th Oscars." Hosted by Jimmy Kimmel. Produced by Michael De Luca and Jennifer Todd. ABC, 4 March 2018.

Omi, Michael, and Howard Winant. *Racial Formation in the United States: From the 1960s to the 1990s*. 1986. New York: Routledge, 2015.

Ortiz Taylor, Sheila. *Coachella*. Albuquerque: University of New Mexico Press, 1998.

Papoulias, Constantina, and Felicity Callard. "Biology's Gift: Interrogating the Turn to Affect." *Body and Society* 16.1 (2010): 29–56.

Paredes, Raymund A. "The Evolution of Chicano Literature." *MELUS* 5.2 (1978): 71–110.

Pérez-Torres, Rafael. *Mestizaje: Critical Uses of Race in Chicano Culture*. Minneapolis: University of Minnesota Press, 2006.

Phelan, Peggy. *Unmarked: The Politics of Performance*. London: Routledge, 1993.

Pina, Michael. "The Archaic, Historical, and Mythicized Dimensions of Aztlán." *Aztlán: Essays on the Chicano Homeland*. Rev. ed. Ed. Rudolfo Anaya et al. Albuquerque: University of New Mexico Press, 2017. 43–76.

Piñata Protest. "Life on the Border." *El Valiente*. Saustex Media, 2013.

———. "Vato Perron." *El Valiente*. Saustex Media, 2013.

Pineda, Cecile. *Face*. 1985. San Antonio, TX: Wings Press, 2003.

Plato. *Timaeus*. Perseus Digital Library. www.perseus.tufts.edu. Accessed 13 March 2017.

Ponjuan, Luis, et al. "Latino Male Ethnic Subgroups: Patterns in College Enrollment and Degree Completion." *New Directions for Higher Education* 2015.172 (Dec. 2015): 59–69.

Ramírez, Catherine. "Afrofuturism/Chicanafuturism: Fictive Kin." *Aztlán: A Journal of Chicano Studies* 33.1 (Spring 2008): 185–94.

Rankine, Claudia. *Citizen: An American Lyric*. Minneapolis: Graywolf, 2014.

Reilly, Katie. "Here Are All the Times Donald Trump Insulted Mexico." *Time*, 31 Aug. 2016. http://time.com.

Ricoeur, Paul. *Time and Narrative*. Chicago: University of Chicago Press, 1984.

Riis, Jacob A. *How the Other Half Lives: Studies among the Tenements of New York*. Mineola, NY: Dover, 1971.

Rivera, Lysa. "Future Histories and Cyborg Labor: Reading Borderlands Science Fiction after NAFTA." *Science Fiction Studies* 39.3 (Nov. 2012): 415–36.

Roberts, John. "Shelby County v. Holder 570 U.S. (2013)." *Justia Law*. https://supreme.justia.com/. Accessed 10 March 2017.

Rodríguez, Juana María. *Sexual Futures, Queer Gestures, and Other Latina Longings*. New York: New York University Press, 2014.

Rodríguez, Richard T. "Being and Belonging: Joey Terrill's Performance of Politics." *Biography* 34.3 (2011): 467–91.

Rogers, Everett M., and Livia Antola. "Telenovelas: A Latin American Success Story." *Journal of Communication* 35.4 (Dec. 1985): 24–35.

Román, Elda María. *Race and Upward Mobility: Seeking, Gatekeeping, and Other Class Strategies in Postwar America*. Palo Alto, CA: Stanford University Press, 2018.

Rosaldo, Renato. "Politics, Patriarchs, and Laughter." *Cultural Critique* 6.2 (1987): 65–86.
Rosler, Martha. "Image Simulations, Computer Manipulations: Some Considerations." *Ten-8* 2.2 (1991).
Rowe, Ken, "Non-Play *Threesomes* Leave One Properly Dumbfounded." *Redwood City Tribune*, 21 Feb. 1977, 9.
Ruiz, Sandra. "Waiting in the Seat of Sensation: The Brown Existentialism of Ryan Rivera." *Women and Performance: A Journal of Feminist Theory* 25.3 (2015): 336–52.
Ruiz, Stefan, and Pablo Helguera. *The Factory of Dreams: Inside Televisa Studios*. Reading, PA: Aperture, 2012.
Saldívar, José David. *Border Matters: Remapping American Cultural Studies*. Berkeley: University of California Press, 1997.
Saldívar, Ramón. *The Borderlands of Culture: Américo Paredes and the Transnational Imaginary*. Durham: Duke University Press, 2006.
———. *Chicano Narrative: The Dialectics of Difference*. Madison: University of Wisconsin Press, 1990.
Samuels, Ellen. *Fantasies of Identification: Disability, Gender, Race*. New York: New York University Press, 2014.
Sánchez, Alberto Sandoval. "Breaking the Silence, Dismantling Taboos: Latino Novels on AIDS." *Journal of Homosexuality* 34.3–4 (1998): 155–75.
Sánchez, Rosaura, and Beatrice Pita. *Lunar Braceros: 2125–2148*. National City, CA: Calaca Press, 2009.
Sánchez y Tapia, José María. "A Trip to Texas in 1828." Trans. Carlos Castañeda. *Southwestern Historical Quarterly* 29.4 (1928): 249–88.
———. *Viaje a Texas en 1828–1829: Diario del Teniente*. Ed. Jorge Flores. Papeles Históricos Mexicanos. Mexico, DF: Porrua, 1939.
Sax, Margaret, et al. "The Origins of Two Purportedly Pre-Columbian Mexican Crystal Skulls." *Journal of Archaeological Science* 35.10 (2008): 2751–60.
Schell, Jonathan. *The Fate of the Earth*. New York: Knopf, 1982.
Seigworth, Gregory J., and Melissa Gregg. "An Inventory of Shimmers." *The Affect Theory Reader*. Ed. Gregory J. Seigworth and Melissa Gregg. Durham: Duke University Press, 2010. 1–29.
Sheldon, Rebekah. "Form/Matter/Chora: Object-Oriented Ontology and Feminist New Materialism." *The Nonhuman Turn*. Ed. Richard Grusin. Minneapolis: University of Minnesota Press, 2015. 193–222.
Shilts, Randy. *And the Band Played On: Politics, People, and the AIDS Epidemic*. New York: St. Martin's, 2007.
Siebers, Tobin. *Disability Theory*. Ann Arbor: University of Michigan Press, 2008.
Skidmore, Thomas E. *Brazil: Five Centuries of Change*. New York: Oxford University Press, 2010.
The Smiths. "Bigmouth Strikes Again." *The Queen Is Dead*. Rough Trade, 1986.
Snyder, Sharon L., and David T. Mitchell. *Cultural Locations of Disability*. Chicago: University of Chicago Press, 2006.

Stepler, Renee, and Anna Brown. "Statistical Portrait of Hispanics in the United States." Pew Research Center's Hispanic Trends Project, 19 Apr. 2016. www.pewhispanic.org.

Stern, Daniel. *The Interpersonal World of the Infant: A View from Psychoanalysis and Developmental Psychology*. New York: Basic Books, 1985.

Treichler, Paula A. *How to Have Theory in an Epidemic: Cultural Chronicles of AIDS*. Durham: Duke University Press, 1999.

US Census Bureau. FFF: Hispanic Heritage Month, 2016. www.census.gov. Accessed 10 March 2017.

Viego, Antonio. *Dead Subjects: Toward a Politics of Loss in Latino Studies*. Durham: Duke University Press, 2007.

Vigil, Ricky. "Mojado Punk's Not Dead: An Interview with Piñata Protest." *SLUG Magazine*, 4 Sept. 2013. www.slugmag.com.

Villa, Raúl. *Barrio-Logos: Space and Place in Urban Chicano Literature and Culture*. Austin: University of Texas Press, 2000.

Villela, Khristaan D., Mary Ellen Miller, and Matthew H. Robb. Introduction to *The Aztec Calendar Stone*. Ed. Khristaan D. Villela and Mary Ellen Miller. Los Angeles: Getty Research Institute, 2010. 1–41.

Walsh, Jane M. "Legend of the Crystal Skulls." *Archaeology Magazine* 61.3 (May–June 2008). http://archive.archaeology.org.

Washington, Harriet A. *Medical Apartheid: The Dark History of Medical Experimentation on Black Americans from Colonial Times to the Present*. New York: Doubleday, 2006.

Wells, Liz. "Thinking about Photography." *Photography: A Critical Introduction*. New York: Routledge, 2000. 9–74.

Wollaeger, Mark A., and Matt Eatough, eds. *The Oxford Handbook of Global Modernisms*. New York: Oxford University Press, 2012.

Yudell, Michael, et al. "Taking Race out of Human Genetics." *Science* 351.6273 (Feb. 2016): 564–65. science.sciencemag.org, doi:10.1126/science.aac4951.

INDEX

abjection, 154
accordion, 156–157. *See also* Del Norte, Álvaro; Piñata Protest
aesthetics: "aesthetic activation," 129–130; Chicanx science fiction and, 128; Latinx dismodern and, 88; neoliberal, 4, 17, 128; punk, 152, 155
affect, 30–31, 34; Chicanx punk and, 152; cognition and, 51–53, 163–164n3; humanities-based thought on, 30, 52; interdisciplinary study of, 52–53; politics and, 17; scientific thought on, 31, 52. *See also* race
Affect Theory Reader, The (Seigworth and Gregg), 34
Afrofuturism, 127–128
Agamben, Giorgio, 126
AIDS, 91–93, 96, 99, 117. *See also* Cuadros, Gil; Morales, Alejandro; Ortiz Taylor, Sheila
Alaimo, Stacy, 20, 92, 95–96, 112, 117–118
Alcoff, Linda, 51–52
Allatson, Paul, 98–99
Anzaldúa, Gloria, 19, 128, 131, 157
assemblage, 18–19, 99, 138
Augustine: "The City of God," 99
authenticity, 92, 96, 112–115, 117
Aztec calendars, 27–29. *See also* Piedra del Sol

Bad Modernisms (Mao and Walkowitz), 86
Barad, Karen, 16
barbasco, 21, 93–97, 117
Barrios, José Luis, 129

Barthes, Roland, 64–65, 68
Beltrán, Cristina, 7, 11, 18, 152
Benjamin, Harry, 95
Benjamin, Walter, 77, 140–143
Bergson, Henri, 32, 35–36, 42, 54–55, 76
Bhabha, Homi, 142
biopolitics, 117, 132, 136–137
blood, 96, 104, 109, 112–113, 115, 132–136, 145, 147, 149, 169n15
body, 18–20, 24, 136; "aesthetic activation" and, 129–130; affect and, 30–31, 34, 51–53; AIDS and, 99, 118; alienated, 131; ancestry and, 148; belief and, 41–42; body politic and, 88; brown, 66–67, 90, 125, 130, 132–133; *chicanidad* and, 96; Chicanx cultural production and, 7; community and, 58, 67; corporatization of, 132–133; disability (*see* disability); duration (*see* duration); "flesh," 87, 165n15; gesture and, 4–5, 11; historical narrative and, 29, 148; humanity and, 74, 88; image and, 60; intent of, 43–44; Latinx dismodern and, 87; mediation and, 21; necropolitics and, 119; as object, 9, 21, 43–44, 74, 84, 98, 131, 135; personhood and, 44; political agency and, 149; pollution and, 136; present absence of, 66–67; race and, 5–6, 21, 32–34, 50–51, 57, 97, 131, 148, 164n10; representation and, 33, 90; *sacer* and, 126, 149; self and, 44, 54, 58, 150; signification and, 20–21, 44; sound and, 74–75; technology and, 21, 127, 129–130, 136–137, 145, 148; transformation and, 104; unruly, 19.

body (*cont.*)
See also Gilb, Dagoberto; knowledge; language; materiality; Pineda, Cecile; sensory experience; space; subjectivity; temporality; text; transcorporeality
Braidotti, Rosi, 120, 126, 137–138, 147, 148–150
Brik, Ossip, 65
Bruce-Novoa, Juan, 72, 85

Callard, Felicity, 52
Candelaria, Cordelia, 161n4
Chen, Mel, 4, 29–31, 34, 47
chicanidad, 10, 13–15, 18, 41, 98, 158
chicanismo, 13, 41
Chicanx: affect and, 24; AIDS and, 91, 118; Chicanafuturism, 127–128; Chicanx studies, 3–4, 53–54, 161–162n4; cultural production, 6–7, 11; experience, 54; "expressway generation" of artists, 98; identity, 41; Latinx trends and, 3; literature, 2, 15–19, 30, 55; punk, 152, 155–157; queerness and, 12–13, 98; science fiction, 119, 127–128; signification and, 7; text, 15–16. See also Cuadros, Gil; *Homeboy Beautiful*; Lunar Braceros; Morales, Alejandro; Ortiz Taylor, Sheila; science fiction
chora, 17, 20, 49, 62, 65, 74, 77, 90, 92, 96–97, 101, 106, 109, 115, 131, 163. See also reading: choratic
Chow, Rey, 162n8
Christie, John, 85
cognition, 30–31, 34–35, 37, 39, 42–43, 47, 52–54, 74, 138, 162n10, 164n3
Colibrí Center for Human Rights, 123–125
Connolly, William, 10–11, 162n10, 163n11
Crudos, Los, 154–155
Cuadros, Gil: *City of God* (1994), 91–92, 96–108, 116–118
"Cuts and Impressions" (Guzmán and León), 11

D'Ammassa, Don, 127
Darío, Rubén, 86
Del Norte, Álvaro, 155–158
Deleuze, Gilles, 53–54
Diawara, Manthia, 32, 164n5
Díaz, Junot, 1–2, 151; *The Brief Wondrous Life of Oscar Wao* (2007), 6–7
disability: body and, 33, 43, 164–165nn7–10, 166n1; identity and, 166n1; race and, 33
discourse: AIDS, 91–93, 116; biomedical, 117; diversity, 91; racial, 32
disidentification, 32, 53–54
Duncombe, Stephen, 15
duration: body and, 27, 32–33, 43–44, 49, 63; narrative and, 36; presence and, 35–36; scientific time and, 45–46, 76; time and, 36–37, 42. See also Bergson, Henri

Ekman, Paul, 52
ethnicity, 3, 5, 34, 41, 50, 85, 91, 96, 114, 161n4, 162n8. See also authenticity

Fellner, Astrid, 85
form, 6–7; body and, 20; content and, 37, 45, 76, 85, 129; "large format" photography, 68; *latinidad* as, 6; repetition and, 73; temporality as, 45, 109–110; text and, 54, 102. See also duration; reading: choratic
free will, 39–40

Galarza, Ernesto, 54
García Canclini, Néstor, 142
gender: dysphoria, 95; femininity, 42; heteronormativity and, 134–135; race and, 42–43, 157; trans, 94–95
gesture, 4–5, 11, 158
Gilb, Dagoberto, 27, 30–33, 51–55, 166n19: "The Death Mask of Pancho Villa" (1993), 29, 33–36, 44; *The Last Known Residence of Mickey Acuña* (1994),

36–44; "please, thank you" (2011), 44–50, 57
González, Marcial, 85–86, 89
Gonzales-Day, Ken, 65–67, 78, 81–84, 86, 90
Guattari, Félix, 53–54
Guerlac, Suzanne, 36

Habell-Pallán, Michelle, 152
Hall, Stuart, 92–93
Hames-García, Michael, 5, 9
Harman, Graham, 16, 51, 164n6, 166n18
Hassig, Ross, 26–29, 163n1
Hayles, N. Katherine, 137
heteronormativity, 19, 95–96, 134–135, 147
Hirschfeld, Magnus, 95
history: of accordion, 156–157; body and, 34, 52–53, 104, 148, 165n11; Chicanx, 103–104; of Chicanx punk, 152; commodification of, 141; of cybernetics, 137; as existential mode, 41–42; future, 127, 129, 132; identity and, 41, 44, 85, 117, 165n11; of photography, 64–65, 77; as present absence, 41; repetition of, 141–142; as temporal hybridity, 142; time and, 36. *See also* Benjamin, Walter; *Lunar Braceros*; lynching; modernism; Morales, Alejandro
Hogan, Ernest, 128–129
Homeboy Beautiful (Terrill/Maricón Collective), 12–15, 17–18, 158
Honma, Todd, 15
Huehls, Mitchum, 41, 130–131, 149
hybridity, 142, 171n10

identity, 89, 164–165n10, 166n19; "affirmative ethics" and, 137; body and, 87; class, 46; Chicanx, 41; ethnicity and, 30, 42, 45, 48, 50, 55; history and, 41; *latinidad* and, 6; Latinx, 1–2; literary studies and, 3; *mexicanidad* and, 155; politics, 88, 165n11; post-, 165n11; queer, 98; race and, 41, 45, 51, 84–85, 165n12; reified, 89; representation and, 33; science fiction and, 127–128. *See also* disability
"illegals," 125–126
indigeneity, 21, 27, 106, 109, 112–113, 115, 117, 133–134, 147. *See also* barbasco

Jameson, Fredric, 65
Johnson, David, 85

Kant, Immanuel, 50–51
King of the Hill (1997–2009), 21–23
knowledge: "AIDS-graphesis," 98; antiracist, 4; belief and, 39–40; body and, 29–30, 32–34, 36, 39, 44, 74; embodied presence and, 16; heteronormativity and, 95–96; history and, 41, 141; *latinidad* and 11; production, 3; race and, 5, 9, 15–16, 32, 130; scientific, 138–139; social experience and, 162n10; technology and, 137; text and, 54–55. *See also* sensory experience

Lacan, Jacques, 11
language: as agential intra-action, 16; authenticity and, 114–115; body and, 30–31, 54, 91; as chora, 97, 115; embodied, 29, 32; feeling and, 30, 53–54; knowledge and, 30, 51; materiality of, 4, 47, 53, 66; *mexicanidad* and, 155; "minor literature" and, 53–54; music and, 1; new materialism and, 16; object-oriented ontology (OOO) and, 15–16; otherness and, 54; as present absence, 114, 116; race and, 4, 9, 15, 30, 32; the real and, 91, 115; representation and, 4, 114; as self, 54; shared, 48–50; sovereignty and, 153–154; temporality and, 47, 165n13; wholeness and, 106; "withdrawal" (Harman) and, 16. *See also* Chen, Mel; Gilb, Dagoberto; racial immanence; reading: choratic; sensory experience; transcorporeality; writing

"Latin@futurism" (Merla-Watson and Olguín), 128
latinidad, 3, 6, 11–12, 151–152
Latinx: AIDS and, 98; "Decade of the Hispanic," 19; identity, 1–2; Latinx dismodern, 88; Latinx studies, 3–4, 10–11, 161–162n3–4; lynching and, 81–83; modernism and, 86–88, 169n16; politics, 7, 18; population, 2–3, 169n12; punk, 152, 154; queer, 12; science fiction, 128; signification and, 7. See also *latinidad*
Latour, Bruno, 17–18, 130–131
Laveaga, Gabriela Soto, 93–94
Levinas, Emmanuel, 168n9
Leys, Ruth, 31, 52, 163–164n3
Libet, Benjamin, 40, 165n14
Limon, José, 85
lingering, 5, 12, 15, 17, 19–20, 27, 29, 55, 157
Lipsitz, George, 99
literary studies: close reading and, 3–4; crisis in, 3; Latinx, 3–4, 161–162n4; multiculturalism and, 4; race and, 3–4. See also modernism; science fiction
Lomas, Laura, 87
Lozano-Hemmer, Rafael, 21, 119–122, 125, 129, 150
Lunar Braceros (Sánchez and Pita), 127, 129–144, 146–149
lynching, 81–83, 170–171n8. See also Gonzales-Day, Ken

Maricón Collective, 12–15
Marker, Russell, 93
Martí, José, 87
mass migrant graves, 125–126
Massumi, Brian, 30–31, 52
materiality: abstraction and, 117, 126; of body, 31, 91–92, 117–118, 125, 145, 149–150; *chicanidad* and, 158; duration and, 47; ethics and, 112, 117; of flesh, 145; of language, 4, 47, 53, 66; metaphor and, 109; physical distinction as, 43; of personhood, 44; of poverty, 37, 51; of race, 5, 9, 15–16, 32, 130; temporality and, 20, 143; writing and, 53, 143, 146. See also new materialism; object; object-oriented ontology
matter, 5, 11, 16–17, 35, 144, 147, 149
Mbembe, Achille, 119
Melamed, Jodi, 4, 130
Meillassoux, Quentin, 32, 164n6
Merleau-Ponty, Maurice, 32, 35, 40, 47, 51–52, 63–64, 165n15, 167–168n6
mestizaje, 19, 104, 134, 157
mexicanidad, 155, 157
Meyerowitz, Joanne, 94–95
Michaels, Walter Benn, 4
Minich, Julie, 92–93, 98, 103
modernism, 83–87: imperial modernity, 87; Latinx dismodern, 88
modernismo, 86–87, 171n12
Morales, Alejandro: *The Rag Doll Plagues* (1992), 127, 129–149
Moya, Paula, 3–4
Muñoz, José, 32

necropolitics, 119, 126, 130
new materialism, 15–16, 47
North American Free Trade Agreement (NAFTA), 22–23, 163n15

object: affect and, 52; body as, 9, 21, 43–44, 74, 84, 98, 131, 135; correlationism, 164n6; cognition and, 35, 42; definition of, 166n18; entanglement of, 117; gendered, 42–43; history as, 141; indigeneity and, 134; philosophy and, 50–51; photography and, 64, 68; racialized, 19, 42–43, 129, 134; subject and, 18, 35–36, 74, 102, 107–108, 112, 130–131, 135; temporality and, 29; thing and, 17–18; text as, 49, 75, 77; transversality, 170n4. See also object-oriented ontology
object-oriented ontology (OOO), 2, 15–16, 51, 166n18

Ortiz Taylor, Sheila: *Coachella* (1998), 21, 91–92, 96–97, 108–118

Papoulias, Constantina, 52
Paredes, Américo, 54, 87
Paredes, Raymund, 161n4
Pérez-Torres, Rafael, 98–99, 103
photography, 64–68, 77–78. *See also* Gonzales-Day, Ken; Ruiz, Stefan
Piedra del Sol (Aztec Sun Stone), 20, 25–29
Piñata Protest, 155, 157. *See also* Del Norte, Álvaro
Pineda, Cecile, 55, 78; *Face* (1985), 20, 57–64, 66–67, 70, 72–81, 84–90, 168n9
Pita, Beatrice. *See* Lunar Braceros
place: body and, 75, 103, 127; chora and, 17; communal sense of, 57, 84, 92; *latinidad* and, 11; temporality and, 139–140, 147–148; things as, 18. *See also* Cuadros, Gil; Ortiz Taylor, Sheila
population: Latinx, 2
posthuman, 2, 126, 137, 148–149
presence, 16, 35–36, 67, 71–72, 81, 144. *See also* Gilb, Dagoberto; Ruiz, Stefan
present absence, 38, 60, 62, 113; body as, 45–46, 66; history as, 41; language as, 114, 116; photography and, 64–66, 81. *See also* Gonzales-Day, Ken; Ruiz, Stefan
punk, 152, 154–155

queer: AIDS discourse and, 93, 98; attachment, 118; *chicanidad*, 12–15, 18, 98; ecology, 95–96, 104, 118; gesture, 11; Latinx and, 12; *mestizaje*, 19; science fiction and, 127; visibility and, 164n8. See also *Homeboy Beautiful*; Maricón Collective

race: affect and, 30–32, 34, 51–52; authenticity and, 114; biology and, 5, 163n13; body and, 5–6, 21, 32–34, 50–51, 57, 97, 131, 148, 164n10; in Brazil, 84; as chora, 20; disease and, 91–92, 98, 109 diversity and, 91, 130; ethnicity and, 34, 50; form and, 6, 9, 84; gender and, 42–43, 157; ideology of, 30, 34, 134; Latinx and, 11; as mode, 50; modernity and, 5, 84; posthumanism and, 2; punk and, 152; reality of, 5–6, 16, 51; representation and, 3–4; science fiction and, 127–128; subjection, 9, 50; as trace, 114; visibility and, 5, 83–85, 114. *See also* disability; AIDS; Cuadros, Gil; knowledge; language; materiality; Ortiz Taylor, Sheila); racial immanence; sensory experience; space; temporality
Racial Formation in the United States (Omi and Winant), 5–6
racial immanence, 17, 21, 32, 34, 37, 41, 55, 152–153, 155, 158
Ramírez, Catherine, 127–128
reading: the body, 21, 51, 58, 131, 144; choratic, 15–18, 32, 45, 53, 66, 106, 130, 152; close, 3–4; "emergent causality" and, 10; as performance of politics, 152; as process of connection, 12; representational, 4, 9, 15, 17, 24, 161–162n4; temporality of, 148; world-building and, 145–146; zines and, 15. *See also* Gilb, Dagoberto; Lunar Braceros; racial immanence; science fiction
repetition, 65–67, 73–74, 80, 92, 96, 102–103, 114–115, 141–143
Ricoeur, Paul, 36, 165n13
Rivera, Lysa, 127
Rodríguez, Juana María, 4, 11
Rodríguez, Richard T., 12
Rosaldo, Renato, 53–54
Rosler, Martha, 65, 77–78
Ruiz, Sandra, 5
Ruiz, Stefan, 65–66, 68, 84; *Factory of Dreams*, 66–72, 78–79, 81

Saldívar, Ramón, 87
Sánchez, Alberto Sandoval, 98

Sánchez, José María, 153–155
Sánchez, Rosaura. *See* Lunar Braceros
Santa Anna, Antonio López de, 8–9, 21–23
science fiction, 127–128. *See also* Lunar Braceros; Morales, Alejandro
self, 117–118: belief and, 42; body and, 44, 54, 58, 150; as differential, 120; duration and, 36; flesh as index of, 88; history and, 41; language and, 54; making, 149; narrative and, 37; other and, 103, 110, 128, 134, 150; relational, 50, 99, 103, 105–106, 117, 120; visual sense of, 64. *See also* identity; sensory experience
sense: bodily, 33; of self, 37, 64, 74, 106, 117; of "sense," 32; of time (*see* duration). *See also* sensory experience
sensory experience: body and, 32–35, 43, 44, 51, 60, 74–75; knowledge and, 31, 35, 39; language and, 20, 34–37, 54, 166n19; race and, 34–35, 50; self and, 74
Sheldon, Rebekah, 17
Shilts, Randy, 92
space: body and, 21, 75, 104, 138, 148, 150; border, 40, 125, 129, 153–154; Chicanx, 98; chora as, 17, 163n14; communal, 98–99, 108, 122; corporatization of, 132, 140; environment, 112; as event, 122; experience of, 119–120; "interactional," 164n7; metaphysics of, 131; place and, 139; race and, 98, 140; self and, 38; sociality of, 139–140, 162n10; speech and, 75; textual, 108; time and/of, 41–43, 49, 107–109, 138–141, 144
Stern, Daniel, 52
Stobbe, John: "The Things They Carried" (2014), 122–125
subject: body and, 5–6, 20, 24, 57, 137–138, 149; of capital, 134; Cartesian, 128; "dead subjects," 10–11; deconstruction of, 102, 126, 130; diversity and, 130; environment and, 120; ethnic, 10, 162n8; identity and, 85, 88, 166n19; interdependent, 120; Latinx politics and, 7; legal, 137; "neoliberal aesthetics" and, 4; object and, 35, 74, 107–108, 112, 130–131, 135; philosophy and, 50–51, 130–131; politics and, 126; punk and, 155; repetition and, 102; representational reading and, 10–11, 17–19; subjection (*see* race); of writing, 7
subject-object relation, 130–131, 135

telenovela, 78
temporality: alternate, 55, 140; ambiguous, 110; assemblage and, 138; authenticity and, 112–113; Aztec, 26–29; body and, 20, 27, 30, 36, 45–46, 49, 66, 108, 127, 138, 142–143, 148; cyclical, 49, 96–97, 111–112; elastic, 27; European, 27; of expectation, 5, 11, 14–15; as form, 45; history and, 41, 141–142; hybrid, 142; identity and, 41; indigeneity and, 27, 112–113, 134; *latinidad* and, 11; linear, 97, 111–112; materiality and, 20, 143; modernism and, 86; possibility and, 138; race and, 5, 20, 112; of reading, 148; the real and, 109–110; sociality of, 138–139; storytelling and, 165n13; text and, 96, 107, 147; of writing, 68. *See also* duration; space
Terrill, Joey. *See Homeboy Beautiful*
text: act and, 100; as active agent, 16; affect and, 57; body and, 15, 29–30, 36, 53, 57, 60, 63, 74–77, 96, 98–99, 101, 106–107, 144–146, 148, 152; as emblem, 77; as event, 18–19; freedom as function of, 106; intertextuality, 102–103, 143; as physical engagement, 12; reader and, 3–4, 6; technology and, 148; as thing, 17–18. *See also* Pineda, Cecile; racial immanence; reading
Theatre of Man, 59–60, 62, 167n2. *See also* Pineda, Cecile
thing, 16–18, 20. *See also* object; object-oriented ontology

time: being and, 45; body and, 27, 36, 45, 49, 63, 107–108, 138, 142–143, 148; brane theory, 138, 140; of capital, 140; colonial, 27, 29; as content and form, 109–110; cyclical, 31, 49, 96; indigenous, 27–28, 109, 112–113, 134; intertextuality and, 143–144; liminal, 11; linear, 14, 21, 28, 36–37, 45–47, 76, 111–113; narrative, 35–36, 109; "of the now," 142; politicization of, 27–28; race and, 112; scientific knowledge and, 138; as sense, 42; sociality of, 139; suspension of, 18, 143, 163n11; time-travel (*see* Lunar Braceros; Morales, Alejandro) unfamiliar and, 45; worldviews and, 109–110; writing and, 75, 143. *See also* duration; lingering; Ortiz Taylor, Sheila; Piedra del Sol; space

transcorporeality, 92, 96, 170n4

transgender, 94–95

Treichler, Paula, 91–93, 117

Vargas, Kathy, 60–62

Viego, Antonio, 10–11

Villa, Raúl, 98

Villa, Francisco "Pancho," 163n2

vision: body and, 5; fragility of, 65; "hierarchies of vision," 4; race and, 5, 114; self and, 64, 166n19; visual experience, 74. *See also* photography; Pineda, Cecile

Wells, Liz, 65

Wollaeger, Mark, 86

writing: about race, 131; act of, 7, 75; "AIDS-graphesis" and, 98; the body, 144–145; choratic, 90, 106; as event, 62, 68, 75; grace and, 76; the real and, 96; time of, 63, 68, 143; as world-making, 145. *See also* language; Pineda, Cecile; text

zines, 15. *See also Homeboy Beautiful*

ABOUT THE AUTHOR

Marissa K. López is Associate Professor of English and Chicana/o Studies at UCLA and author of *Chicano Nations: The Hemispheric Origins of Mexican American Literature* (New York University Press, 2011). She is the former director of UCLA's Chicana/o Studies Research Center, former vice president of the Latina/o Studies Association, and current chair of the MLA's prize committee for the best book in Chicana/o and Latina/o Literary and Cultural Studies.

www.ingramcontent.com/pod-product-compliance
Lightning Source LLC
Chambersburg PA
CBHW020411080526
44584CB00014B/1273